BEGINNER'S FRENCH

BEGINNER'S FRENCH

MARIE-ROSE CARRÉ

HIPPOCRENE BOOKS, INC.
NEW YORK

For information, address:
Hippocrene Books, Inc.
171 Madison Avenue
New York, NY 10016

Library of Congress Cataloging-in-Publication Data

Carré, Marie-Rose.
Beginner's French / Marie-Rose Carré
p. cm.
ISBN 0-7818-0863-4
1. French language—Textbooks for foreign speakers—English. I. Title.

PC2129.E5 C3785 2001
448.2'421—dc21 2001039140
CIP

Printed in the United States of America.

CONTENTS

FRANCE

GEOGRAPHY

France is a country of 58 million inhabitants over an area of about 50,000 square kilometers. It is bordered in the north by **La Manche**, also called the English Channel, in the northeast by Belgium and Luxembourg, in the east by Germany, Switzerland, and Italy, in the south by the Mediterranean and Spain, and in the west by the Atlantic Ocean. The capital of the country is **Paris** (9.3 million inhabitants). For administrative purposes the country is divided into 92 departments, grouped in 22 regions. The main cities are **Strasbourg**, **Bordeaux**, **Toulouse**, **Marseille**, **Lyon**, **Lille**, and **Nantes**.

There are four main rivers: the **Seine**, the **Rhône**, the **Loire**, and the **Garonne**.

The territory is made up of plains and mountains. On the eastern border are the **Jura** and the **Alps**. On the southwestern border the **Pyrénées** extend from the Mediterranean to the Atlantic. In the center of the country is the **Massif Central**, with a chain of extinct volcanoes, a granitic mass in the north and a region of limestone hills in the south, where Roquefort cheese is ripened in vast underground caves. This is the great region of mineral waters and spas.

To the north, **Normandy** with its coast along the Channel is a region of pastures and apple trees, producing milk and cream and famous for its cheeses, the best known of these being the *Camembert*. **Brittany**, to the west, is a rocky peninsula with the Channel along its northern coast and the Atlantic to the south. It has many fishing ports and supplies fish and shellfish to most of the country. The coast has numerous shipbuilding enterprises as well. The **Loire Valley**, extending south of these regions, enjoys a particularly mild climate, good for fruit production and wines of great distinction. With its many Renaissance "chateaux" it attracts millions of tourists. It is considered as the region of France where the best, most harmonious French is spoken. Going south, we find a countryside of rich cultures and vineyards, where one of the towns is named **Cognac**. Then there is **Bordeaux** and its region, which have been famous for their wines since the fifteenth century. Across a region of pines growing in sandy soil we reach the **Pyrénées** and the Spanish border. Then going east across a region of hills, where geese are raised for the production of foie gras and truffles can be found in the woods, we reach **Toulouse**. The Concorde was built here and the Airbus production plants are a major activity. This is the south of the country with a much warmer climate than the north. The Mediterranean coast attracts many vacationers. **Marseille** is an important commercial port and has been since the fourth century B.C. when Phoenicians settled there. The rest of the coast is the **Riviera**, a paradise for retirees and a recourse for summer tourists when cold and rain spoil the summer vacations in the north. Heading north, the **Alps** offer magnificent landscapes and great skiing in the winter. And the **Rhône Valley**, parallel to the Alps, has manufacturing industries, chemical and pharmaceutical, as well as extensive vineyards on the southern hills of **Provence** and **Haute Provence**. **Grenoble** and **Lyon** are the most important cities of this area. North of Lyon the famous wine regions of **Burgundy**, **Champagne**, and **Alsace** with Beaujolais, Nuits St. George and many other vineyards have been producing remarkable wines since the Middle Ages. A priest, Dom Perignon (1639–1715), invented the process for making champagne here. Over the centuries, this eastern part of the country has been ravaged by many wars, but always springs back to life. Continuing through the northern plains, one comes to the Channel, where the Chunnel has its station in **Calais**. Going south from Calais, one can reach in one hour, by high-speed train, **Paris**.

CLIMATE

With seas on three of its borders, and two ranges of high mountains on the others, France has a great variety of climates. Normandy in the northern part is lush and green with rich pastures. Brittany also has a mild climate but the soil is rocky. The center regions of the country have climates with more marked extremes, colder in the winter, warmer in the summer. In the southern regions, winter is shorter, with temperatures slightly higher and summers decidedly warmer. Temperatures range from 35 or 40° Fahrenheit to 75 to 80° in summer. The Mediterranean coast, **la Côte d'Azur**, has practically no rain between June and October.

HISTORY

French history goes back to 5,000 B.C. and numerous works of art testify to the cultural activity of these faraway times. Magnificent pictures in caves are dated to 300 centuries B.C. Celtic tribes invaded the territory about ten centuries B.C. and starting sometime in the sixth century B.C., Greek and Phoenician traders established trading posts and cities on the southern coast. Gaul entered history with Julius Caesar's Gaellic wars (58–52 B.C.) and became a Roman province during the first century A.D. Trade routes, administrative policies, and culture spread throughout the territory. The first monasteries date to the fifth century. Merovius, king of the Salian Franks, defeated Attila the Hun in the year 451 and the supreme authority became a king. In 496, Clovis was baptized in Reims and became the first king of the Franks living in and around Lutetia (later to become Paris from the name of the Parisii who inhabited the region). Then followed centuries of development of cities, extension of arable lands, constructions of castles and ramparts, and wars, including the one hundred years war between the French and the English that concluded with the burning at the stake of Joan of Arc in 1431. King succeeded king, each one fighting to hold on to his possessions and to enlarge the territory that he controlled. Starting from the thirteenth century, each king attempted to expand the country to the size and borders of what eventually would be modern France.

François I became king in 1515 and went to fight in Italy. On his return to France he encouraged the development of the arts, inviting several painters and sculptors to come to work for him, in particular Leonardo da Vinci, who gave him the Mona Lisa. He also built magnificent "chateaux," such as Chambord, as country residences and gathered around him a "court" of aristocratic men and women, giving them many festivities for which numerous artists were hired. In 1539, an Ordinance established a modern law system and mandated the use of French, instead of Latin, in administrative documents. François I reigned until 1547.

In 1541 Calvin published his *Institutes of the Christian Religion* and Protestantism started to spread in the country. The tension between Catholics and Protestants soon erupted into civil war, which went on, with periods of calm and atrocious violence, until 1589 when Henri of Bearn (a province on the Spanish border), who was a protestant, became a catholic and king of France as Henri IV. He started to reorganize the country, promised peasants and workers "a chicken in the pot every Sunday" and stabilized economic and political powers and relations between the government and the people. He was assassinated in Paris in 1610.

The seventeenth and eighteenth centuries were a period during which, with the help of their ministers, the kings, Louis XIII, Louis XIV, Louis XV, and Louis XVI, strengthened the power of the administration over the nobility. With the expansion of manufacturing and trade, a powerful, increasingly rich and educated middle class developed. At the same time, the kings and their courts were spending vast sums of money on luxury items and on art, to decorate their "chateaux" and mansions. Wars to defend the territory and to expand it also required enormous expenditures. But none of these rulers could establish a strict and well-balanced taxation system. Toward the end of the eighteenth century, the state was practically bankrupt and the people manifested their opposition to the absolutism of the government by storming the old medieval prison that was its symbol: the Bastille, on July 14, 1789. The Revolution had started and under the influence of the numerous political thinkers of the century, Montesquieu, Voltaire, Diderot, Rousseau and many others, assemblies were elected to elaborate a Bill of Rights that applied to every citizen in the country. King Louis XVI was tried, condemned to death, and guillotined on January 23, 1793. But with violent rivalry between factions, the revolutionary ideal was in great danger, at the same time as the nation itself was threatened by all the monarchies of Europe. The strong man needed to reestablish order in the cities and resist the attacks on the borders was a general of Corsican origin, Napoléon Buonaparte, who, coming back after winning a series of battles against the Austrians and the British, proclaimed himself First Consul and soon after, Emperor of the French People. But in 1812, after a disastrous campaign to conquer Russia, he was sent into exile to the island of St. Elena, where he died.

XIXth Century

The nineteenth century evolved with a succession of kings trying to govern by decrees, without the assent of elected assemblies. This led to three revolutions. In July 1830, Charles X was deposed and Louis Philippe became king. In 1848, the monarchy was overthrown and the Republic was proclaimed. Louis Napoléon (Napoléon Buonaparte's nephew) was elected president but in 1852 he dissolved the assembly and proclaimed himself emperor. His reign was marked by widespread modernization of the road system, expansion of the railroad network and extensive urban renewal in the city of Paris. In 1870 war was declared on Prussia. Louis Napoléon was deposed soon after in a period of socialist insurrection, and the Third Republic was proclaimed. Several months later, France was invaded and Paris occupied. In 1871, France surrendered and an armistice was signed. France lost Lorraine and Alsace, two provinces on the German border.

Events to Note

1783 First balloon flight by the Montgolfier brothers
1795 France adopts the metric system
1837 First passenger train service
1884 Trade unions recognized
1885 Pasteur discovers a vaccination for rabies and proves the existence of germs and microbes
1889 Eiffel Tower inaugurated
1895 Confédération Général du Travail founded to obtain regulations on working conditions
1905 Law on the separation of Church and State

XXth Century

The years from 1900 to 1910 are called *La Belle Epoque* and were a period of great intellectual and artistic activity for the middle class. Meanwhile, workers were organizing associations and unions to establish their rights.

In 1914 the First World War broke out between France and Germany, with use of new weapons that caused enormous loss of life. Armistice was accepted by the Germans on November 11, 1918. The years that followed saw the dictators taking power in Europe, Franco in Spain, Mussolini in Italy, Hitler in Germany, and frequent manifestations of social unrest in France. In 1935, the socialist Léon Blum formed the Popular Front government that gave all workers the forty-hour workweek, several weeks of paid vacations, medical insurance, etc.

In 1939 the Second World War began. France was invaded and occupied by the German armies in 1940. In June 1941, General de Gaulle formed the Free French Forces and declared that the true French government was in exile in London. Resistance was organized on the territory and many men and women escaped from France to rejoin the Free French Forces. In 1944, the Allies landed in Normandy and Paris was liberated by French troops under General de Gaulle. In 1945 Armistice was declared. In 1946, the Fourth Republic was established, and replaced by the Fifth Republic, whose constitution was written by General de Gaulle, with provisions to avoid frequent changes of Ministers. The period of decolonization started at the end of the 1950s. The Algerian crisis started in 1958. In 1962 de Gaulle decided in favor of Algerian independence. In 1968, de Gaulle, then president, retired after a referendum that was not widely supported. He died in 1970.

Soon after the end of the Second World War, France and Germany's heads of state started working on the organization of a European Economic Community that would join all the countries of Europe into a common market, abolishing all trade barriers and using a common currency, the Euro, that will be launched in 2002.

Presidents since 1970, elected for seven years:

1969 Georges Pompidou
1974 Valery Giscard d'Estaing
1981 François Mitterand
1988 Re-election of F. Mitterand
1995 Jacques Chirac

Events to Note

1946 Women gain the right to vote
1947 National Medicare Coverage organized
1954 French colonies, Tunisia, Morocco and Indo-China gain their independence
1981 TGV (train à grande vitesse) starts service to Lyon: It will develop during the next 20 years
1988 Edith Cresson, first woman Prime Minister in France
1999 Electoral lists must present an equal number of men and women candidates

ARTS AND CULTURE

The cultural heritage of France is so vast, rich and varied, and museums so numerous everywhere that travelers should buy a guidebook to find general information and precisions on the period they are interested in. For exhibits and museum offerings, and activities in music, theater or cinema, weekly publications such as *La Semaine de Paris* will give all necessary details and can be found at any newsstand.

Paris is a city of wide avenues and many squares and gardens, with extended perspectives and innumerable artistic details, such as, for example, wrought iron railings on the facades of buildings. Taking a sight-seeing bus tour and following its route on a map of the city is a good way to get a first acquaintance with the layout of the town, relying on the most conspicuous monuments to imagine its organization. A trip on the Bateaux-Mouche* that go up and down the Seine, from the Pont de l'Alma to the Ile de la Cité and the Notre Dame cathedral, will give you another view of the bridges and of the succession of buildings along the river. Walking and riding the many buses that crisscross the city will put you in direct contact with the people on their way to work or to shop or going to school. If you find yourself going by a covered market, go in and observe the many types of food that are sold there. Even in winter, you will come across open-air markets, active from 7 A.M. to 1 P.M.

When you want to go as fast as possible from one point to another, you will use the subway or *métro*, signaled on the sidewalk by the sign Ⓜ. A weekly or monthly "orange card" enables you to ride as many times as you want with a single valid ticket—from Monday to the following Sunday, or from the first to the last day of the month (see Practical Details – Paris).

Mouche means "fly" but actually is the name of the first organizer of this novel way of sight-seeing.

Paris offers interesting sights for everyone: palaces such as the Louvre, of course, where the kings of France lived until the Revolution of 1789, but also the Conciergerie where Marie-Antoinette was a prisoner before being beheaded, or the Palais Royal, built for the king's brother, the scene of many impassioned arguments during the Revolution and now a peaceful courtyard with flowers and fountains surrounded by an arcaded gallery. All over town, you will find squares, gardens and parks, such as the Luxembourg gardens extending around the Palais du Luxembourg built by Queen Catherine de Médicis in the sixteenth century, and now the seat of the Senate. There are the Tuileries, between the Louvre and the Place de la Concorde (which was the site of the guillotine during the Revolution), the Parc Monceau, the Parc Montsouris, the Parc of the Buttes Chaumont and several others with statuary and beautiful flowerbeds from spring to late autumn. Many are the churches: on the Ile de la Cité, the first settlement of the Parisii, Notre Dame de Paris, miraculously cleaned in 1999, is a gothic cathedral. St. Germain l'Auxerrois was built in romanesque style, St. Sulpice in seventeenth-century style, the Madeleine of the eighteenth looks like a Greek temple, and the Sacré Coeur on top of the Montmartre hill has neo-byzantine domes. And then, of course, in a category by itself, there is the Eiffel Tower, placed on the Champ de Mars where soldiers from the Ecole Militaire, built in the seventeenth century, used to learn the arts of war, and that is now a large playground for children. The tower of metal built by Eiffel for the 1900 World Fair was judged too ugly to keep its place among the monuments of the city and was saved only because in 1918 a radio station was installed at its very top, the highest point in Paris.

Strolling along the Seine you will notice displays of books and many images of various types, set in big green boxes hung on the parapets above the river. You are looking at the *bouquinistes* established there since the nineteenth century. Books and pictures, often not classified, invite you to browse.

For idle strolling between shops displaying every imaginable type of objects, even buttons cut from discarded uniforms of the Paris fire department, *les pompiers*, you will go, but only on Saturday, Sunday and

Monday, to Le Marché Aux Puces, at the Porte de Clignancourt, straight ahead from the subway station, going north. It is a vast market, occupying several blocks of low buildings. It offers an immense variety of secondhand items. One section specializes in good quality "antiques" including crystal chandeliers and silverware. One can count on it to be full of surprises and satisfying discoveries.

Museums are numerous enough to meet the interests of everyone. The Louvre has doubled the length of its galleries in the last five years. At the Porte de la Villette is the Palais des Sciences and nearby, you will find the Musée de la Musique. Back in the center of town, a block away from the Louvre is the Musée des Arts Décoratifs and the Musée de la Mode, presenting fashions through the centuries. The Musée de Cluny is devoted to the art of the Middle Ages, the Musée d'Orsay, in a building that was a railway station, shows works of the nineteenth century, and the Musée d'Art Moderne and the Centre Pompidou specialize in contemporary art, starting at the beginning of the twentieth century. From the upper terrace of the latter, there is a magnificent view of the roofs of Paris. In the section of town called Le Marais, close to the Seine, an elegant townhouse of the seventeenth century has been turned into a very interesting Musée de la Ville de Paris. Another large, beautiful seventeenth-century building houses the works of Picasso. There are several other museums established in the very house where the artist lived: Delacroix, Gustave Moreau, Braque and others.

From mid-June to mid-September, Paris has fewer activities, mostly in theater and music, although of course all museums, movie houses and a few theaters stay open through the summer. While foreign tourists come to Paris in huge numbers, the French move out to go to the provinces, seashore, mountains or countryside for their four-week vacations. This means that cultural activities start everywhere in towns, villages and around chateaux and historical monuments. Traditions are revived and spectacles organized: plays, classical and modern, in open-air theaters, concerts and festivals. In settings where historical events took place, such as Versailles, some chateaux in the Loire valley and many other sites, evenings of *Son et Lumière* (Sound and Light) shows are given; voices with musical background tell the story of the place while lights evoke the scenes described. All of these shows are given in several languages every evening. Festivals are innumerable, all over the country. The most famous ones are the Theater Festival in Avignon, and the Opéra in Aix en Provence. Seats should be booked well ahead of time. The Office du Tourisme on the Avenue des Champs-Elysées in Paris (75006) will have all necessary information about the festivals all over the country and will send you booklets upon request.

Just as interesting as theatrical activities are the landscapes and natural beauties found on the territory: sandy beaches, as in the Charentes, rocky coastline as in Brittany, pine forests in the Landes, green mountains in the Pyrénées, snowy crests and peaks in the Alps, and the very magnificent caves of the southern Massif Central and the Périgord, such as the famous Lascaux, the "Sistine Chapel" of prehistoric times.

PRACTICAL DETAILS – PARIS

Transport in Paris

Buses and the Subway (RATP, Régie Autonome des Transports Parisiens):

- Tickets are purchased in subway stations, and are good for both the bus and métro.
- Passes for 2, 3, and 5 days, or a week or a month are available.
- Books of 20 single ride tickets are available.
- Pocket maps for both bus and métro are available at the ticket windows or in newspaper kiosks.
- A big Ⓜ (for métro) indicates a subway station on the sidewalk.
- RER (Reseau Express Regional):
    - A fast, express train with its own tracks. It stops only at a few stations on the line, and goes far out of town to the suburbs including Versailles.
    - A special ticket must be bought for RER rides.
- At bus stops you will find the itinerary of each line that stops there.

Taxis

- Taxis operate 24 hours a day.
- You can order a taxi by phone for any time of the day or night:
  Alpha Taxis: 01.45.85.85.85
  G7: 01.47.39.47.39
  Taxis Bleus: 01.49.36.10.10

Airports

ROISSY CHARLES DE GAULLE
- For international transatlantic flights
- 45 minutes to one hour north of Paris

- Connected to Paris by:
  - Air France Bus – shuttle service
  - RER line B3
  - Taxi

ORLY

- For charter, continental and African flights
- Connected to Paris by:
  - Air France Bus – shuttle service
  - RER
  - Taxi

Trains

- Operated by the **SNCF** – Société Nationale des Chemins de Fer Français
- 6 railway stations in Paris, each one with its special sector
- Grandes Lignes – for long distance travel
- Banlieue – for suburban destinations
- Tickets and reservations:
  - Your ticket will indicate the name of the station from where your train will depart.
  - Before boarding the train you must validate your ticket by getting it punched in one of the orange machines that are on the quay.
- You will find the number of the platform of departure for your train on the big panels in the hall of the station.
- Trains leave exactly on time.
- If you are going to take a TGV (*train à grande vitesse*—high-speed train) you must have an assigned seat. It is a good idea to book a seat well ahead of time because these trains are often full.

Cars

- There are numerous rental agencies, and these can be found in the phone book. If you book in the United States, you will benefit from a better rate.

- Gas: about four times more expensive than in the United States
- Traffic rules:
  - The cars coming from your right have the right of way in all circumstances except if there is a sign to the contrary.
  - Wide avenues in the cities have a separate lane on the right reserved for buses and taxis. It must be respected.
  - No turns on red.

Shopping

- Stores are open from 9:00 A.M. to 7:00 P.M., in general, and closed on Sunday.
- Supermarkets stay open until 9:00 P.M. and are closed on Sunday.
- Most hairdressers, and some shops that are open on Sunday are closed on Monday.
- In each section of town, small markets offer all of the main staples and stay open 7 days a week until 10:00 at night.

INTRODUCTION TO THE LANGUAGE

HOW TO USE THE TEXTS AND TRANSLATIONS

Each lesson begins with a French "dialogue" and its English translation on the opposite page. Each text is translated as closely as possible to the French original so as you check the meaning of the words, the sentence in French should "make sense." At the beginning, you should work on only a few lines of the text, 10–12 lines for example. Then re-read the text in French, several times without looking at the English original, so that the text in the foreign language has meaning, by itself, for you. As you proceed in the grammar lessons, you should go back to the remaining parts of the previous texts. Re-read the part that you have worked on and go further in the text.

When you have acquired a good knowledge of grammatical vocabulary and rules, you should use the French texts to identify in them the elements of grammar and syntax that you have learned, forms of verbs, constructions with prepositions, order of words, meaning of verb tenses, etc. It will help to establish categories and note expressions in these categories in your notebook.

A third use of the text and their translations, when you have a good grasp of grammar forms and rules, is to compare the French texts and their translations and observe how the French expression differs from what seems to be a similar English expression. For example:

In English:	Look at this.
In French:	Regardez cela. (no translation of at)
In English:	This is yours?
In French:	Ceci est à vous?

In learning a language, one has to form expressions according to the habits of that language, and contrary to one's own language habits. For example:

Lesson 1:	I have been studying French for a year.
	J'apprends le français depuis un an.
In English:	compound past + present participle + *for*
In French:	present tense + *depuis* (since)

Building vocabulary is also essential. Following each dialogue is a list of the vocabulary used in the text, with English translation. Expressions are included in this list, as well as different verb forms. Noun gender and article are also provided. As the lessons progress, only new vocabulary is included in the lists. The glossary at the end of the book can be referred to for the meaning of a word.

ALPHABET AND PRONUNCIATION

a	as in m**a**t
b	as in **b**at
c + vowel **e** or **i**	**s** as in **s**ound
c + vowel **a**, **o**, or **u**	**k** as in **k**ind
ç	**s** as in **s**ound
d	as in **d**ent
e	as in **uh** (short, dull, almost mute sound)
é	as in pl**ay**, but not rounded
è	as in b**e**t
ê	same as **è**
f	as in **f**ire
g + vowel **e** or **i**	as in **j**ournal
g + vowel **a**, **o**, or **u**	as in **g**ull
h	mute
i	as in scr**ea**m
j	as in **j**oke (without any "d" sound)
k	as in **k**ilt
l	as in **l**ong
m	as in **m**an
n	as in **n**ine
o	as in c**o**ld
p	as in **p**aste
q	as in **c**ool
r	as in **r**ose, but from the back of the throat
s	as in **s**ea
s between vowels	as in si**z**e
t	as in **t**one
u	as in **u**bris, like German **ü**
v	as in **v**erb
w	same as **v**, but when followed by the sound "ee" it is pronounced like **w** in **w**eekend

x	as in ta**x**
y	as in **i**
z	as in **z**oo

There are additional accented letters, but pronunciation does not change significantly (à, â, î, ô, ù, û).

REMARKS ON PRONUNCIATION

General Remarks

In the French language each letter or combination of letters, such as diphthongs, is pronounced with only *one* sound. There is no slight sound of a "d" or "t" before another consonant, for example, *joli* (pretty) – joh-lee.

Each syllable of the word is pronounced with the same accent, and the exact value of its letters.

goú – ver – ne – ment (government)
la vil – le est gran – de (the town/city is big)

Combinations of Letters: Diphthongs & Triphthongs

Some groups of two or more vowels are pronounced as a single sound; the letters are said jointly.

combination	*approximate pronunciation*	*example*
ai	ay, eh (short, not rounded)	fr**ai**s (fresh)
au & **eau**	o	**au**to (car), **eau** (water)
eu & **oeu**	uh, euh (formed by pursing both lips)	nev**eu** (nephew), c**oeu**r (heart)
ia	ya	part**ia**l (partial)
ie	ye / ee (at the end of a word)	le m**ie**n (mine) / am**ie** (friend)
io	yo	port**io**n (portion)
oi	w as in **wa**gon	**oi**e (goose)
ou	oo as in y**ou**	b**ou**e (mud)

Note: In the pronunciation of words ending in *tion*, which are very numerous in English and in French, the sound of the last syllable is *sion*, for example, *portion* (portion) is pronounced por-**s**-ion (no "sh" sound).

Consonants

- **th** is pronouced like **t**
- **ch** is pronounced like **sh** in English
- **ph** is pronounced as an **f**
- **bl**, **cl**, **fl**, and **vl** are pronounced as one sound, with no sound between the letters
- **gn**: the "g" is not pronounced and a "nie" sound is formed, ex. i**gn**orant (ignorant), approximately pronounced ee-nyo-rahn.

Nasal Vowels

These vowel sounds are formed by a combination of a vowel with an **n** (or **m** in front of **b**, **p**, or **m**) followed by a consonant or at the end of a word. They are pronounced as a single sound and the vowel is nasalized. The sound "n" disappears.

vowels	*pronunciation*	*example*
a + **n** (**m**)	**an** (ahn)	**an**tique (antique)
e + **n** (**m**)	**en** (like **an**) / like "th**an**k" at the end of a word, with no final *n* sound	**en**trée (entry) / bi**en** (good)
i + **n** (**m**)	**in** (like final **en**)	br**in** (tiny bit)
oi + **n** (**m**)	**oi + en**	m**oin**s (less)
ai + **n** (**m**)	like final **en**	Améric**ain** (american)
o + **n** (**m**)	nasalized **o** (ohn), with no *n* sound	garç**on** (boy)
u + **n** (**m**)	nasalized **u** (uhn), with no *n* sound	**un** (one), h**um**ble (humble)

Note: Practice of these sounds with a native speaker is highly recommended.

Forms and Sounds of the Letter "E"

The letter **e** has three sounds according to the accent placed on it.

No accent: the sound is mute. It is used to pronounce the consonant that precedes the **e**.

absente – absent

Note: The final (**e**)**s** or **x** of the plural of nouns and adjectives is never pronounced, but the "s" is heard if the next word starts with a vowel.

*les livr**es*** – the books (no *s* sound)
*les livr**es** en vente* – the books on sale (*s* is heard, and combines with *en*)
*les cheveu**x** au vent* – hair in the wind (*z* is heard, and combines with *au*)

The é: An acute accent (´) is placed on the **e**. It is pronounced like English "may" but shorter.

The same sound is found in the pronunciation of:

- the plural articles: *les* (the), *des* (some) – (no *s* sound)
- the ending **er** of infinitive verbs, nouns and adjectives: *aimer* (to love), *jardinier* (gardener), *coutumier* (customary)
- the ending **ez** for the second person plural of all verbs: *vous aimez* (you love)
- the ending **et** for nouns and adjectives: *chalet* (mountain cottage), *fluet* (thin)
- the ending **ai** in verbs: *je voudrai* (I would want)

The è: A grave accent (`) is placed on the **e**. It is pronounced like English "bet." In some cases the accent is a "circonflex" (^) and the sound is the same as for the *è*.

mère – mother
être – to be

Note: **E** is pronounced with the sound of **è** when it is followed by two consonants, unless the first one is an **m** or an **n**.

essentiel – essential (sounds like *è*)
lecteur – reader (sounds like *è*)

- **X** is considered as a double consonant. In the word *exorcisme* (exorcism), the first *e* has the *è* sound.

- The trema (¨) is used to indicate that a letter must be pronounced:

  Noël – Christmas: the *o* and the *e* are heard separately.

  In the case of endings in *gue*, the trema indicates that the *u* must be pronounced (and the *ë* stays mute).

  aigu (*m.*) – sharp: *aiguë* (*f.*) the *u* must be heard.

Exceptions

femme (woman) – pronounced "f**a**mme"
sens (sense, meaning) – pronounced "sen**s**"
tous (all) – pronounced "tou**s**"
cher (dear) – pronounced "ch**er**"
ennemi (enemy) – pronounced "enne-mee" (no nasalization)

Particularities

- **H** at the beginning of a word can be "mute" or "hard":

  Mute *h* does not count.

  des hommes – some men: pronounced "dézomme"
  l'homme – the man: pronounced "lomme"

Hard *h* has no sound but counts as a consonant.

le haricot – the bean: pronounced "le arico"
les haricots – the beans: pronounced "lé arico"

- **C** is pronounced **ss** before **e**, **i** and **y**.
- **Ç** (with a cedilla) is pronounced **ss** before **a**, **o** and **u**.

le ciel – the sky (sounds like "siel")
la leçon – the lesson (sounds like "lessohn")*

- **C** is pronounced **k** before **a**, **o** and **u**.

le café – the coffee (kah-feh)
le colonel – the colonel (koh-loh-nel)
cueillir – to pick (kuh-yir)

- **G** is pronounced **j** before **e**, **i** and **y**.

rougir – to blush (roo-jeer)
nous mangeons – we eat (noo mahn-john)*

- **G** has a guttural sound "**g**(**u**)" before **a**, **o** and **u**.

gomme – gum (gumm)
mangue – mango (mahn-gue)*

*Nasalized, no final n sound.

ABBREVIATIONS

d.o.	direct object
i.o.	indirect object
f.	feminine
for.	formal
inf.	informal
interr.	interrogative
intr.	intransitive
lit.	literally
m.	masculine
nt.	neuter
pl.	plural
refl.	reflexive
sg.	singular
tr.	transitive

LESSON ONE

DIALOGUE

Dans L'Avion New York-Paris

PAUL: Pardon, monsieur, est-ce que ce... Ceci est à vous?

ROBERT: Ah! Mon écharpe! Oui, c'est mon écharpe! Merci, merci beaucoup.

PAUL: J'entends que vous parlez français. Je n'ai pas encore parlé avec un vrai Français. Vous me comprenez?

ROBERT: Oui, je vous comprends très bien. Alors vous allez à Paris? Et pour la première fois?

PAUL: Oui, pour la première fois. Mais j'étudie le français depuis un an, très sérieusement, chaque jour. Presque chaque jour. Avec des cassettes, des chansons, et beaucoup d'information sur l'Internet. Je suis marié maintenant. Ma femme dort en ce moment. Depuis longtemps nous voulons connaître la France.

ROBERT: J'espère que le temps sera beau, le ciel bleu et l'air agréable pour votre séjour parce qu'à Paris, les promenades à pied à travers la ville sont très intéressantes. On part le matin, on prend un café au lait et un croissant à la terrasse d'un café.

PAUL: La terrasse? Qu'est-ce que c'est: la terrasse d'un café?

ROBERT: En France, les restaurants ont le droit de mettre des chaises et des tables sur une partie du trottoir. Il faut laisser un espace pour les gens qui passent, bien sûr, et ces chaises et tables dehors, s'appellent 'la terrasse'.

PAUL: Ah! Je comprends. *Il sort son carnet.* 'Terrasse' avec deux 's'?

In the New York-Paris Plane

PAUL: Excuse me, sir, is this... This is yours?

ROBERT: Ah! My scarf! Yes, it's my scarf! Thank you, thank you very much.

PAUL: I hear you speaking French. I have not yet spoken with a real French man. Do you understand me?

ROBERT: Yes, I understand you very well. Then, you are going to Paris? And for the first time?

PAUL: Yes, for the first time. But I have been studying French for a year, very seriously, every day. Almost every day. With cassettes, songs and much information on the Internet. I am married now. My wife is sleeping right now. For a long time we have wanted to know France.

ROBERT: I hope that the weather will be good, the sky blue and the air pleasant for your stay because in Paris, walks through the city are very interesting. You start in the morning, you take a cup of coffee with milk and a croissant on the terrace of a café.

PAUL: The terrace? What is that: the terrace of a café?

ROBERT: In France, restaurants have the right to put some chairs and tables on part of the sidewalk. They must leave some space for pedestrians, of course, and those chairs and tables are called "the terrace."

PAUL: Ah! I understand. *He takes out his notebook. Terrasse* with two "s"?

Robert: Oui, et deux 'r'.

Paul: Je dois inscrire tous les mots que je ne connais pas.

Robert: Très bonne idée! C'est ce que je devrais faire en anglais. Et vous mettez l'article féminin ou masculin devant le nom, pour les apprendre ensemble.

Paul: C'est ce que je vais faire. La terrasse! La terrasse d'un café.

Robert: Yes, and two "r."

Paul: I must write down all the words that I don't know.

Robert: Very good idea! That's what I must do in English. And you put the article, feminine or masculine, before the noun to learn them together.

Paul: That's what I am going to do. The terrace! The terrace of a café.

VOCABULARY

à	at; to
à Paris	to Paris
à pied	on foot
à travers	across
agréable	pleasant
air, l' *m.*	air
alors	then
an, un *m.*	one year
anglais	English
article, l' *m.*	article
avec	with
avion, l' *m.*	airplane
beau	beautiful
beaucoup de	many
bien sûr	of course
café, un *m.*	(a) coffee
café au lait, un *m.*	(a) coffee with milk
carnet, le *m.*	notebook
cassettes, des *f.*	(some) cassettes
ces	these, those
c'est ce que	that is what
chaises, des *f.*	(some) chairs
chansons, des *f.*	(some) songs
chaque	every, each
ciel, le *m.*	sky
clair	clear
connaître	to know
croissant, un *m.*	(a) "croissant"
dans	in
dehors	outside
de mettre	to place

depuis	for
des	some
deux	two
devant	before
dort	is sleeping/is asleep
droit, le *m.*	right
d'un café	of a café
du trottoir	of the sidewalk
écharpe, l' *f.*	scarf
en ce moment	right now
ensemble	together
espace, un *m.*	(a) space
est à vous	is yours
est-ce que ce/ceci	is this
et	and
faire	to do
féminin	feminine
femme, la *f.*	wife
français	French
Français, un *m.*	(a) Frenchman
gens, les *m.*	people
il faut	it is necessary
il sort	he takes out
inscrire	to write down
je/j'	I
j'entends	I hear
j'espère que	I hope that
j'étudie	I have been studying
je comprends	I understand
je dois	I must
je n'ai pas parlé	I have not spoken
je ne connais pas	I do not know
je suis marié	I am married
je vais faire	I am going to do
jour, le *m.*	day

laisser	to leave
les apprendre	to learn them
longtemps	for a long time
ma	my
maintenant	now
mais	but
masculin	masculine
matin, le *m.*	in the morning
me	me, to me
merci beaucoup	thank you very much
mon	my
monsieur	sir
mots, les *m.*	words
ne ... pas encore	not yet
nom, le *m.*	noun
nous voulons	we have wanted
on	one/we
on prend	one takes
ont	have
ou	or
oui, c'est...	yes, it is...
parce qu(e)'	because
pardon	excuse me
part	goes
partie, une *f.*	(a) part
passent	walk by
photos, les *f.*	pictures (photographs)
pour	for
première fois, la *f.*	first time
presque	almost
promenades, les *f.*	walks
que	that
qu'est-ce que c'est	what is that
qui	who
restaurants, les *m.*	restaurants

s'appellent	are called
séjour, le *m.*	visit
sera	will be
son	his
sont	are
sur	on
tables, des *f.*	(some) tables
temps, le *m.*	weather
terrasse, la *f.*	terrace
tous	all
très bien	very well
très bonne idée	very good idea
très intéressantes	very interesting
très sérieusement	very seriously
ville	city, town
vous	you
vous allez	you are going to
vous comprenez	you understand
vous mettez	you put
vous parlez	you speak
vrai	true, real

GRAMMAR

The Present Tense and the Imperative

Personal Subject Pronouns

The personal subject pronouns are always used with the verb.

	singular	*plural*
1st pers.	je (I)	nous (we)
2nd pers.	tu (you)	vous (you)
3rd pers.	il/elle (he/she)	ils/elles (they (*m.*)/they (*f.*))

Note: The second person plural *vous* is also used to address one person in a respectful way.

Present Tense Conjugation of Regular Verbs

There are three types of verbs, each with a different ending in the infinitive: *er*, *ir* and *re*.

- Present tense conjugation of ER verbs:

Endings	*chanter* (to sing)	
-e	je chante	(I sing)
-es	tu chantes	(you sing)
-e	il/elle chante	(he/she sings)
-ons	nous chantons	(we sing)
-ez	vous chantez	(you *pl.* sing)
-ent	ils/elles chantent	(they *m./f.* sing)

• IR verbs:

There are two categories of *ir* verbs. Their conjugations are different, and a dictionary must be consulted to know the category to which the verb belongs. (For irregular verbs see Appendix.)

Endings	*finir* (to finish)	
-is	je finis	(I finish)
-is	tu finis	(you finish)
-it	il/elle finit	(he/she finishes)
-issons	nous finissons	(we finish)
-issez	vous finissez	(you *pl.* finish)
-issent	ils/elles finissent	(they *m./f.* finish)

Endings	*dormir* (to sleep)	
-s	je dors	(I sleep)
-s	tu dors	(you sleep)
-t	il/elle dort	(he/she sleeps)
-ons	nous dormons	(we sleep)
-ez	vous dormez	(you *pl.* sleep)
-ent	ils/elles dorment	(they *m./f.* sleep)

• RE verbs:

Endings	*vendre* (to sell)	
-s	je vends	(I sell)
-s	tu vends	(you sell)
-d/t	il/elle vend	(he/she sells)
-ons	nous vendons	(we sell)
-ez	vous vendez	(you *pl.* sell)
-ent	ils/elles vendent	(they *m./f.* sell)

Note: The third person singular *d* ending is used for verbs with the infinitive ending *dre*.

Negative Form

The negative is formed by adding *ne* immediately before the verb and *pas* immediately after.

Je ne chante pas. – I do not sing.
Je ne finis pas. – I do not finish.
Je ne vends pas. – I do not sell.

Interrogative Form

The interrogative can be formed by placing *est-ce que* (is) at the beginning of a sentence or by placing the subject after the verb. A *-t-* is placed for ease of pronunciation between a mute *e* and a pronoun starting with a vowel.

Est-ce que je chante?/Chante-t-il?
Am I singing?/Does he sing?

Est-ce que je finis?/Finit-il?
Am I finishing?/Does he finish?

Est-ce que je vends?/Vend-il?
Am I selling?/Does he sell?

Negative Interrogative Form

The negative question is formed by placing *est-ce que* before the verb in the negative form or by placing *ne* before the verb and *pas* after the subject.

Est-ce que je ne chante pas?/Ne chante-t-il pas?
Am I not singing?/Does he not sing?

Est-ce que je ne finis pas?/Ne finit-il pas?
Am I not finishing?/Does he not finish?

Est-ce que je ne vends pas?/Ne vend-il pas?
Am I not selling?/Does he not sell?

Note: The present tense is an equivalent construction for the English "I am doing this." The use of the gerundive to indicate that the action is ongoing does not exist in French and such ideas are expressed by the use of the present tense, or by the use of the expression: *être en train de...* (*lit.* "to be in the process of...") when you want to insist on the process going on.

Present Participle

The present participle is the form of the verb corresponding to the English verb form ending in "ing." It is formed with the radical of the imperfect tense (see Lesson Two), by replacing the *ions* ending of the 1st person plural with the ending *ant.*

vendre (to sell) – vend-ions – vendant (selling)
finir (to finish) – finiss-ions – finissant (finishing)

Three verbs have an irregular present participle:

avoir (to have) – ayant (having)
être (to be) – étant (being)
savoir (to know) – sachant (knowing)

This participle has a past form: the compound present participle. It is composed of the present participle of the auxiliary + past participle of the verb conjugated (see Lesson Two on forming the past participle).

ayant aimé (having liked)
étant venu (having come)

Uses

The present participle can be used:

- as a noun

  le courant – the current

- as an adjective

  une personne charmante – a charming person

- as a verb (either used alone or preceded by the preposition *en*, equivalent to the English "by")

  It is used to convey the meaning that two actions take place at the same time:

  En travaillant dur, il s'est fatigué.
  By working hard, he became tired.

  Or to signify that one action takes place immediately before another:

  Prenant son livre, il s'est mis à lire.
  Taking his book, he started to read.

The past form of the present participle is used to indicate that there is an interval between the first and the second action in the sentence, exactly as in English.

Ayant dormi très tard, il a manqué son train.
Having slept very late, he missed his train.

Ayant aimé cette maison, il l'a achetée.
Having liked this house, he bought it.

Present Tense Irregularities - Changes in Spelling

- When the ending is a mute *e*, the preceding *e* becomes *è*.

  Je me lève. – I get up.
  Tu te lèves. – You get up.
  Il se lève. – He gets up.
  Ils se lèvent. – They get up.

- For verbs whose infinitive ends with *eler* and *eter*, the consonant *l* or *t* is doubled before the present tense endings with a mute *e*.

  appeler – j'appelle, tu appelles, il/elle appelle, ils/elles appellent
  But: nous appelons, vous appelez (I call, etc.)
  jeter – je jette, tu jettes, il/elle jette, ils/elles jettent
  But: nous jetons, vous jetez (I throw, etc.)

  Exception: *acheter* – j'achète (I buy)

- In verbs ending with *ayer*, *oyer* and *uyer*, the *y* becomes *i* before mute endings.

  payer – je paie (I pay)
  nettoyer – je nettoie (I clean)
  essuyer – j'essuie (I wipe)

- In verbs ending in *cer*, when conjugated *c* becomes *ç* to preserve the soft sound.

  commencer – nous commençons (we start)

- In verbs ending in *ger*, an *e* is placed after the *g*, when the ending starts with *o* or *a* (past tense only).

  changer – nous changeons (we change)
  ils changeaient (they changed)

- In verbs ending with a consonant and *re*, the *re* is dropped:

  vendre – je vends (to sell)

- If the verb ends with a *pre*, a *t* must be added in the three singular persons of the present tense (after the *re* is dropped).

  interrompre – j'interrompt, tu interrompt, il/elle interrompt
  But: nous interrompons, vous interrompez, ils/elles interrompent (I interrupt, etc.)

- Verbs ending in *re* or *oir*: some of these conjugations are irregular and are given in the Appendix.

Uses

The present indicative is used to express an action or a state of mind existing at the present moment:

Je travaille. – I am working./I work.

- To express a fact or an idea which is always true, sometimes in the form of a proverb.

  La liberté est nécessaire à l'humanité.
  Liberty is necessary for the people.

  Pierre qui roule n'amasse pas mousse.
  Rolling stone gathers no moss.

- To express an immediate past or future.

  Nous sommes là dans cinq minutes.
  We will be there in five minutes.

J'arrive de Paris.
I have just arrived from Paris.

Je pars pour Paris.
I am leaving for Paris.

- To express a future after a conditional *si* (if).

Je partirai si tu pars.
I will go away if you go away.

Si tu pars, je pars!
If you leave, I leave!

Special Constructions

- With venir de + verb infinitive: to express the idea of the recent past.

Il vient d'arriver de Paris.
He has just arrived from Paris.

- With aller + verb infinitive: to express the idea of the near future.

Il va arriver demain.
He is going to arrive tomorrow.

These two verbs (*aller* and *venir*) are used with these meanings in the present and imperfect indicative only.

Note: The adverb "just" with a temporal meaning is *never* used in French.

- With *depuis* (since) to express the idea that an action started in the past continues up to the present.

Depuis combien de temps dort-il? Trois heures.
How long has he been sleeping? For three hours.

Note: The English preposition "for" must be replaced by *depuis*. The usual equivalent of "for," *pour* in French, must *never* be used before an expression of time.

- Equivalents of *depuis*

Equivalents of *depuis* are also used with the present tense to signify an event started in the past that continues up to the present.

Il y a ... que:
Il y a trois heures que je vous attends.
I have been waiting for you for three hours.

Cela fait... :
Cela fait combien de temps que vous m'attendez?
How long have you been waiting for me?
Je vous attends depuis dix minutes.
I have been waiting for you for ten minutes.

Voilà ... que:
(used only for an answer)
Voilà dix minutes que je vous attends.
I have been waiting for you for ten minutes.

The Imperative

The imperative is the verb form used to give an order.

FORMS

The imperative mode has three forms: second person singular, first person plural, and second person plural. For all verbs (regular and irregular) these are taken from the present indicative, and are conjugated without a subject pronoun.

aimer – to like
aime (like)
aimons (let's like
aimez (like – you *pl.*)

finir – to end
finis (finish)
finissons (let's finish)
finissez (finish – you *pl.*)

faire – to do
fais (do)
faisons (let's do)
faites (do – you *pl.*)

aller – to go
va (go)
allons (let's go)
allez (go – you *pl.*)

vendre – to sell
vends (sell)
vendons (let's sell)
vendez (sell – you *pl.*)

Note: The *-s* ending is omitted from the forms of all verbs ending in *-es* and *-as* in the 2nd person singular of the present indicative.

aller – va
aimer – aime
ouvrir – ouvre

This *-s* is used when the verb is followed by the pronouns *y* and *en*.

Vas-y! – Go!
Donnes-en. – Give some.

EXCEPTIONS

- The following verbs take these forms in the imperative:

être – to be
sois (be)

avoir – to have
aie (have)

soyons (let's be)
soyez (be – you *pl.*)

ayons (let's have)
ayez (have – you *pl.*)

savoir – to know
sache (know)
sachons (let's know)
sachez (know – you *pl.*)

vouloir – to want
veuille (want)
veuillons (let's want)
veuillez (want – you *pl.*)

NEGATIVE IMPERATIVE

The negative imperative is formed like the negative present, by adding *ne* before the verb and *pas* after it.

Ne fume pas. – Don't smoke.
Ne mangeons pas. – Let's not eat.

See Lesson Three for the usage of object pronouns with the imperative form.

EXERCISES

I. Conjugate and repeat aloud the following verbs in the present tense, then write the forms in the following persons.

1. arriver (nous)
2. changer (vous)
3. acheter (elle)
4. étudier (ils)
5. appeler (tu)
6. espérer (je)
7. finir (vous)
8. dormir (elle)
9. partir (vous)
10. bâtir (nous)
11. venir (il)
12. pouvoir (elles)
13. vouloir (tu)
14. recevoir (il)
15. perdre (nous)

II. Translate the following expressions.

1. He is singing. (chanter)
2. Is she studying? (étudier)
3. I am not sleeping. (dormir)
4. He cannot. (pouvoir)
5. Isn't she coming? (venir)
6. She is losing. (perdre)
7. They are not building. (bâtir)
8. We are leaving. (partir)
9. Is she arriving? (arriver)
10. It is being born. (naître)

III. Translate into English. Note the changes in the construction of the sentence.

1. Depuis combien de temps dort-elle? (dormir)
2. Elle dort depuis trois (3) heures.
3. Depuis quand voyagent-ils en France? (voyager)
4. Ils voyagent depuis quatre (4) semaines.
5. Il y a combien d'années que vous le connaissez? (connaître)
6. Je le connais depuis dix (10) ans.

7. Cela fait combien de jours qu'il travaille ici? (travailler)
8. Cela fait cinq (5) jours qu'il travaille ici.
9. Voilà trente (30) minutes que je vous appelle. (appeler)

IV. Answer the following questions in French.

1. How long have you been reading? (lire)
2. How long has she been working? (travailler)
3. How long has she been playing? (jouer)
4. How long have you been traveling? (voyager)

V. Give the affirmative and negative imperative forms in all three persons for the following verbs.

1. chanter (to sing)
2. dormir (to sleep)
3. manger (to eat)
4. aller (to go)
5. être (to be)
6. voir (to see)
7. attendre (to wait)
8. courir (to run)
9. craindre (to fear)
10. défendre (to defend)
11. faire (to do)
12. dire (to say)

LESSON TWO

DIALOGUE

Présentations

Paul: Ah! Voilà le moment de déjeuner. Macaroni au jambon ou poulet? Je vais prendre le poulet. Avec du vin? Mais oui, du vin rouge.

Robert: C'est du poulet en sauce tomate. Donc c'est parfait.

Paul: Et aussi de l'eau. Je vais passer ce plateau à ma femme. Elle est réveillée. Je vous présente ma femme, Louise. Elle parle bien français. Mon nom est Paul. C'est un bon nom français, n'est-ce pas?

Robert: Oui, certainement. Je m'appelle Robert Duchamp. Mais vous savez, en France, le prénom n'est pas employé avec les personnes qui ne sont pas de votre famille ou des amis intimes.

Paul: Ah! Non? Pourquoi?

Robert: Parce que les rapports entre les personnes sont plus formels. C'est la politesse apprise depuis l'enfance.

Paul: Ah! Alors, qu'est-ce qu'il faut dire?

Robert: On emploie le nom de famille, comme pour moi, Duchamp.

Paul: Et pour nous Smith...

Robert: C'est ça! Mais avant le nom, on met 'monsieur' ou 'madame'.

Paul: Et si elle n'est pas mariée? 'Mademoiselle'?

Introductions

Paul: Ah! Now is the time for lunch. Macaroni and ham or chicken? I am going to take the chicken. With wine? Oh yes, red wine.

Robert: It is chicken in tomato sauce. So, it is perfect.

Paul: And also some water. I will pass this tray to my wife. She is awake. Let me introduce my wife, Louise. She speaks French quite well. My name is Paul. It is a good French name, isn't it?

Robert: Yes, certainly. My name is Robert Duchamp. But, you know, in France, first names are not used with people who are not in your family, or close friends.

Paul: Ah! Really? Why?

Robert: Because relationships with people are more formal. It is the politeness learned in your early years.

Paul: Ah! Then what should one say?

Robert: You use the family name, as for me, Duchamp.

Paul: And for us, Smith...

Robert: Exactly! But before the name, you put "mister" or "Mrs."

Paul: Or, if she is not married? "Miss"?

ROBERT: Exactement! Et à votre femme, je dis 'bonjour, madame Smith'.

PAUL: Il faut prendre l'habitude. Et une autre question: pour dire 'tu' ou le 'vous' formel à quelqu'un?

ROBERT: C'est une question difficile. Mais la meilleure solution, c'est de dire 'vous' à tout le monde.

PAUL: A tout le monde?

ROBERT: Oui, à chaque personne à qui vous vous adressez.

PAUL: Et aux petits enfants?

ROBERT: Si vous rencontrez des enfants très jeunes, il est mieux de leur dire 'tu'. C'est bizarre de leur dire 'vous', mais vous ne devez pas vous habituer au 'tu' et vous ne direz pas 'tu' à un homme ou à une dame que vous venez de rencontrer.

PAUL: Le français a des obstacles.

ROBERT: Comme toutes les langues!

ROBERT: Exactly! And to your wife I say "hello, Mrs. Smith."

PAUL: One must get used to it. And another question: to use *tu* or the formel *vous* with someone?

ROBERT: It is a difficult question. But the best solution is to say *vous* to everybody.

PAUL: To everybody?

ROBERT: Yes, to every person you will speak with.

PAUL: And to little children?

ROBERT: If you meet very young children, it is better to say *tu* to them. It sounds strange to say *vous* to them, but you must not get used to *tu* so that you will not use it with a man or a lady you have just met.

PAUL: The French language has obstacles.

ROBERT: As do all languages!

VOCABULARY

à ma femme	to my wife
à quelqu'un	to someone
à qui	to whom
amis, des *m.*	friends
apprise	learned
au jambon	with ham
autre	other
aux petits enfants	to small children
avant	before
bon nom, un *m.*	(a) good name
bonjour, madame	good day, madam
certainement	certainly
c'est bizarre	it is strange
c'est ça	that's it
c'est parfait	it is perfect
chaque personne	each person
comme	as; just as
dame, une *f.*	(a) woman
de l'eau	some water
déjeuner, le *m.*	lunch
depuis	since
difficile	difficult
dire	to say
donc	so
du poulet	some chicken
du vin	some wine
elle	she
elle est réveillée	she is awake
elle parle bien	she speaks well
en	in
en sauce tomate	in tomato sauce

enfance, l' *m.*	early years/childhood
entre	between
et aussi	and also
exactement	exactly
famille, la *f.*	family
formel	formal
homme, un *m.*	(a) man
il	it; he
il est mieux de	it is better to
intimes	close *pl.*
je	I
je dis	I say
je m'appelle	my name is
je vais passer	I am going to pass
je vous présente	let me introduce you to
leur dire	to say to them
macaroni, le *m.*	macaroni
madame	"madam"
mademoiselle	"miss"
mais	but
meilleure, la *f.*	the best
moment, le *m.*	moment
mon nom	my name
n'est pas employé	is not used
n'est-ce pas?	isn't it so?
ne sont pas de	are not of
obstacles, des *m.*	obstacles
on emploie	we use
on met	one puts
ou	or
parce que	because
personnes, les *f.*	persons
plus formels	more formal *pl.*
politesse, la *f.*	politeness
pourquoi?	why?

prendre l'habitude	to become used to
prénom, le *m.*	first name
qu'est ce qu'il faut	what must one
qui	who
rapports, les *m.*	rapports, relations
rencontrer	to meet
rouge	red
si	if
solution, la *f.*	solution
sont	are
tout le monde	everybody
toutes les langues	all the languages
très jeunes	very young
tu	you
voilà	here is
voilà le moment	now is the time
votre	your
vous ne devez pas	you must not
vous ne direz pas	you will not say
vous rencontrez	you meet
vous savez	you know
vous venez de	you have just
vous vous adressez	you speak to, you address

GRAMMAR

Tenses Expressing Past Actions: The Imperfect and the Past Perfect

When we talk to other people, we tell them very often about past actions, situations, thoughts. There are two tenses in French to express the past: the imperfect and the past perfect.

The Imperfect Tense

FORMS

Endings are added to the radical of the verb (the root or stem), which is obtained by removing the *ons* ending from the 1st person plural form of the present tense. All verbs, regular and irregular, follow this pattern except for the verb *être* (to be).

The imperfect is called the *imparfait* in French.

Imperfect endings:

	singular	*plural*
1st pers.	-ais	-ions
2nd pers.	-ais	-iez
3rd pers.	-ait	-aient

Examples:

In the present tense: *finir* (to finish) – *nous finissons* (we finish)

In the imperfect tense:

je finissais (I was finishing)
tu finissais (you were finishing)
il/elle finissait (he/she was finishing)
nous finissions (we were finishing)
vous finissiez (you *pl.* were finishing)
ils/elles finissaient (they *m./f.* were finishing)

In the present tense: *vendre* (to sell) – *nous vendons* (we sell)

In the imperfect tense:

je vendais (I was selling)
tu vendais (you were selling)
il/elle vendait (he/she was selling)
nous vendions (we were selling)
vous vendiez (you *pl.* were selling)
ils/elles vendaient (they *m./f.* were selling)

So the imperfect tense is always regular once you know the first person form. But you need to know the present tense form of the verb you want to use, and some of these are irregular.

traduire (to translate)
Present: nous traduisons
Imperfect: nous traduisions

Imperfect of être (to be)

This form is irregular and must be memorized.

j'étais (I was)
tu étais (you were)

il/elle était (he/she was)
nous étions (we were)
vous étiez (you were)
ils/elles étaient (they were)

The Past Perfect

As in English it is a compound tense. Its name in French is *passé composé* (compound past). It is made up of two words, using *avoir* or *être* in the present tense as an auxiliary + the past participle of the meaningful verb.

Avoir is the most commonly used auxiliary.
Etre is used in certain well-defined cases (see below).

FORMS

parler (to talk, to speak)

j'ai parlé (I spoke)
tu as parlé (you spoke)
il/elle a parlé (he/she spoke)
nous avons parlé (we spoke)
vous avez parlé (you *pl.* spoke)
ils/elles ont parlé (they *m./f.* spoke)

CONSTRUCTIONS

In these forms the auxiliary is the verb and the past participle is the adjective. The past participle is formed by taking the root of the verb and adding *é* for *er* verbs and adding *i* for *ir* verbs. Many past participles are irregular and must be learned individually (see Appendix for a selection of irregular verbs). When the verb *avoir* is used as auxiliary, there is no agreement between subject and verb.

Negative Form

Ne ... pas on either side of the verb.

Je n'ai pas parlé. – I did not talk.

Interrogative Form

The subject is placed after the verb.

Ai-je parlé? – Did I speak?
A-t-il parlé? – Did he speak?

Interrogative Negative Form

N'ai-je pas parlé? – Didn't I speak?
N'a-t-il pas parlé? – Didn't he speak?

With Object Pronouns

The past participle agrees with the gender and number of the object pronoun only when the pronoun comes before the verb (object pronouns are presented in Lesson Three).

J'ai donné ces fleurs (*f.*) *à Marie.*
I gave these flowers to Mary.
Je les ai données à Marie.
I gave them to Mary.
J'ai donné ces fleurs que j'ai aimées.
I gave these flowers that I liked.

With Direct and Indirect Object Pronouns

Direct and indirect object pronouns are placed before the verb.

J'ai donné ce cadeau à Marie.
I gave this present to Mary.
Je le lui ai donné. (*le*: d.o./*lui*: i.o.)
I gave it to her.

As-tu donné ce cadeau à Marie?
Did you give the present to Mary?
Le lui as-tu donné?
Did you give it to her?

N'as-tu pas donné ce cadeau à Marie?
Didn't you give this present to Mary?
Ne le lui as-tu pas donné?
Didn't you give it to her?

CONJUGATION WITH *ETRE*

The auxiliary *être* is used in two types of conjugations. The past participle agrees with the subject in number and gender.

I. Sixteen verbs of motion

aller	monter	partir	revenir
arriver	mourir	passer	sortir
descendre	naître	rester	tomber
entrer	parvenir	retourner	venir

All other verbs of motion take *avoir.*

Note: When the verbs *monter* and *descendre* have a direct object they are conjugated with *avoir.*

Je suis vite descendu.
I quickly went downstairs.

Il a lentement descendu l'escalier.
He slowly went down the stairs.

Note: You will notice in these examples the place of the adverb between the subject and the verb in English. In French, this construction is absolutely impossible. Compare the sentences in English and in French, where the adverb is placed after the verb.

II. Reflexive verbs

These are verbs preceded by two pronouns of the same person: one a subject and the other an object pronoun.

se lever (to get up)
il se levait – he used to get up
il s'est levé – he got up

These verbs indicate that the subject (first pronoun) makes the action on himself (second pronoun – direct object).

Uses of These Tenses

When you want to express something that has happened in the past, you have to choose one of these two tenses, that is you must decide what is the quality of the action or situation that you want to relate – according to the meaning of these two tenses.

• The past perfect gives the idea that the verb relates an action done once and finished within the limits of time that it implies.

Elle a ouvert la porte.
She opened the door.

J'ai bien dormi.
I slept well.

J'ai travaillé pendant 3 heures.
I worked for 3 hours.

Il a été riche pendant à peu près 10 ans.
He was rich for 10 years or so.

In the first two examples the verb itself suggests the limits of the action. In the second two examples a limited time period is given.

• The imperfect is used in all other cases. It implies that a situation exists but does not depend on limitations in time.

description:

Elle était belle.
She was beautiful.

L'examen était difficile.
The exam was difficult.

situation without time limits:

A cette époque, il travaillait beaucoup.
At that time, he worked a lot.

Particular Uses

A contrast is established between the meanings of the two tenses in sentences indicating that an event took place at a certain moment when another situation was going on.

Nous regardions la télévision quand il est entré.
We were watching television when he came in.
[imperfect] [past perfect]

- Expression of Habitual or Repeated Action

In English, a repeated action is expressed with a verb preceded by the auxiliary "would," which seems to be the same form that expresses a conditional mode.

I would do this if you would do that.
In summer I would go fishing every day.

In French the two expressions are not similar. The use of the conditional to express "habit," or repeated action, does not convey the intended meaning. The imperfect must be used.

En été, j'allais à la pêche très souvent.
In summer I would go fishing very often.

Il chantait quand il prenait sa douche.
He would sing when he took his shower.

Bien des fois, j'allais me promener avec elle.
Many times I would go walking with her.

But if the number of times is expressed, each "time" representing an action done and finished, then the past perfect is used.

Trois ou quatre fois je suis allé me promener avec elle.
Three or four times I went walking with her.

The number of times does not matter.

Mille fois, je lui ai parlé de cela.
A thousand times, I talked to her about it.

Rules

- Equivalent of "for" + expression of time past

  As you can see in the example "I worked for three hours," the preposition "for" in this case is not translated by *pour* as it usually is. In front of expressions of periods of time its equivalent in French is *pendant.*

- Equivalent of the word "times" in expressions of repetition: *fois*

  Je l'ai fait cinq fois.
  I did it five times.

- *Le temps,* the French equivalent of the word "time" always means "a period of time."

  J'ai le temps de faire ceci.
  I have time to do this.

- The expression *être en train de* + infinitive can be used in the imperfect to emphasize the continuity of the action. It cannot be used with the past perfect.

  J'étais en train de travailler quand il est venu.
  I was working when he came.

- Expression of an action started in the past and continuing up to the present

  To express the idea that an action is started in the past and continued up to the present, a sentence must be constructed according to rigorous rules. By observing the following examples in English and in French you will see that the two languages use a different system to convey this idea.

1. At the beginning of the sentence an expression of time must be used, such as:

   Voilà ... que + verb
   Cela fait ... que + verb
   Il y a ... que + verb
   (It has been ... that)

2. These expressions are followed by the indication of the length of the period during which something has, or has not, taken place.

   Voilà trois jours que je travaille.
   (*lit.* It has been three days that I am working.)
   I have been working for three days.

   The verb indicates what has or has not taken place.

3. The tense of the verb indicates the moment when the action did or did not take place.

   Present: *Voilà dix jours qu'il travaille à son livre.* (up to the present time)

   Past: (up to a moment in the past)

   Il y avait dix jours qu'il travaillait à son livre quand... (imperfect)
   It had been ten days that he had worked on his book when...

   Il y a eu huit jours aujourd'hui qu'il n'a pas travaillé. (past perfect)
   (*lit.* It has been eight days today that he has not worked.)
   As of today, he has not worked for eight days.

   Cela faisait huit jours qu'il n'avait pas travaillé. (imperfect and pluperfect)
   (*lit.* It had been eight days that he had not worked.)
   He had not been working for eight days.

• Uses of *depuis* (since)

Depuis + expression of time is used to mark the beginning of a period during which something has or hasn't happened, and its ending in the present time.

Je ne l'ai pas vu depuis huit jours.
I have not seen him in eight days.
Il travaille à son livre depuis trois mois.
He has been working on his book for three months.

The tense used is the present to indicate that the action is still going on or the past perfect to indicate that the time past is a definite period terminating with the moment mentioned.

System of Tenses

When a sentence starts with a verb in the past, all the subsequent verbs in the sentence must be in one of the past tenses.

Il a dit qu'il faisait beau.
He said the weather was fine.

EXERCISES

I. Identify the infinitive of the following verbs. Write the imperfect form of the verb for the odd numbers and the past perfect form for the even numbers.

1. tu finis
2. je souris
3. je connais
4. ils font
5. il comprend
6. ils s'arrêtent
7. nous voyons
8. j'entre
9. vous engagez
10. nous partons
11. ils appellent
12. tu es
13. elle a
14. elle aperçoit
15. vous buvez

II. Fill in the blanks with the imperfect form of the verb given. Each verb expresses a condition without given limits of time.

1. Je ______ (finir) mon voyage quand il est venu.
2. Le voyage ______ (ne pas être) très long.
3. Mais ______ (il y a) des moments très intéressants.
4. Pendant la journée nous ______ (marcher) dans la forêt.
5. C'______ (être) fatigant mais très beau.
6. Le soir nous ______ (se reposer) et nous ______ (manger) un bon dîner.
7. Les membres du groupe ______ (porter) de gros sacs.
8. Un garçon ______ (faire) des remarques très amusantes.
9. Les jours ______ (passer) vite.
10. Et le dernier jour ______ (arriver). Il ______ (falloir) retourner en ville.

III. Fill in the blanks with the past perfect. Each action is given as started and finished.

1. Hier je ______ (revenir) et mon ami ______ (venir) me voir.
2. Je lui ______ (dire): le voyage ______ (ne pas être) très long.

3. Mais ______ (il y a) des moments très intéressants.
4. Chaque (every) jour, nous ______ (marcher) dans la forêt.
5. Ça ______ (être) fatigant mais très beau.
6. Le soir nous ______ (se reposer) et nous ______ (manger) un bon dîner.
7. Les jours______ (passer) vite.
8. Le dernier jour ______ (arriver) et il ______ (falloir) revenir en ville.

LESSON THREE

DIALOGUE

Conversation Sur Quelques Détails Pratiques

LOUISE: Je crois que j'ai fait une petite sieste. Il fait très chaud dans cet avion. Merci, mademoiselle. Je prendrai bien un verre d'eau. Un grand verre d'eau gazeuse. Ah! Elle est bien fraîche.

PAUL: Ah! Voilà les nouvelles sur l'écran. Et la météo!

LOUISE: Il fait beau, à Paris?

L'HOTESSE: Oui, madame, il fait du soleil et la température est de 24°.

LOUISE: 24°? Au mois de juin? Il gèle, il neige?

L'HOTESSE: Non, madame, le soleil brille, avec quelques nuages. Et 24 degrés est une température très agréable en centigrades, parce qu'il gèle à la température de 0° et l'eau boût à la tempèrature de 100°.

LOUISE: Est-ce qu'il ne donnent pas la température en Fahrenheit en France? Est-ce qu'on peut trouver un thermomètre en Fahrenheit?

L'HOTESSE: Peut-être au BHV. Ils ont tout au BHV!

LOUISE: Le BHV?

L'HOTESSE: C'est un des Grands Magasins de Paris. C'est le Bazar de l'Hôtel de Ville, sur la place de l'Hôtel de Ville, qui est la Mairie de Paris et non pas un hôtel.

Conversation On Several Practical Details

LOUISE: I think that I took a nap. It is very warm on this plane. Thank you, miss. I would love a glass of water. A tall glass of sparkling water. Ah! It is nice and cool.

PAUL: Ah! There are news on the screen. And the weather report!

LOUISE: Good weather in Paris?

HOSTESS: Yes, Mrs., it is sunny and the temperature is 24°.

LOUISE: 24°? In June? It is freezing, it is snowing?

HOSTESS: No, Mrs., the sun shines, with a few clouds. And 24° is a very pleasant temperature in centigrades, because freezing is at 0° and water boils at 100°.

LOUISE: Don't they give temperatures in degrees Fahrenheit in France? Can one find a thermometer in Fahrenheit?

HOSTESS: Maybe at the BHV. They have everything at the BHV!

LOUISE: The BHV?

HOSTESS: It is one of the department stores in Paris. It is the Bazaar of the Hotel de Ville, on the square of the Hotel de Ville, which is the Paris town hall, and not a hotel.

LOUISE: On n'a pas apporté de thermomètre!

L'HOTESSE: Pour faire la conversion de centigrades en Fahrenheit, c'est très simple. 10° au-dessus de O° C sont équivalents à 18° Fahrenheit au-dessus de 32° F. Vous changez 10° en 18°, et vous ajoutez 32°. Pour 24° vous avez deux fois et demi 10°, donc deux fois 18° plus 9°. 45° plus 32° font 77 degrés F. Un temps agréable pour une promenade!

PAUL: Ah! Maintenant c'est à 26° C.

LOUISE: Tu comprends, Paul?

PAUL: Oui. Les Français ne font pas les choses comme les autres!

L'HOTESSE: Ou le contraire, cher monsieur, le contraire.

LOUISE: Ah! Oui, c'est vrai! Et les autres mesures?

L'HOTESSE: Toutes différentes! Toutes du système métrique!

PAUL: Ah, oui je sais, les kilomètres, les kilogrammes, les litres, les demi-litres...

LOUISE: Et les mesures pour les vêtements? Pour les chaussures?

L'HOTESSE: Oui, madame, les tailles du 36 au 54, les pointures pour les chaussures... Mais ne vous inquiétez pas, dans les Grands Magasins, Le Printemps, Les Galeries Lafayettes, ils vous donneront des feuilles avec tous les renseignements nécessaires.

LOUISE: We did not bring a thermometer!

HOSTESS: Making the conversion from centigrades to Fahrenheit is very simple. Each 10° Celsius above O° are equivalent to 18° Fahrenheit above 32° F. So you add two blocks of 18° starting with 32° for the same number of blocks of 10° C. For 24° you have twice 10° and one half, so twice 18° plus 9°. 45° plus 32° F gives you 77° F. Good weather for a walk!

PAUL: Ah! Now it is 26° C.

LOUISE: You understand, Paul?

PAUL: Yes. The French do not do things like everybody else!

HOSTESS: On the contrary, dear sir, on the contrary.

LOUISE: Ah! Yes, that's true! And the other measuring units?

HOSTESS: All different! All in the metric system!

PAUL: Ah, yes I know, kilometers, kilograms, liters, half-liters...

LOUISE: And sizes for clothes? For shoes?

HOSTESS: Yes, Mrs., sizes from 36 to 54, and for shoes... But don't worry, in the big department stores, Le Printemps, Les Galeries Lafayettes, they will give you leaflets with all the necessary information.

VOCABULARY

ajoutez	add
au-dessus de	above
au mois	in the month
autres, les *m.*	others
autres mesures, les *f.*	other measurements
boût	boils
brille	is shining
c'est vrai	it is true
cet avion	this plane
changez	you change
chaussures, les *f.*	shoes
choses, les *f.*	things
comme	as
contraire, le *m.*	opposite
conversion, la *f.*	conversion
dans	in
de 24°	is 24°
demi-litres	half-liters
deux fois	twice
du 36 au 54	from 36 to 54
écran, l' *m.*	screen
en centigrades	in centigrades
est-ce que	is (question)
et demi	and a half
feuilles, des *f.*	papers, leaflets
font	make
fraîche	fresh
gazeuse	bubbly
Grand Magasin, le *m.*	department store
Hôtel de Ville, l' *m.*	town hall
il fait beau	the weather is fine

il fait chaud	it is hot
il fait du soleil	the sun is shining
il gèle	it is freezing
il neige	it is snowing
ils vous donneront	they will give you
j'ai fait	I took
je crois	I believe
je prendrai bien	I would like
je sais	I know
juin	June
kilomètres, les *m.*	kilometers
litres, les *m.*	liters
mairie, la *f.*	town hall
météo, la *f.*	weather report
ne font pas	do not do
ne vous inquiétez pas	don't worry
nécessaires	necessary
nouvelles, les *f.*	news
nuages, les *m.*	clouds
on n'a pas apporté	we did not bring
on peut	one can
petite	short
place, la *f.*	square
pointures, les *f.*	shoe sizes
pour faire	to make
quelques	a few
renseignements, les *m.*	information
sieste, la *f.*	siesta, nap
simple	simple
soleil, le *m.*	sun
système métrique, le *m.*	metric system
tailles, les *f.*	sizes
température, la *f.*	temperature
tout	everything
toutes différentes	all different

très	very
trouver	to find
tu comprends	you understand
verre d'eau, un *m.*	(a) glass of water
vêtements, les *m.*	clothing

GRAMMAR

Personal Pronouns

Personal pronouns replace nouns as objects of verbs and are placed before the verb.

Direct and Indirect Objects

In a sentence a verb is followed by one or several nouns called "objects" of this verb.

Il donne le livre à son ami.
He gives the book to his friend.

- When the noun follows the verb without a preposition the noun is a direct object.
- When there is a preposition, as in *à son ami*, the object is an indirect object.
- When the noun has been expressed, if it has to be repeated a personal pronoun is used in its place. This personal pronoun is placed between the subject and the verb.

  Il donne le livre (d.o.) *à son ami* (i.o.).
  Il le (d.o.) *lui* (i.o.) *donne.*

Personal pronouns represent the word they replace so they have to be of the same gender and number.

- In compound tenses, the past participle agrees with the direct object pronoun placed before the verb.

FORMS

Direct and indirect objects:

	1st person	*2nd person*
sg.	me	te
pl.	nous	vous

These pronouns are used as reflexive pronouns or as ordinary pronouns to represent direct or indirect objects.

	3rd person: Reflexive	*Non-reflexive d.o.*	*Non-reflexive i.o.*
sg.	se	le (*m.*)/la (*f.*)	lui
pl.	se	les (*m./f.*)	leur

Object of place: *y*
Object with preposition *de*: *en*

CONSTRUCTIONS

The form chosen to represent the noun (*d.o.*) must be placed immediately before the verb. In the interrogative construction it must also stay before the verb. (See chart below.)

Il donne le livre à son amie.
He gives the book to his friend.

Il le lui donne.
He gives it to her. (*lit.* he it to her gives)

Le lui donne-t-il?
Does he give it to her? (*lit.* it to her does give he)

Note: The object pronoun is never placed after the verb as it is in English.

Order of Object Pronouns

This order is always followed in a sentence, although not all of these types of pronouns will be included: subject, object, direct object, indirect object.

je	me	le	lui	y	en
tu	te	la	leur		
il/elle	se	les			
nous	nous				
vous	vous				
ils/elles	se				

Pronoun Y

Y replaces an object with the preposition *à* that refers to a thing.

Il est à Paris. Il y est.
He is in Paris. He is there.

Il ajoute ce livre à ses autres livres.
He adds this book to his other books.
Il y ajoute ce livre.
He adds this book to them.

Pronoun EN

En replaces any object with the preposition *de* that refers to a thing. There is no agreement between *en* and the past participle.

Il a acheté des pommes.
He bought some apples.
Il en a acheté. (no agreement)
He bought some.

Il revient de Paris.
He is back from Paris.
Il en revient.
He comes back from there.

Tu parles de ton voyage.
You speak of your trip.
J'en parle.
I speak of it.

CONSTRUCTION

En must be placed before the verb when the object of the verb is an expression of quantity in which the noun is understood but not expressed.

J'ai acheté des pommes. Combien? J'en ai acheté six.
I bought some apples. How many? I bought six (of them).

Nous avons un peu de lait. Non, nous en avons assez.
We have a little milk left. No, we have enough.

Avez-vous un parapluie? Non, je n'en ai pas!
Do you have an umbrella? No, I don't have one!

The best way to learn this construction is to listen to French people speaking and to hear the *en*, that is placed automatically in front of the verb when it is used to denote a quantity after it. This is done even when the object is *un*.

J'ai besoin d'un crayon. En voilà un.
I need a pencil. Here is one.

There are many idiomatic expressions that are formed with *y* and *en*. Some examples of these are:

vas-y, allez-y – go for it, start
y compris – including
ça y est – that's it, it's done
s'y faire – to resign oneself, to accept
s'y prendre bien/mal – to go about it well/badly
s'en aller – to go, to leave
en avoir assez (de) – to have had enough (of)
s'en faire – to worry (about something)
ne plus en pouvoir – to be at the end of one's rope
s'en tirer – to get out of a difficult situation

Construction with the Imperative Verb Form

Affirmative verb form: imperative verb + pronoun

Donne-moi ce livre.
Give me this book.

Disjunctive pronouns are used with the imperative verb form:

	singular	*plural*
1st	moi (d.o./i.o.)	nous (*m./f.*) (d.o./i.o.)
2nd	toi (d.o./i.o.)	vous (*m./f.*) (d.o./i.o.)
3rd	le (*m.*)/la (*f.*) (d.o.)	les (*m./f.*) (d.o.)
	lui (*m./f.*) (i.o.)	leur (*m./f.*) (i.o.)

These pronouns follow the imperative verb and are preceded by any other pronouns, except *en*. The affirmative imperative is the only case when *me* and *te* become *moi* and *toi*.

Donne les moi. Donne les lui. Donne les leur.
Give them to me. Give them to him/her. Give them to them.

The pronoun *en* replacing an expression with *de* or *des* is always placed last.

Donne moi de ça. – Give me some of that.
Donne m'en. Donne lui en. Donne t'en.
Give me some. Give him some. Give yourself some.

Note: *Moi* becomes *m'* in front of a vowel.

Negative Form

In the negative imperative the pronouns stay in front of the verb and the order of object pronouns is the same as in the normal conjugation of the verb.

Ne m'en donne pas. – Don't give me any.
Ne le lui dis pas. – Don't tell him.

EXERCISES

I. Place the pronoun with the verb.

1. Je veux (le)
2. Je ne veux pas (les)
3. Veux-tu? (en)
4. Donne (lui)
5. As-tu parlé? (lui)
6. N'as-tu pas parlé? (lui)
7. Il va dire (le)
8. Il ne va pas dire (les)
9. Je prends (lui) (la)
10. Je ne prends pas (lui) (la)
11. Ils ont vu (y) (le)
12. Ils n'ont pas vu (y) (le)
13. Parlez (moi)
14. Mettez (me) (en)
15. Elle a pris (y) (en)
16. Elle n'a pas pris (y) (en)

II. Translate the following sentences placing the pronouns in the right order, according to the pattern given.

Les belles photos de nos vacances.

1. I give them to him.
2. I don't give them to him.
3. I give some of them (*en*) to them.
4. Give some to him.
5. He gives some to us.
6. He does not give any to them.
7. Does he give you some?
8. He does not give me any.

III. Write a short sentence to answer the questions, replacing at least one word with a pronoun.

1. Etes-vous à la maison?
2. Aime-t-elle le coq au vin?
3. Allez-vous parler à votre ami?
4. A-t-elle parlé de son projet à ses amis?

5. Vas-tu nous présenter ton père?
6. Voulez-vous un pain au chocolat?
7. Voulez-vous un gateau aux amandes?
8. Vas-tu aller en ville avec tes camarades?
9. Croyons-nous son histoire?
10. Combien de francs as-tu maintenant?

IV. Replace the underlined words by a pronoun and place the pronoun according to the rule.

1. Donne-lui ce livre.
2. Donne-le à ton ami.
3. Venez leur raconter cette histoire (*f.*).
4. Dites-moi votre nom.
5. Chantez-nous des chansons.
6. Allons chercher des tomates.
7. Venez à mon magasin.
8. Envoyez-moi des lettres.
9. Ne donnez pas de bonbon à cette enfant.
10. Ecris une lettre à tes amis.

V. Change the negative imperative to the affirmative form, placing the pronouns according to the rule.

1. Ne vous en allez pas.
2. Ne nous y envoyez pas.
3. Ne la lui disons pas.
4. Ne lui en faisons pas.
5. Ne nous la demande pas.
6. Ne vous en occupez pas.
7. Ne m'en donne pas une.
8. Ne les lui prends pas.
9. Ne me les laissez pas.
10. Ne leur en prenez pas.

LESSON FOUR

DIALOGUE

Arrivée A Roissy

PAUL: Tu vois quelque chose?

LOUISE: De la campagne, mais très vague.

PAUL: Dis-moi quand tu verras la Tour Eiffel.

ROBERT: Non, c'est regrettable, vous n'allez pas voir la Tour Eiffel. L'aéroport Charles de Gaulle est au nord de Paris, sur la route vers Lille, et à coté de la ville de Senlis. Donc on ne voit pas Paris depuis les airs. Et en allant à Paris depuis Roissy, la ville de l'aéroport, on ne voit pas la Tour Eiffel non plus. On voit des gratte-ciel avant d'arriver en ville, mais rien de vraiment intéressant. Sauf peut-être que le bus passe près de l'aéroport du Bourget...

LOUISE: Le Bourget, c'est quoi?

ROBERT: C'est là que Charles Lindberg a atterri, en 1927, venant de New York dans son avion The Spirit of St. Louis, la première traversée de l'Atlantique en avion.

PAUL: Ah! Extraordinaire! Et nous, quand nous atterrissons, tout à l'heure, qu'est-ce que nous faisons?

ROBERT: Oui, c'est un peu bizarre. Il faut faire très attention aux plaques avec les flèches. Vous aurez un long corridor qui descend, qui est un tapis roulant. Puis vous avez une file d'attente devant le contrôle des passeports. Au-dessus des guichets une plaque dit: EU Nationaux, citoyens de l'union européene, et une autre plaque dit Non EU Nationaux. C'est pour vous. Le douanier met un tampon avec la date d'entrée sur votre passeport. Et ça y est, vous êtes en France!

Arrival At Roissy

PAUL: You see something?

LOUISE: Countryside, but very vague.

PAUL: Tell me when you see the Eiffel Tower.

ROBERT: No, it's too bad, but you are not going to see the Eiffel Tower. The Charles de Gaulle airport is north of Paris, on the road to Lille and close to the city of Senlis. So you do not see Paris from the air. And going to Paris from Roissy, the village next to the airport, you do not see the Eiffel Tower either. You see some big skyscrapers before getting into town, but nothing really interesting. Except perhaps that the bus drives close to Le Bourget airport…

LOUISE: Le Bourget, what is that?

ROBERT: That is where Charles Lindberg landed, in 1927, coming from New York with his plane The Spirit of St. Louis, the first crossing of the Atlantic by plane.

PAUL: Ah! Extraordinary! And for us, when we land, very shortly, what do we do?

ROBERT: Yes, it is a little strange. You must pay great attention to the signs with arrows. You will have a long downhill corridor with a walking escalator. Then you have a line of people waiting for passport control. One sign above the booths says EU Nationals, citizens of the European Union, and another sign says Non EU Nationals. That's for you. The officer stamps your passport with the date of entry. And that's it, you are in France!

PAUL: Et après on va prendre nos bagages. Et après? Pour aller à Paris?

ROBERT: Vous avez de grosses valises?

PAUL: Oui, assez grosses!

ROBERT: Alors, il faut prendre l'autobus. Vous sortez avec votre chariot et vous allez prendre votre billet que vous devez payer en francs, bien sur. Dans quel hôtel avez-vous des réservations?

LOUISE: C'est dans l'hôtel Ibis, rue des Plantes, dans le XIVème arrondissement.

ROBERT: Alors il faut prendre l'autobus pour Montparnasse. Il s'arrête à coté de la Gare Montparnasse et ensuite vous prenez un taxi. L'Ibis n'est pas loin.

PAUL: Et ça y est, on va descendre. Mais j'ai tellement soif! Et toi aussi, Laura? Ah! L'hôtesse nous apporte un verre d'eau. Merci, madame! Et au revoir monsieur, et merci des renseignements.

PAUL: And after that we go to get our luggage. And after that? To get to Paris?

ROBERT: Do you have heavy suitcases?

PAUL: Yes, quite heavy!

ROBERT: Then you should take the bus. You go out with your cart and you go to take your ticket, which you must pay for in francs of course. In what hotel do you have reservations?

PAUL: At the Hotel Ibis, on the "Street of the Plants" in the 14th Arrondissement.

ROBERT: Then you must take the bus for Montparnasse. It stops close to the Montparnasse train station and then you take a taxi. The Ibis is not far from there.

PAUL: And that's it, we are about to land. But I am so thirsty! And you too, Louise? Ah! The hostess is bringing us a glass of water. Thank you, *madame*! And good-bye, *monsieur*, and thank you for all the information.

VOCABULARY

a atterri	landed
à coté de	beside, close to
aéroport, l' *m.*	airport
airs, les *m.*	the air
arrondissement, un *m.*	(a) section (of a city)
assez	quite
au nord de	to the north of
autobus, l' *m.*	bus
billet, le *m.*	ticket
ça y est	that's it
campagne, la *f.*	countryside
ces guichets-là	those windows/booths
c'est là que	this is where
c'est pour vous	it is for you
c'est quoi	it is what
chariot, le *m.*	cart
contrôle des passeports, le *m.*	passport control
dans quel hôtel	in what hotel
date d'entrée, la *f.*	date of entry
de grosses valises	heavy suitcases
depuis	from
des réservations	reservations
descend	go down
devant	in front of
dis-moi	tell me
donc	so
douanier	customs officer
en allant à	going to
en avion	by airplane
ensuite	after that
et après	and afterwards

et après?	and then?
extraordinaire	extraordinary
faire attention	to pay attention
file d'attente, une *f.*	(a) waiting line
flèches, les *f.*	arrows
gare, la *f.*	train station
guichets, les *m.*	windows/booths
il faut	it is necessary
il s'arrête	he stops
j'ai tellement soif	I am so thirsty
la ville de	the city of
long corridor, un *m.*	(a) long corridor
mais	but
met	puts
n'est pas loin	is not far
Nationaux, les *m.*	residents
non plus	neither
nos bagages	our luggage
nous atterrissons	we land
nous faisons	we do
on ne voit pas	one does not see/we do not see
on va prendre	you go to take
plaque, la *f.*	sign
première, la *f.*	the first
près de	close to
puis	then
quand	when
quelque chose	something
qu'est-ce que	what is it that
regrettable	too bad
rue, la *f.*	street
sur la route	on the road
tampon, un *m.*	(a) stamp
tapis roulant, un *m.*	(a) moving sidewalk
Tour Eiffel, la *f.*	Eiffel Tower

tout à l'heure	in a short time
traversée, la *f.*	crossing
très	very
tu verras	you will see
tu vois	you see
un peu	(a) little
vague	vague
venant de	coming from
vers	toward
votre	your
vous aurez	you will have
vous n'allez pas voir	you are not going to see
vous sortez	you go out

GRAMMAR

Articles

There are three categories of articles: the definite article (le, la, les), the indefinite article (un, une, des) and the partitive article (du, de la, des). These articles indicate the gender of the noun, masculine or feminine.

FORMS

	masculine	*feminine*
sg.	le, un, du (de + le)	la, une, de la
pl.	les, des (de + les)	les, des

Note: à + le = au
à + les = aux

USES

These forms of the article are used to express two very different ideas.

The Definite Article

le (*m.*), la (*f.*), les (*pl.*) (*m./f.*)

This form is used to indicate that you are giving the noun following it a general and total meaning.

La liberté est nécéssaire.
Liberty is necessary.

Les pommes sont bonnes pour nous.
Apples are good for us.

This second example refers to everything called apple. You will notice that in English there is no article used for this meaning.

La pomme rouge est belle.
The red apple is beautiful.

Uses

The definite article is used for:

- Designating a person or object that is singled out in its category: *passez moi le verre* (pass me the glass).

- Titles: *Le Président de la République* (The President of the Republic), *Monsieur le Directeur* (Mister the Director) but: not before *monsieur, madame, mademoiselle.*

- Before geographical names of mountains, rivers, etc.: *Le Mont Blanc, La Seine.*

- Before names of languages or disciplines: *la biologie, la chimie; le français, le russe.*

- Before the names of the seasons: *le printemps, l'hiver* (spring, winter).

- To indicate the price of something by measure or weight: *les pommes coûtent 15 francs le kilo* (apples cost 15 francs a kilo).

- To give a date: *c'est le 15 mars* (it's the fifteenth of March).

- Before the name of the days of the week in the expression of an habitual action: *il se promène le samedi* (he takes a walk on Saturdays).

The Indefinite and Partitive Articles

un (*m.*), une (*f.*), du (*m.*), de la (*f.*), des (*pl.*) (*m./f.*)

These forms of the article are used every time you select a certain amount out of the whole represented by the noun.

J'achète une voiture.
I am buying a car.

Tu achètes des pommes.
You buy apples.

Tu lui donnes de l'affection.
You give her love.

You will notice that in English there is no article for this meaning.

CONSTRUCTIONS WITH *DE*

- After a negative verb the partitives *des, du, de la* become *de.*

  Il ne mange pas de pommes.
  He doesn't eat any apples.

- After all expressions of quantity:

  adverbs: beaucoup de (many), peu de (few), combien de (how many), etc.
  nouns: famille (family), classe (class), sac (bag), masse (mass), douzaine (dozen), etc.
  adjectives: plein de (full of), couvert de (covered with), rempli de (filled with), etc.

verbs: garnir de (to fill up), combler de (to fill to the brim), remplir de (to fill with), etc.

Note: In English many of these expressions use "with" for these meanings. In French *de* is used and never *avec* (with).

- Before a noun which is the object of another noun and gives the quality of that noun:

  une maison de pierre – a house made of stone
  le livre de lecture – the book used for reading

- Before a noun preceded by an adjective:

  il m'a donné des fleurs rouges – he gave me (some) red flowers
  But: *il m'a donné de belles fleurs* – he gave me beautiful flowers

EXERCISES

I. Place the correct article before the following nouns, indicating if they are masculine or feminine.

definite article

1. livre
2. autobus
3. trains
4. composition
5. activité
6. chapeau
7. cousines
8. vie
9. homme
10. eau

indefinite article

1. livres
2. chapeaux
3. soleil
4. action
5. bonheur
6. temps
7. bonté
8. sourires
9. confiance
10. amitiés

II. In the following sentences, fill in the blanks with the correct article.

1. Tu prends _______ pomme.
2. Tu prends _______ livre qui est sur la table.
3. Il prend _______ légumes pour le diner.
4. _______ tomates sont bonnes pendant _______ été.
5. _______ français est _______ langue difficile.
6. _______ Français aiment beaucoup _______ bon vin.
7. Nous n'avons pas _______ lait ni _______ café.
8. _______ samedi, nous faisons _______ longue promenade.
9. J'aime _______ promenades quand _______ temps est beau.
10. Ne prenons pas _______ tomates!

11. La table est couverte ______ fruits divers.
12. Une famille ______ lapins mange ______ salade dans ______ jardin.

III. Translate into French.

1. Take an apple.
2. Don't buy tomatoes.
3. On Saturday we do not work.
4. Do you like vegetables?
5. Do you eat vegetables?
6. The weather is good for a walk.
7. In summer we take walks.
8. Do you like wine?

LESSON FIVE

DIALOGUE

A l'Hôtel Ibis

PAUL: Nous voilà à Paris. Je trouve cet hôtel agréable et notre chambre ouvre sur la cour intérieure. Ce sera très calme.

LOUISE: Mais où sommes-nous dans Paris? Nous sommes près de quoi?

PAUL: Voici une carte. Et voilà la Rue des Plantes. Veux-tu aller à la Place d'Alésia? Il doit y avoir des restaurants. Demain, nous achèterons le Guide Michelin; le rouge pour les restaurants, et le vert pour les monuments. Ton père nous l'a recommandé. Pour ce soir, partons à la découverte.

Ils marchent en se tenant par la main. Ils regardent les plaques bleues au coin de chaque rue.

PAUL: Regarde! Rue d'Alésia! Et la Place? Tout droit? A droite? A gauche? Je vais demander à ce monsieur: Pardon, monsieur, la Place d'Alésia, s'il vous plaît?

MONSIEUR: Je ne suis pas du quartier, mais je crois que c'est là-bas. A droite et puis tout droit.

LOUISE: Il faut faire attention pour retrouver notre hôtel.

PAUL: Nous demanderons notre chemin. Ça marche!

LOUISE: Beaucoup de magasins! Tous fermés à cette heure. Oh! Regarde ce manteau!

At the Ibis Hotel

PAUL: Here we are in Paris. I find this hotel pleasant and our room opens on the inside courtyard. It will be very quiet.

LOUISE: But where are we in Paris? What are we close to?

PAUL: Here is a map. And here is the Rue des Plantes. Do you want to go to the Place d'Alésia? There must be some restaurants there. Tomorrow we will buy the Guide Michelin; the red one for the restaurants and the green one for the monuments. Your father recommended it. For tonight, let's go and explore.

They walk holding hands. They look at the blue plaques at the corner of each street.

PAUL: Look! Rue d'Alésia! And the square? Straight ahead? To the right? To the left? I am going to ask this gentleman: Excuse me, *monsieur*, the Place d'Alésia, please?

MONSIEUR: Well, I do not live around here, but I think it is over there. To your right and then straight ahead.

LOUISE: We must pay attention to how to get back to our hotel.

PAUL: We will ask our way. It works!

LOUISE: Many stores! All closed at this hour. Oh! Look at this coat!

PAUL: Et voilà un café avec une terrasse!

LOUISE: La place d'Alésia! Quelle circulation! Toutes ces voitures!

PAUL: Et un restaurant qui a l'air bien. Tiens, ils mettent le menu dehors. On peut lire et décider si on aime la nourriture qu'ils offrent.

LOUISE: Et aussi combien elle coûte. Regarde, il y a un petit restaurant italien à côté! Des pâtes, de la pizza...

PAUL: Mais nous sommes en France! Notre premier soir en France!

LOUISE: Ça ne t'impressionne pas ces hommes avec leur costume noir, leur tablier blanc, et ces assiettes garnies qu'ils portent sur leurs mains?

PAUL: Comme dans les images de La Belle Epoque! C'est notre Belle Epoque! Allons-y!

Paul prend une bavette de boeuf aux échalottes et Louise une sole normande avec de la crème. Pour dessert, une Tarte Tatin, puis deux express. Ils rentrent à leur hôtel après une promenade tranquille.

PAUL: And here is a café with a terrace!

LOUISE: The Alésia square! Look at the traffic! All these cars!

PAUL: And a restaurant that seems all right. Look, they put a menu outside. We can read and decide if we like the food they offer.

LOUISE: And also how much it costs. Look, there is a small Italian restaurant next door! Pasta, pizza...

PAUL: But we are in France! Our first evening in France!

LOUISE: They do not seem intimidating to you, these men with their black suits, their long white aprons and those well-garnished plates they carry on their hands?

PAUL: As in the paintings of the Belle Epoque! It is our own Belle Epoque! Let's go in!

Paul takes a skirt steak with shallots and Louise a sole Normand style, baked in cream. For dessert, a Tarte Tatin, then two espressos. They return to their hotel after a leisurely walk.

VOCABULARY

à	in
acheter	to buy
agréable	pleasant
aller à	to go to
aller à la découverte	to explore
Belle Epoque, la *f.*	(1895–1910)
carte, la *f.*	map
ce	this
cet	this (in front of a vowel)
chambre, la *f.*	room
chemin, le *m.*	way, path
circulation, la *f.*	traffic
coin, le *m.*	corner
cour, la *f.*	courtyard
dans	in
demain	tomorrow
des Plantes	of the Plants
doit y avoir	there must be
droit	straight
et	and
être	to be
faire attention	to pay attention
fermés	closed
gauche, la *f.*	left (direction)
guide Michelin, le *m.*	Michelin guidebook
hôtel, l' *m.*	hotel
il	there
il y a	there are
images, les *f.*	images, paintings
intérieure	interior
intimidant	intimidating
je	I

l'(e)	it
magasins, les *m.*	stores
mais	but
manteau, le *m.*	coat
monuments, les *m.*	monuments
notre	our
nourriture, la *f.*	food
nous	we
nous voilà	here we are
où	where
ouvrir	to open
partir	to go
père, le *m.*	father
place, la *f.*	town square
pour	for
près de	near
quoi	what
recommander	to recommend
regarde	look
restaurants, des *m.*	some restaurants
rouge, le *m.*	the red one
rue, la *f.*	street
se tenant par la main	holding hands
soir, le *m.*	evening
sur	on
Tarte Tatin	(a type of apple pie)
ton	your
tranquille	leisurely, calm
trouver	to find
tu	you
vert, le *m.*	the green one
voici	here is
voilà	there is
vouloir	to want
y	there

GRAMMAR

Interrogative Words and Constructions

The simplest way of forming an interrogative sentence is to place the expression *est-ce que...* (*lit.* is it that...) at the beginning of a declarative sentence.

Il chante une chanson d'amour.
He sings a love song.
Est-ce qu'il chante une chanson d'amour?
Is he singing a love song?

Note: The interrogative construction is always placed at the beginning of the sentence and all the verbs that follow retain the plain declarative form:

Est-ce que	il chante?
[interrogative]	[declarative]
Récite-t-il le poême	qu'il a appris?
[interrogative]	[declarative]

Is he reciting the poem that he learned?

Interrogative Construction

I. subject of the verb: a pronoun

The subject pronoun goes after the verb.

ELLE chante une chanson.
Interr. *Chante-t-elle une chanson?*

II. subject of the verb: a noun

When the subject of the sentence is a noun, this noun is placed in front of the verb and a subject pronoun agreeing with the noun subject must be placed after the verb.

MARIE chante une chanson.
Interr. *Marie chante-t-elle une chanson?*

Indirect Interrogation

Certain verbs are used to ask a question indirectly. In this case the interrogative word is *si*, the equivalent of the English "if."

Je demande si vous êtes d'accord avec moi.
I ask if you agree with me.

Interrogative Pronouns: qui and que

The two interrogative pronouns *qui* (who) and *que* (what) ask a question about:

QUI...? A person. *Qui êtes-vous?* – Who are you?
QUE...? A thing. *Que chantez-vous?* – What do you sing?

These pronouns are invariable.

- *Qui* can be preceded by a preposition.

Avec qui êtes-vous parti? – With whom did you leave?

- *Qui* can be the object of the verb.

  Qui avez-vous rencontré? – Who did you meet?
  Par qui êtes-vous envoyé? – By whom are you sent?

- *Que*: *Qu'est-ce que c'est?* – What is it?

- When *que* is preceded by a preposition it becomes *quoi*.

  Pourquoi? – why?
  Avec quoi fais-tu cela? – With what do you do that?
  De quoi as-tu besoin? – What do you need?
  En quoi croyez-vous? – What do you believe in?

  Note: In French, a preposition is always placed before a noun or pronoun and can never be moved to the end of a sentence by itself.

  English: What do you do it with?
  French: Avec quoi le faites-vous?

Interrogative Adverbs

After the interrogative word, such as an adverb, the verb is always inverted when the subject is a pronoun: verb + subject. When the subject is a noun, the subject remains before the verb and a pronoun agreeing with the subject is placed after the verb.

Asking questions about:

Time: *Quand êtes-vous libre?* – When are you free?
Quand Marie est-elle libre? – When is Mary free?

Cause: *Pourquoi êtes-vous triste?* – Why are you sad?

Manner: *Comment êtes-vous arrivé?* – How did you arrive?

Place: *Où êtes-vous arrivé?* – Where did you arrive?

Measure: *Combien avez-vous payé?* – How much did you pay?

The interrogative construction of the verb is used in all cases.

Interrogative Adjective: quel

The interrogative adjective *quel* (what, which) precedes a noun to ask a question about it.

Quel jour êtes-vous arrivé?
What day did you arrive?

FORMS

m. sg.	QUEL	*m. pl.*	QUELS
f. sg.	QUELLE	*f. pl.*	QUELLES

The adjective agrees with the gender and number of the noun.

Quelles pommes avez-vous achetées?
Which apples did you buy?

Interrogative Pronoun: lequel

FORMS

m. sg.	LEQUEL	*m. pl.*	LESQUELS
f. sg.	LAQUELLE	*f. pl.*	LESQUELLES

These pronouns are composed of the article + *quel*. So when they are preceded by the preposition *à* or *de*, the preposition combines with the article.

de + lequel = duquel
à + lequel = auquel

This pronoun is used to ask a question about a choice expressed by a noun. The pronoun must agree with the noun expressing the choice.

Voici des fleurs. <u>Lesquelles</u> sont pour vous?
Here are the flowers. Which ones are for you?

Interrogative Expressions with Relative Pronouns

Persons: Qui est-ce qui...
Qui est-ce que...
preposition + qui est-ce que...

Things: Qu'est-ce qui...
Qu'est-ce que...

The rules given in the preceding paragraphs apply to these expressions:

<u>Qui</u>: interrogative pronoun for persons

- Qui est-ce qui...

  Qui est-ce qui vous ennuie? – Who is it that annoys you?

  The second *qui* is a relative pronoun and the subject of the verb that follows.

  Qui est-ce qui est à la porte?
  Who is it who is at the door?

- Qui est-ce que...

  Que is the relative pronoun direct object form and must be the direct object of the verb that follows it.

  Qui est-ce que j'entends à la porte?
  Who is it that I hear at the door?

Que: interrogative pronoun for things

- Qu'est-ce que...

  Qu'est-ce que vous achetez? – What is it that you are buying?
  Qu'achetez-vous? – What are you buying?

- Qu'est-ce qui...

  Qu'est-ce qui vous amuse?
  What is it that amuses you?

Constructions with Prepositions

The preposition must be placed at the beginning of the expression, just before the interrogative pronoun.

De qui est-ce que vous parlez?
About whom are you speaking?

A qui est-ce que vous parlez?
To whom are you talking?

De quoi parlez-vous?
What are you talking about?

EXERCISES

I. Turn the following sentences into interrogative sentences using *est-ce que...* for only one sentence.

1. Il invente beaucoup de machines.
2. La jeune fille a ouvert la fenêtre.
3. Tu n'as pas compris son intention.
4. Il ne pourra pas vous aider.
5. Elle ne le recommencera pas.
6. Vous n'y pensez plus maintenant.
7. L'exercice est très difficile.
8. Mes amis vont acheter cette maison.

II. Write questions to which the following sentences are an answer, using *quand*, *comment*, and other interrogative words.

1. Je serai à la bibliotheque dans une heure.
2. Nous partirons pour Paris.
3. Il va sortir à 9 heures.
4. Cette jeune fille part en ballon.
5. Cet homme a gagné des millions.
6. Mon camarade rentre ce soir.
7. Elle pleure parce qu'elle a perdu son chat.
8. Son père va très bien.

III. Use an interrogative pronoun matching the indication between parentheses at the beginning of each sentence.

1. ________ voyez-vous? (un homme)
2. ________ achètes-tu? (des oranges)
3. ________ parles-tu? (à)
4. ________ travaille-t-il? (pour M. Dupont)

5. ________ feras-tu cela? (avec cet instrument)
6. ________ mettez-vous cela? (dans une boîte)
7. ________ avez-vous confiance? (en un bon gouvernment)
8. ________ ne pouvez-vous pas travailler? (sans un bon stylo)

LESSON SIX

DIALOGUE

Deuxième Journée A Paris

PAUL: Qu'est-ce que tu veux faire aujourd'hui?

LOUISE: Ce que tu voudras, mais quelque chose d'intéressant.

PAUL: Bien sûr. Tu es fatiguée?

LOUISE: Non, j'ai bien dormi. Quelle heure est-il?

PAUL: Il est onze heures du matin!

LOUISE: Onze heures?

PAUL: Mais oui! Tu entends la cloche de l'église? ...trois, quatre, cinq, six, sept, huit, neuf, dix, onze. Elle sonne toute la journée comme ça?

LOUISE: Je crois qu'elle ne sonne pas pendant la nuit parce que moi, j'étais réveillée à cinq heures et je n'ai rien entendu avant huit heures. Mais ma montre disait: onze heures.

PAUL: Ça s'appelle le décalage horaire, n'est-ce pas? Nous avons sauté six heures de notre vie. Il est vraiment quelle heure?

LOUISE: A ma montre il est cinq heures, mais il faut que je la change. Nous sautons par dessus six heures et il est onze heures ici. Il faudra aller prendre un café et un croissant dans un bar. Je sais où il y en a un. Et le marchand de journaux est à côté. Nous achèterons un journal, le Figaro ou le Monde, et nous aurons l'air tout à fait français.

Second Day In Paris

Paul: What do you want to do today?

Louise: Whatever you want, but something interesting.

Paul: Of course. Are you tired?

Louise: No, I slept well. What time is it?

Paul: It is eleven o'clock!

Louise: Eleven?

Paul: Yes, of course! Do you hear the church bells? ...three, four, five, six, seven, eight, nine, ten, eleven. Do they ring all day like that?

Louise: I think that it does not ring during the night because I was awake at five o'clock, and I did not hear anything before eight. But my watch said: eleven.

Paul: This is called jet lag, isn't it? We skipped over six hours of our lives. What time is it really?

Louise: By my watch it is five o'clock but I must adjust it. We skip over six hours and it is eleven here. We should go to have a croissant and coffee in a bar. I know where there is one. And the newsstand is next to it. We will buy a newspaper, the Figaro or the Monde, and we will look totally French.

PAUL: Mais en retard sur l'horaire normal! Ecoute, voilà la cloche de l'église qui sonne encore.

LOUISE: Oui, un seul coup. Il est onze heures et demie. C'est pratique, ça! Et si l'on veut l'heure exacte, on peut téléphoner à l'horloge parlante. Elle te dira 'au quatrième top il sera exactement onze heures trentre quatre minutes' et tu mettras ta montre à l'heure.

PAUL: Et aussi notre pendulette de voyage. Demain matin nous serons sérieux et nous nous lèverons assez tôt pour avoir du temps dans la matinée. A huit heures du matin?

LOUISE: D'accord. C'est raisonnable. Et maintenant, quel temps fait-il dehors? Je vois du soleil, et je vois des nuages. Est-ce qu'il fait chaud? Est-ce qu'il fait froid? Il faut nous acheter un thermomètre. Mets ça sur une liste!

PAUL: Et traduire les centigrades en degrées Fahrenheit?

LOUISE: Bien sûr. Je veux savoir si j'ai besoin d'un tricot, d'une veste, d'un manteau...

PAUL: Ou d'un imperméable, et d'un parapluie. Voilà des nuages...

LOUISE: Eh bien, en route!

PAUL: But behind schedule! Listen, the church bell is ringing again.

LOUISE: Yes, one time only. It is half past eleven. How convenient! And if you want the exact time, you can telephone the talking clock. It will tell you "at the fourth beep it will be exactly thirty-four minutes past eleven" and you will set your watch at the right time.

PAUL: And also our travel clock. Tomorrow morning we will be serious and we will get up early enough to have time during the morning. At eight o'clock?

LOUISE: All right. It is reasonable. And now, what is the weather outside? I see sunshine and I see clouds. Is it warm? Is it cold? We must buy a thermometer. Put that on a list!

PAUL: And calculate centigrades into degrees Fahrenheit?

LOUISE: Of course. I want to know if I need a sweater, a jacket, a coat...

PAUL: Or a raincoat, and an umbrella. There are some clouds...

LOUISE: Well, let's go!

VOCABULARY

à l'heure	on time
acheter	to buy
au quatrième	at the fourth
aujourd'hui	today
avant	before
avoir besoin de	to need
bar, le *m.*	bar
bien	well
bien sûr	of course
ça	this, that
ce que	what
centigrades	centigrades
changer	to set it straight, change
cinq	five
cloche, la *f.*	bell
coup, le *m.*	stroke
croire	to believe
croissant, le *m.*	croissant
d'accord	all right
décalage horaire, le *m.*	jet lag
dehors	outside
demain	tomorrow
dire	to say
dix	ten
dormir	to sleep
du matin	in the morning
église, l' *f.*	church
en	in
en Fahrenheit	into Fahrenheit
en retard sur	late for, behind
en route	let's go

entendre	to hear
et demie	and a half
être fatigué	to be tired
être réveillé	to be awake
exact	exact
faire	to do
français	French
heures, les *f.*	hours
horaire, l' *m.*	schedule
horloge, l' *f.*	clock
huit	eight
il est	it is
il fait chaud	it is warm
il fait froid	it is cold
imperméable	raincoat
intéressant	interesting
journal, le *m.*	newspaper
la	it *f.*
manteau, le *m.*	coat
moi	I
montre, la *f.*	watch
n'est-ce pas?	isn't it so?
neuf	nine
normal	normal
notre vie	our life
nous	we
nuages, les *m.*	clouds
nuit, la *f.*	night
onze	eleven
ou	or
parapluie	umbrella
parce que	because
par-dessus	over
parlante	talking
pendant	during

pendulette, la *f.*	alarm clock
pratique	practical
qu'est-ce que...	what... (question)
quatre	four
quel temps fait-il	how is the weather
quelle heure	what time
quelque chose de	something
qui	which
raisonnable	reasonable
rien	nothing
s'appeler	to be called
sauter	to skip
se lever	to get up
sept	seven
sérieux	serious
si	if
six	six
soleil, le *m.*	sun
sonner	to strike, to ring
sur une liste	on a list
téléphoner à	to telephone
thermomètre, le *m.*	thermometer
top, un *m.*	beep, buzz, signal
tout à fait	entirely
toute la journée	all day long
traduire	to translate
tricot, le *m.*	sweater
trois	three
un seul	a single
veste, la *f.*	jacket
voir	to see
vouloir	to want
voyage, le *m.*	trip
vraiment	really

GRAMMAR

Relative Pronouns

Forms

Qui, Que – Dont
Who, Whom – Whose
Which – Of which
That

Relative pronouns are used, in English as in French, to link two sentences in which the same noun appears.

Paul est un charmant jeune homme.
Paul is a charming young man.
Paul est mon ami.
Paul is my friend.

Paul, qui est mon ami, est un charmant jeune homme.
Paul, who is my friend, is a charming young man.

J'attends mon amie Marie.
I am waiting for my friend Marie.
Mon amie Marie est une jeune fille intelligente.
My friend Marie is an intelligent young girl.

Mon amie Marie, que j'attends, est une jeune fille intelligente.
My friend Marie, who I am waiting for, is an intelligent young girl.

Qui – masculine, feminine, singular, plural – is used as the subject of the verb that follows it, or as the indirect object of the verb, preceded by a preposition.

Que – masculine, feminine, singular, plural – is used as the direct object of the verb that follows it.

Rules

The form of the relative pronoun to be used depends on the construction of the verb that follows it. Certain verbs are constructed with direct objects; these are marked as transitive (*tr.*) in dictionaries. Others take prepositions such as *à* or *de* and are marked as intransitive (*intr.*) in dictionaries.

attendre (*tr.*) – to wait
telephoner à (*intr.*) – to telephone someone
parler de (*intr.*) – to talk about someone or something

Relative Pronouns with Prepositions

qui – for persons
lequel, lesquels – for things (*m.*)
laquelle, lesquelles – for things (*f.*)
dont – for persons and things

The preposition is placed before the pronoun. The preposition depends on the construction of the verb that follows it.

Qui, lequel

- Persons

La personne à qui j'ai parlé n'est pas ici aujourd'hui.
The person I spoke to is not here today.

La personne pour qui j'ai travaillé n'est pas ici aujourd'hui.
The person for whom I worked is not here today.

La personne <u>*avec*</u> *qui j'ai travaillé n'est pas ici aujourd'hui.*
The person with whom I worked is not here today.

• Things

La maison que tu vois là-bas est la maison de mes parents.
The house (that) you see over there is the house of my parents.

La maison <u>*dans*</u> *laquelle j'habite est très confortable.*
The house in which I live is very comfortable.

La compagnie <u>*pour*</u> *laquelle je travaille est très petite.*
The company I work for is very small.

DONT – for persons and things

Replaces an object with *de*, whatever the meaning of the object.

Les questions dont il a parlé sont très importantes. (parler de)
The questions about which he talked are very important.

Les personnes dont elle a parlé sont très généreuses. (parler de)
The people she talked about are very generous.

RULE

In a sentence with two verbs the *relative pronoun* must always be used, with its preceding preposition when needed, before the second verb. The *preposition* cannot be placed at the end of the sentence, as it is in English, and the *relative pronoun* cannot be omitted. Practicing these constructions by repeating the above examples as many times as necessary will make you familiar with the proper construction.

Antecedents, or "what comes before"

A relative pronoun refers to the noun or pronoun that comes immediately before it. This noun or pronoun is its necessary antecedent.

La personne que je vois venir marche vite.
The person whom I see coming walks fast.

La maison blanche que vous voyez là-bas est jolie.
The white house (that) I see over there is pretty.

La maison de mes amis que vous voyez là-bas est jolie.
My friends' house that you see over there is pretty.

In sentences in which there is no antecedent noun, a pronoun is placed before the relative pronoun. This pronoun is a demonstrative pronoun and never a direct translation of the English "the one who...," "the one that..."

Celui que vous voyez...
The one you see...

Demonstrative Pronouns

	singular	*plural*
m.	celui	ceux
f.	celle	celles
nt.	ce	ceux

The variable forms are used when there is a noun to refer to in the sentence. The demonstrative form will agree with the gender and number of the noun last mentioned. Note that the demonstrative pronoun is placed immediately before the relative pronoun.

J'apporterai des fleurs (f. pl.). Quelles sont *<u>celles</u>* *que tu préfères?*
I will bring flowers. What are the ones that you prefer?

J'ai trois livres (m. pl.). Tu prendras *<u>celui</u>* *que tu préfères.*
I have three books. You will take the one (that) you prefer.

When there is no noun in the sentence the neuter pronoun *ce* is placed before the relative pronoun.

Voici ce que je comprends.
Here is what I understand.

Ce que je veux, c'est cette voiture.
The one I want is this car.

Note: Demonstrative pronouns are reviewed in Lesson Twelve.

EXERCISES

I. Fill in the blanks with *qui* if the verb does not have a subject, or *que* if the verb has a subject and the *que* is a direct object.

1. Voilà une question _______ est très importante.
2. Voilà une question _______ nous trouvons importante.
3. Vous avez acheté un livre _______ vous voulez lire dans le train?
4. Vous avez acheté un livre _______ vous intéresse?
5. Connais-tu la personne _______ nous a repondu?
6. Connais-tu l'homme _______ je vois entrer dans la salle?

II. Complete the following sentences with *dont* and the verb given, conjugated as needed.

1. Elle a acheté la veste _______ (avoir envie de).
2. Elle m'a donné le livre _______ (parler ensemble) (de).
3. Il arrive d'un pays _______ (ignorer l'existence) (de).
4. C'est le problème _______ (faire une etude) (de).
5. Je ne connais pas le pays _______ (venir) (de).
6. Vous ne comprenez pas la situation _______ (s'occuper) (de).
7. Voilà la chose _______ (avoir besoin) (de).
8. C'est une action _______ (se souvenir) (de).
9. Donnez moi une idée _______ (pouvoir se servir) (de).
10. Ce n'est pas moi _______ (entendre la voix) (de).

III. To practice the uses of *qui* (referring to a person after a preposition), write a sentence using the following verbs with a relative clause after the preposition.

Ex. faire ... avec
Jean est la personne avec qui je fais ce travail.

1. aller chez
2. se disputer avec
3. rendre visite à
4. travailler pour
5. rester auprès de
6. se présenter devant
7. se tenir derrière
8. compter sur

LESSON SEVEN

DIALOGUE

Jardins du Luxembourg

PAUL: Le ciel est bleu et je vois en bas dans la cour une femme en robe rose. Il doit faire chaud et bon dehors. Allons nous promener dans les jardins du Luxembourg.

LOUISE: Le guide dit qu'ils sont beaux. Il y a un grand palais...

PAUL: Nous verrons le palais quand nous serons là-bas.

LOUISE: Prenons l'autobus, c'est plus agréable que le métro. On peut voir les rues, les bâtiments, et tous les gens qui marchent, tous français.

PAUL: Tous français? Oh! Non! Il y a des gens de toutes les origines, de toutes les couleurs de peau, de toutes les nationalités, à Paris; certains viennent d'autres pays d'Europe, mais aussi d'Afrique, et d'Asie. Des jeunes et des vieux, des riches... Mais attends! Où est l'arrêt d'autobus? Et avant de le prendre, il faut avoir un billet... Et les billets se vendent dans les stations de métro. Voilà l'escalier pour aller sous-terre, et voilà le guichet avec une queue. Attendons!

LOUISE: Regarde ce qu'on dit ici. C'est une carte d'abonnement pour un mois, n'est-ce-pas?

PAUL: Oui. Je vais en prendre deux et payer avec ma carte Visa.

LOUISE: C'est très bien, mais il faut une photo. Allons à la cabine de Photomaton. Un sourire, cinq minutes, et la voilà! Oh là là comme je suis horrible!

Luxembourg Gardens

PAUL: The sky is blue and down there in the courtyard I see a woman in a pink dress. It must be warm and nice outside. Let's go for a stroll in the Luxembourg Gardens.

LOUISE: The guidebook says that they are beautiful. There is a vast palace...

PAUL: We will see the palace when we are there.

LOUISE: Let's take the bus, it is more pleasant than the subway. One can see the streets, the buildings, and all the people walking, all French.

PAUL: All French? Oh! No! There are people of every origin, every skin color, every nationality in Paris; some come from other countries in Europe, and many also from Africa and Asia. Young and old, rich and... But wait! Where is the bus stop? And before taking it, one must have a ticket. And tickets are sold in subway stations. Here are the stairs to go underground and there is a line in front of the window. Let's wait!

LOUISE: Look at what it says here. This is a pass for one month, isn't it?

PAUL: Yes. I am going to take two, and pay with my Visa card.

LOUISE: Fine, but we need a photo. Let's go to the photo booth. A smile, five minutes, and here it is! Oh no! How horrible I look!

Paul: Mais non, mais non! Et puis, qu'est-ce que ça fait? Voilà ma photo. J'ai l'air si bizarre! Tu veux épouser un type comme ça?

Louise: Bien sûr! Avec plaisir! Et merci madame. Avec ça, nous allons chercher l'autobus 38. Je le vois qui arrive. Ah! Service Partiel! Qu'est-ce que ça veut dire? Pardon, monsieur, vous allez aux Jardins du Luxembourg... Ah, non, pardon, au Luxembourg? Bon, très bien.

Paul: Tiens, écoute ça. Il y a une voix qui annonce l'arrêt suivant. Quand la voix dira 'Auguste Comte' ce sera l'arrêt après. On appuie sur le bouton pour ouvrir la porte, et on descend.

Louise: Et en face de nous, une grande grille, et un jardin public. C'est le Luxembourg!

Paul: Quels arbres magnifiques. Ils sont très vieux, n'est-ce pas?

Louise: On a organisé le parc au commencement du dix-septième siècle, quand on a construit ce chateau pour la reine Marie de Médicis, femme du roi Henri IV. Certains de ces arbres ont des centaines d'années.

Paul: Et toutes ces statues! Et un grand bassin, avec beaucoup d'enfants tout autour. Et beaucoup de bateaux qui flottent sur l'eau.

Louise: Allons nous asseoir à l'ombre et admirer la scène, avec toutes les belles fleurs et les élégantes perspectives.

PAUL: No, not at all! Besides, what does it matter? Here is my photo. I look so odd! Would you marry a guy like this?

LOUISE: Of course! With pleasure! And thank you, *madame*. With that, we are going to look for Bus 38. I see it coming. Ah! Limited Service! What does that mean? Excuse me, *monsieur*, are you going to the Luxembourg Gardens? Ah no, excuse me, to the Luxembourg? Good, very well.

PAUL: Well, listen to that. There is a voice that announces the next stop. When the voice says "Auguste Comte" it will be the next stop. You press the button to make the door open, and one gets off.

LOUISE: And just ahead of us, a great wall of grillwork, and a public garden. It's the Luxembourg!

PAUL: What magnificent trees. They are very old, aren't they?

LOUISE: The park was designed at the beginning of the seventeenth century, when the castle was built for the Queen Marie de Medicis, wife of Henry the IVth. Some of these trees are several hundred years old.

PAUL: And all these statues! And this large pond with so many children all around. And many boats floating on the water.

LOUISE: Let's sit in the shade and admire the scene, with all the bright flowers and the elegant perspectives.

VOCABULARY

à l'ombre	in the shade
admirer	to admire
année, l' *f.*	year
annoncer	to announce
appuyer	to push
après	after
arbre, l' *m.*	tree
arrêt, l' *m.*	stop
Auguste Comte	(name of a street)
avant de	before
avec plaisir	with pleasure
bassin, le *m.*	basin
bateau, le *m.*	boat
bâtiment, le *m.*	building
beau	beautiful
beaucoup de	many
billet, le *m.*	ticket
bizarre	bizarre, strange
bouton, le *m.*	button
cabine, la *f.*	booth
carte, la *f.*	card
carte d'abonnement, la *f.*	membership card/ticket
certains de	some of
chateau, le *m.*	castle
ciel, le *m.*	sky
comme je suis	how ... I am
commencement, le *m.*	beginning
construire	to build
couleur, la *f.*	color
dehors	outside
centaines, des *f.*	hundreds

descendre	to step out
dire	to say
eau, l' *f.*	water
écouter	to listen
élégante	elegant
en	in; of them
en bas	down there
en face de	in front of
épouser	to marry
escalier, l' *m.*	stairs
Europe	Europe
faire bon	nice weather (*lit.* to do good)
femme, la *f.*	the woman
fleur, la *f.*	flower
flotter	to float
gens, les *m.*	people
grand	large
grille, la *f.*	grillwork fence
guichet, le *m.*	window, booth
horrible	horrible
jardin public, le *m.*	public garden
jardins, les *m.*	gardens
jeune	young
enfant, l' *m.*	child
escalier, l' *m.*	stairs
marcher	to walk
mois, le *m.*	month
nationalité, la *f.*	nationality
organiser	to organize
origine, l' *f.*	origin
palais, le *m.*	palace
parc, le *m.*	park
payer	to pay
pays, le *m.*	country
peau, la *f.*	skin

perspective, la *f.*	perspective
photo	picture (photograph)
photomaton, le *m.*	photo booth
porte, la *f.*	door
qu'est-ce que ça fait	what does it matter
qu'est-ce que ça veut dire	what does that mean
quand	when
quels	what
queue, la *f.*	line
reine, la *f.*	queen
riche	rich
robe, la *f.*	dress
roi, le *m.*	king
rose	pink
s'asseoir	to sit down
se promener	to walk
se vendre	to be sold
service partiel, le *m.*	partial service
siècle, le *m.*	century
sourire, le *m.*	smile
sous-terre	underground
station de métro, la *f.*	subway station
statue, la *f.*	statue
suivant	next
tous	all
tout autour	all around
très	very
type, le *m.*	guy
vieux	old
voix, la *f.*	voice
dix-septième	seventeenth

GRAMMAR

The Future Tense

Conjugation

The future tense of regular verbs is formed by adding the present tense endings of *avoir* to the infinitive form of the verb. In verbs with a final *e* in the infinitive, such as *vendre*, that *e* is dropped.

Endings:

	singular	*plural*
1st	-ai	-ons
2nd	-as	-ez
3rd	-a	-ont

aimer (to love)	*vendre* (to sell)
j'aimerai (I will love)	je vendrai (I will sell)
tu aimeras	tu vendras
il/elle aimera	il/elle vendra
nous aimerons	nous vendrons
vous aimerez	vous vendrez
ils/elles aimeront	ils/elles vendrons

Many verbs have an irregular radical in the future tense but once you know the first person form the same radical is used for all persons (see Appendix).

voir (to see)
je verrai, tu verras, il/elle verra, nous verrons, vous verrez, ils/elles verront (I will see, etc.)

Uses

- The future expresses an action or a situation that will come after a certain amount of time.

- If this action comes after a short time the verb *aller* is used in the present tense before the verb in the infinitive.

  Je vais partir avec mes amis.
  I am going to go with my friends.

- The future is always used after the conjunctions of time when they introduce a sentence that refers to the future.

  quand, lorsque – when
  aussitôt que – as soon as
  dès que – as soon as
  pendant que – while
  tandis que – while
  tant que – as long as

  Je serai ici quand vous arriverez.
  I will be here when you arrive.

  Note: In English the verb remains in the present, while in French the future tense must be used.

- The future is used in conversation to avoid giving a direct order to someone.

  Vous finirez ce travail pour demain, s'il vous plaît.
  Please have this work finished for tomorrow.

- The future is used after verbs that indicate that one asks a question to oneself or someone else: *se demander* (to wonder), *ne pas savoir* (not to know), *s'inquieter* (to worry)—and these sentences are constructed with an interrogative *si* (if). *Si* is elided to *s'* in front of *i*.

Je me demande s'il viendra.
I wonder if he will come.

Je ne sais pas s'il sera content.
I do not know if he will be pleased.

EXERCISES

I. Alternating persons in the singular and plural, give the future forms of the following verbs, then learn these forms by heart.

1. avoir
2. être
3. aller
4. courir
5. envoyer
6. savoir
7. faire
8. devoir
9. croire
10. falloir
11. mourir
12. pleuvoir
13. pouvoir
14. s'asseoir
15. tenir
16. venir
17. voir
18. valoir

II. Fill in the blanks with the appropriate forms of the future, except where the future should not be used.

1. Comme il ne le ______ (voir) pas, il ne le ______ (savoir) pas.
2. Si vous ne ______ (se lever) pas, vous ______ (être) en retard.
3. Si elle est vraiment gentille, nous ______ (aller) avec elle au cinéma.
4. Nous nous demandons si elle ______ (savoir) résoudre ce problème.
5. Vous ______ (donner) de vos nouvelles dès que vous le ______ (pouvoir).
6. Si tu te______ (perdre) que ______ (faire) tu?
7. Crois-tu qu'il ______ (venir) demain?
8. Elle vous ______ (voir) quand elle (avoir) le temps.
9. Nous ______ (s'en aller) quand vous ______ (finir).
10. Vous ______ (se coucher) dès que vous ______ (avoir) envie de dormir.

III. Complete the following sentences, noting the tenses used.

1. Je partirai quand...
2. Je partirai si...
3. Je vous verrai...
4. Je vous verrai si...
5. Nous vous écrirons si...
6. Nous vous écrirons quand...
7. Ils vous répondront quand...
8. Nous vous répondrons si...

LESSON EIGHT

DIALOGUE

Visitons La Tour Eiffel

PAUL: Nous voilà en route pour Le Printemps, un grand magasin où tu veux faire des achats.

LOUISE: Et toi aussi, j'espère. Tu vas acheter des cadeaux pour tes deux neveux, et pour ta mère, et pour...

PAUL: Pour les neveux, un T-shirt avec Paris et la Tour...

LOUISE: Mais nous n'avons pas encore vu la Tour Eiffel! A quoi pensons-nous?

PAUL: Tu veux y aller maintenant?

LOUISE: Oui, oui. On peut prendre un autre autobus? Avec notre carte, nous pouvons circuler partout. Descendons. Nous sommes près de la Seine, la Tour Eiffel est près de la Seine aussi, donc si nous prenons un autobus qui va dans cette direction, nous serons plus près. Et avec ce beau temps, ce sera un plaisir de marcher.

PAUL: Je croyais qu'on pouvait voir la tour, si haute, de partout à Paris, mais je ne l'ai pas encore aperçue.

LOUISE: Enfin, la voilà là-bas, regarde! Mais le conducteur dit qu'il faut descendre ici et aller tout droit à pied le long du quai.

PAUL: Belle promenade! Mais pourquoi cette tour s'appelle-t-elle Eiffel?

Let's Go To The Eiffel Tower

PAUL: Here we are on our way to the Printemps, a department store, where you want to buy lots of things.

LOUISE: And you too, I hope. You are going to buy presents for your two nephews, for your mother, and for...

PAUL: For the nephews, a T-shirt with Paris and the Tower...

LOUISE: But we have not yet seen the Eiffel Tower! What are we thinking?

PAUL: Do you want to go now?

LOUISE: Yes, yes. Can we take another bus? With our pass, we can go anywhere. Let's get off. We are close to the Seine, the Eiffel Tower is close to the Seine as well, so if we take a bus that goes in that direction, we will be closer. With this nice weather, it will be a pleasure to walk.

PAUL: I thought that you could see the tower, so tall, from everywhere in Paris, but I have not yet had a glimpse of it.

LOUISE: Finally, there it is over there, look! But the driver says that we must get off here and walk straight ahead along the quay.

PAUL: Beautiful walk! But why is this tower called Eiffel?

LOUISE: Tu connais le poème qui dit 'sous le pont Mirabeau, coule la Seine...'?

PAUL: Ah, mais oui! Je l'ai appris, mais je ne le sais plus.

LOUISE: Moi non plus, mais la Seine, la voilà! Elle coule toujours!

PAUL: Et Eiffel?

LOUISE: C'était un ingénieur du XIXème siècle à l'esprit moderne, qui s'appellait Gustave Eiffel. Il travaillait avec du métal, pas avec de la pierre. Il a reçu un contrat pour construire un monument original pour l'exposition universelle de 1889, un monument qui représente le progrès de la révolution industrielle.

PAUL: Et il a bien réussi! Elle est célèbre partout dans le monde.

LOUISE: Mais à son époque, les gens n'ont pas pensé cela. Ils ont trouvé que c'était un objet ridicule, qu'on ne pouvait pas la laisser à côté des beaux monuments de pierre de la ville.

PAUL: Ils voulaient la détruire?

LOUISE: Bien sûr! Des pétitions, des protestations dans les journaux!

PAUL: Et ils n'ont pas réussi?

LOUISE: Chaque année la démolition était pour l'année suivante. Et la voilà devant nous!

PAUL: Elle est très élégante. Maintenant, montons jusqu'en haut!

LOUISE: Do you know the poem that says "under the Mirabeau bridge is flowing the Seine..."?

PAUL: Oh yes! I learned it, but I do not know it anymore.

LOUISE: Me either, but the Seine, here it is! Still flowing!

PAUL: And Eiffel?

LOUISE: He was an engineer of the XIXth century with a modern mind, who was named Gustave Eiffel. He worked with metal, not stone. He received a contract to build an original monument for the Universal Exhibition of 1889, a monument that would represent the progress of the industrial revolution.

PAUL: He was very successful! It is known all over the world.

LOUISE: But at the time, the people did not think so. They found it a ridiculous object that could not be left beside the beautiful stone monuments of the city.

PAUL: They wanted to destroy it?

LOUISE: Of course! Petitions, protests in the newspapers!

PAUL: And they did not succeed?

LOUISE: Each year, its demolition was postponed until the next year. And here it is before us!

PAUL: It is very elegant. Now let's go to the top!

VOCABULARY

à coté de	beside
à l'esprit moderne	with a modern mind
à pied	on foot
à quoi pensons-nous	what are we thinking about
à son époque	in his time
apercevoir	to catch a glimpse of
apprendre	to learn
bien sûr	of course
cadeau, le *m.*	present
célèbre	famous
circuler	to ride, go
conducteur, le *m.*	driver
connaître	to know
contrat, le *m.*	contract
couler	to flow
croire	to believe
détruire	to destroy
en route pour	on the way to
espérer	to hope
exposition universelle, l' *f.*	World Fair
faire des achats	to do some shopping
gens, les *m.*	people
grand magasin, le *m.*	department store
ingénieur, l' *m.*	engineer
jusqu'en haut	up to the top
laisser	to leave
le long de	along
maintenant	right now
mère, la *f.*	mother
métal, le *m.*	metal
Mirabeau	(name of bridge)

moi non plus	me neither
monde, le *m.*	world
monter	to climb
ne ... plus	no longer
neveu, le *m.*	nephew
nous voilà	here we are
objet, l' *m.*	object
partout	everywhere
pas encore	not yet
pétitions, les *f.*	petitions
pierre, la *f.*	stone
poème, le *m.*	poem
pont, le *m.*	bridge
près de	near
progrès, le *m.*	progress
protestations, les *f.*	protests
quai, le *m.*	quay
recevoir	to receive
réussir	to succeed
révolution industrielle, la *f.*	Industrial Revolution
ridicule	ridiculous
Seine, la *f.*	the Seine river
si haut	so tall
sous	under
toujours	still
tour, la *f.*	tower
travailler	to work
trouver	to find
tu vas acheter	you are going to buy
un autre	another
ville, la *f.*	city
XIXème siècle, le *m.*	nineteenth century

GRAMMAR

Nouns

The noun is a word that designates a person or a thing. It can be masculine or feminine. It takes the plural ending when necessary. Nouns are in most cases preceded by an article (see Lesson Four). The singular form of the article, *la* or *le*, indicates the gender of the noun. So the article and noun should be learned together.

Gender and Agreement

Since in a sentence the noun is commonly linked with adjectives, or replaced by pronouns, it is absolutely essential to know its gender to make the necessary agreements.

There are no rules that establish distinct categories of masculine and feminine nouns. Most categories have exceptions.

masculine nouns	*feminine nouns*
names of persons or animals of the masculine sex: *un homme* (a man), *un garçon* (a boy), *un chat* (a cat), etc.	names of persons of the feminine sex: *une femme* (a woman), *une fille* (a girl), *une mère* (a mother), *une chienne* (a dog), *une chatte* (a cat), etc.
words ending in: -age: *un garage* (a garage), *un langage* (a language), *un âge* (an age), but: *<u>une</u> image* (an image) -al: *un journal* (a newspaper), *un mal* (a pain), *un canal* (a canal), etc.	words ending in: -tion: *une élection* (an election), *une traduction* (a translation) -ale: *une capitale* (a capital), *une céréale* (a cereal)

Two Genders with Different Meanings

un livre (a book) – *une livre* (a half kilo, a pound)
un manche (a handle) – *une manche* (a sleeve)
un mode (a mode) – *une mode* (what is fashionable)
un poste (a job in an administration) – *une poste* (a post office)
un vase (a vase) – *la vase* (mud)
un voile (a veil) – *une voile* (a sail)

Feminine Form of Nouns

An *e* is added at the end but there are often modifications of the preceding syllable.

un cousin – une cousine (a cousin)
un avocat – une avocate (a lawyer)

But:
un médecin (a doctor) – no feminine form (*une médecine* – a remedy)
un professeur – une (femme) professeur (a professor)
un acteur – une actrice (an actor)
un lecteur – une lectrice (a reader)
un conducteur – une conductrice (a driver)
un maître – une maîtresse (a teacher)
un loup – une louve (a wolf)
Etc.

Some pairs are made of different words:

un oncle (an uncle) – *une tante* (an aunt)
un coq (a rooster) – *une poule* (a hen)
un mouton (a sheep) – *une brebis* (an ewe)

un cheval (a male horse) – *une jument* (a female horse)
un cochon (a pig) – *une truie* (a sow)

Note: Many names of animals do not distinguish between masculine and feminine: *un rat* (a rat), *un crapaud* (a toad), *une tarentule* (a tarantula), *un serpent* (a snake).

Plural Forms

- The plural of nouns generally is marked by adding an *s* or an *x* at the end of the word: *la ville* (the town), *les villes; un feu* (a fire), *des feux.*

- Nouns ending in *s* or *x* or *z* remain the same in the plural, such as: *un fils* (a son), *des fils* (sons); *du houx* (holly), *des houx* (hollies); *un nez* (a nose), *des nez* (noses).

- Nouns ending in *eu, au, eau,* or *oeu* take an *x* in the plural: *un cheveu* (a hair), *des cheveux* (hairs); *un bateau* (a boat), *des bateaux* (boats); *un voeu* (a wish), *des voeux* (wishes).

- Nouns ending in *ou* take an *s,* except seven of them that take an *x*: *bijou* (jewel), *bijoux; caillou* (pebble), *cailloux; chou* (cabbage), *choux; genou* (knee), *genoux; hibou* (owl), *hiboux; joujou* (toy), *joujoux; pou* (lice), *poux.* This list should be memorized.

- Nouns ending in *al* and *ail* take an *x*: *un canal* (a canal), *des canaux; un travail* (a job), *des travaux.*

  Exceptions: *un récital* (a recital), *des récitals; un festival* (a festival), *des festivals*

- Some nouns are always used in the plural: *les vacances* (vacation time), *les gens* (people), *les mathématiques* (mathematics), *les provisions* (supplies).

- Some plurals are irregular: *un oeil* (an eye), *des yeux; un ciel* (a sky), *des cieux; un jeune homme* (a young man), *des jeunes gens.*

  Note: A family name never takes a plural form: *Les Dupont Dupond.*

Nouns of National Origin

These nouns take a capital letter: *un Américain, un Français,* but the corresponding adjective does not: *une femme française.*

EXERCISES

I. Place *le, la* or *les* in front of the following words, and indicate the gender when *les* is used.

1. bureau
2. maison
3. cieux
4. nation
5. gouvernement
6. voiture
7. maladie
8. têtes
9. châteaux
10. parti
11. bontés
12. famille
13. capitalisme
14. tête
15. yeux
16. main
17. chevaux
18. musée
19. peur
20. rêve
21. pouvoirs
22. société
23. permission
24. ordre
25. vendredi
26. écriture
27. prix
28. largeur
29. eaux
30. oiseau

II. Write the following sentences in the plural.

1. Regardez cette eau bleue.
2. Il a l'oreille fine.
3. Le chat est un animal rusé.
4. C'est un bel homme.
5. C'est un garçon courageux.
6. Ce moteur est usé.
7. C'est un vieil ami.
8. Elle a l'oeil alerte.

III. Rewrite these sentences, changing the masculine nouns to a feminine noun and the feminine nouns to a masculine one.

1. Il sort avec sa cousine. (He goes out with his cousin.)
2. Cet enfant a de bons maîtres. (This child has good teachers.)
3. Elles engageront une avocate. (They will engage a lawyer.)

4. Mon oncle ne va pas venir demain. (My uncle will not come tomorrow.)
5. Les actrices jouent une comédie ce soir. (The actresses play a comedy tonight.)
6. Les lecteurs sont nombreux. (The readers are numerous.)
7. Je n'ai pas confiance dans ce conducteur. (I have no confidence in this driver.)
8. Avez-vous un médecin habile? (Do you have a good doctor?)
9. J'ai entendu la louve cette nuit. (I heard the she-wolf last night.)
10. J'ai vu un cheval dans le pré. (I saw a horse in the meadow.)

LESSON NINE

DIALOGUE

Promenade Dans Le Marais

PAUL: J'ai téléphoné à mon cousin Jean-Pierre, mais je n'ai pas eu de réponse. Donc j'ai laissé un message sur son répondeur. J'ai pensé lui proposer une promenade dans le Marais. Il fait un temps parfait pour flâner dans un quartier historique de Paris.

LOUISE: Et les courses dans le Grand Magasin?

PAUL: Plus tard. Nous avons le temps.

LOUISE: Et c'est quoi ce quartier?

PAUL: Le Marais, c'est...

LOUISE: Le dictionnaire dit que c'est un endroit plein d'eau sale et de grenouilles...

PAUL: Ça, c'était vrai il y a quatre cents ans. Et justement, au commencement de ces quatre cents ans, la ville de Paris avait besoin d'espace pour construire des maisons. Et on a fait des canaux, on a asséché le terrain. On a fait des rues, et construit des maisons, des maisons belles et riches, et d'autres maisons pour les 'bourgeois', la classe des commerçants, qui pouvaient acheter un appartement.

LOUISE: Et des gens vivent dans ces maisons maintenant?

PAUL: Allons les voir. Nous allons rencontrer Jean-Pierre à la Place des Vosges. Le mieux est de prendre le métro et de changer à Châtelet, pour la station St. Paul.

Jean-Pierre, je te présente ma femme Louise.

A Stroll In The Marais

PAUL: I called my cousin Jean-Pierre, but I did not get an answer so I left a message on his answering machine. I wanted to propose to him a walk around the Marais. The weather is perfect for a stroll in a historic section of Paris.

LOUISE: And our errands at the department store?

PAUL: Later. We have time.

LOUISE: And what is this section?

PAUL: Le Marais, the marshland, it is...

LOUISE: The dictionary says it is a place full of dirty water and frogs...

PAUL: That was true four hundred years ago. And precisely, at the beginning of those four hundred years, the city of Paris needed space to build houses. And they made canals and drained the land. They made streets and built houses, beautiful and rich townhouses and other houses for the "bourgeois," the middle class of merchants who could buy apartments.

LOUISE: And people live in those houses now?

PAUL: Let's go and see them. We are going to meet Jean-Pierre at the Place des Vosges. The best thing is to take the subway and change at Châtelet, for the St. Paul stop.
Jean-Pierre, let me introduce my wife, Louise.

LOUISE: Bonjour Jean-Pierre. Ah! J'aime beaucoup cette Place des Vosges. Toutes les maisons sont pareilles, en briques roses, avec de grandes fenêtres, et le tour des fenêtres est en pierre blanche. Et toutes les maisons ont trois étages et forment un mur autour de la place!

PAUL: Oui, avec des arcades au niveau de la rue pour marcher sans avoir la pluie sur la tête.

JEAN-PIERRE: J'aimerais bien habiter ici, et j'irais promener mon chien dans le parc.

LOUISE: Oui! Et tu sais qui habitait dans le coin là-bas? Victor Hugo, l'auteur de *Les Misérables* et de beaucoup d'autres livres!

JEAN-PIERRE: Et à l'autre coin de l'arcade, il y a un très bon restaurant où je vous invite pour le déjeuner.

LOUISE: Merci Jean-Pierre!

Louise: Good morning, Jean-Pierre. Oh! I love this Place des Vosges. All the houses are alike, made of pink brick with tall windows, and the border of the windows is made of white stone. And all the houses have three stories and form a wall around the square!

Paul: Yes, with arcades at the level of the street so as to walk without having rain on your head.

Jean-Pierre: I would like to live here, and I would walk my dog in the park.

Louise: Yes, and do you know who lived in that corner over there? Victor Hugo, the author of *Les Misérables* and many other books.

Jean-Pierre: And in this other corner of the arcade, there is a very good restaurant where I am inviting you for lunch.

Louise: Thank you, Jean-Pierre!

VOCABULARY

appartement, l' *m.*	apartment
assécher	to drain
auteur, l' *m.*	author
avoir besoin de	to need
brique, la *f.*	brick
canal, le *m.*	canal
changer à	to change
coin, le *m.*	corner
commerçant, le *m.*	businessman
courses, les *f.*	errands
cousin, le *m.*	cousin
dictionnaire, le *m.*	dictionary
endroit, l' *m.*	place
espace, l' *m.*	space
étage, l' *m.*	floor, story
fenêtre, la *f.*	window
flâner	to stroll
grenouille, la *f.*	frog
historique	historical
il y a...	...ago
inviter	to invite
justement	precisely
laisser	to leave
maison, la *f.*	house
Marais, le *m.*	(a section of Paris)
message, le *m.*	message
mieux est...	the best way is...
niveau, le *m.*	level
pareil	alike
parfait	perfect
plein de	full of

pluie, la *f.*	rain
plus tard	later
présenter	to introduce
proposer	to propose
quartier, le *m.*	section, neighborhood
quatre cents	four hundred
répondeur, le *m.*	answering machine
réponse, la *f.*	answer
terrain, le *m.*	terrain
tête, la *f.*	head
tour, la *f.*	tower
vivre	to live
vrai	true

GRAMMAR

Adjectives

Adjectives are words qualifying a noun. Their form varies with the gender and number of the nouns they qualify. They take a different form for the feminine and the plural nouns. They are modified in the same way if they qualify the subject of the verb "to be."

Il est grand. Elle est grande.
He is big. She is big.
Ils sont grands. Elles sont grandes.
They are big (*m.*). They are big (*f.*).

Forms

The masculine of the adjective being given, the feminine form is obtained by adding an *e* at the end of the word.

petit – petite (small)
brillant – brillante (brilliant)

Note: Adjectives ending in *gu* take an umlaut sign over the *e* (ë) to point out that the *u* should be pronounced.

aigu – aiguë (sharp)
ambigu – ambiguë (ambiguous)

- Adjectives ending in *e* keep the same form in the feminine.

  une femme aimable – a pleasant woman
  un homme aimable – a pleasant man

- Five adjectives change form in the singular when placed in front of a noun that starts with a vowel or a mute *h*: *beau* (beautiful), *bel*; *nouveau* (new), *nouvel*; *fou* (crazy), *fol*; *mou* (soft), *mol*; *vieux* (old), *vieil*.

un bel homme – a handsome man
un vieil ami – an old friend
un fol espoir – a foolish hope

- The feminine of these five adjectives is based on this form of the words: *belle, nouvelle, folle, molle, vieille.*

une belle femme – a beautiful woman
une nouvelle lampe – a new lamp
une folle idée – a crazy idea

Other Changes of Endings from Masculine to Feminine

er – ère
premier – première (first)
cher – chère (costly)

f – ve
naïf – naïve (naive)
furtif – furtive (furtive)

x – se
heureux – heureuse (happy)

eur – euse
voleur – voleuse (thievish)

teur – trice
exportateur – exportatrice (exporting)

- Adjectives ending in a vowel + consonant in most cases double the consonant before the final *e*.

gentil – gentille (nice)
pareil – pareille (similar)
ancien – ancienne (ancient)

Note: There are many exceptions in which the consonant is not doubled:

petit – petite (small)
fin – fine (fine)
mauvais – mauvaise (bad)

- Irregular endings:

blanc – blanche (white)
sec – sèche (dry)
frais – fraîche (fresh)
public – publique (public)
favori – favorite (favorite)
grec – grecque (Greek)
malin – maligne (shrewd)
long – longue (long)
roux – rousse (reddish)
faux – fausse (false)
doux – douce (sweet)

- Adjectives of color are invariable if the color is the name of a plant, or if the qualifying adjective is made up of two words.

une robe marron – a "chestnut-brown" dress
des chemises mauve clair – light mauve shirts
des yeux bleu clair – light blue eyes

The Plural of Adjectives

Forms

The mark of the plural is, as for nouns, an *s* added to the masculine or feminine form of the word.

SPECIAL CASES

- If there is an *s* or an *x* at the end of the adjective there will be no change in the masculine form, but the feminine plural form will need an *s* ending.

  précis (precise)
  sg.: *précis* (*m.*), *précise* (*f.*)
  pl.: *précis* (*m.*), *précises* (*f.*)

  précieux (precious)
  sg.: *précieux* (*m.*), *précieuse* (*f.*)
  pl.: *précieux* (*m.*), *précieuses* (*f.*)

- Adjectives ending in *eau* take an *x* ending in the masculine plural form and an *s* ending in the feminine plural form.

  beau (beautiful)
  sg.: *beau* (*m.*), *belle* (*f.*)
  pl.: *beaux* (*m.*), *belles* (*f.*)

  nouveau (new)
  sg.: *nouveau* (*m.*), *nouvelle* (*f.*)
  pl.: *nouveaux* (*m.*), *nouvelles* (*f.*)

- Endings in *al* become *aux* (for masculine adjectives only).

  normal (normal)
  sg.: *normal* (*m.*), *normale* (*f.*)
  pl.: *normaux* (*m.*), *normales* (*f.*)

Agreement

Adjectives agree in number and gender with the nouns or pronouns they qualify.

les jolies jeunes filles – the pretty young ladies
les roses sont blanches – the roses are white

If an adjective qualifies several nouns of which one or more is masculine, the adjective must be in the masculine plural form.

les forts jeunes hommes et femmes – the strong young men and women

Note: The adjective stays unchanged:

I. After the expression *c'est* even if *ce* represents plural nouns.

   Ces montagnes sont très magnifiques. C'est très beau!
   These mountains are magnificent. It is very beautiful!

II. When it qualifies the verb in expressions such as: *coûter cher* (to cost a high price); *être bon marché* (to be inexpensive); and other expressions such as *travailler dur* (to work hard), *parler fort* (to speak loudly) and *parler bas* (to speak softly).

   ces robes coûtent très cher – these dresses cost a lot/are very expensive
   ces voyages ne sont pas bon marché – these trips are not cheap

Position of the Adjective in the Sentence

According to its meaning, the adjective comes after or before the noun.

AFTER THE NOUN

- When it gives the noun a distinctive quality so that the noun is placed in a category.

nationality: *un chanteur français* – a French singer
religion: *une famille catholique* – a Catholic family
social class: *des habitudes bourgeoises* – middle-class way of life
political: *le parti socialiste* – the socialist party

- When the adjective is modified by an adverb of two or more syllables or followed by an object.

un travail difficile à finir – a work hard to finish
un garçon très fort en biologie – a young man very strong in biology
un paysage vraiment idyllique – a really idyllic landscape

BEFORE THE NOUN

- When the adjective is short (one or two syllables) and usually associated with the noun.

une vieille chapelle – an old chapel
mon autre soeur – my other sister
une bonne promenade – a good stroll

When two adjectives are used with a noun one can be before and the other after.

un grand homme admirable – a great and admirable man

Some adjectives have distinct meanings according to their placement after or before the noun.

- Placed after the noun, the adjective has its practical proper meaning.

- Placed before the noun, the adjective has a figurative meaning.

un homme grand – a tall man
un grand homme – a great man

un bâtiment ancien – an old building
un ancien ami – a former friend

Adjectives with two different meanings, according to place:

adjective	*concrete meaning*	*abstract meaning*
ancien	un monument ancien (an ancient building)	une ancienne usine (a former factory)
brave	un homme brave (a brave man)	un brave homme (a good man)
certain	un résultat certain (a sure result)	une certaine idée (a certain idea)
cher	une robe chère (an expensive dress)	une chère amie (a dear friend)
dernier	l'an dernier (last year)	la dernière année (the final year)
différent	un projet différent (a different project)	différentes situations (different situations)
drôle	une histoire drôle (a funny story)	une drôle d'histoire (a peculiar story)
grand	un homme grand (a tall man)	un grand homme (a great man)
même	l'honnêteté même (honesty itself)	la même personne (the same person)

nouveau	un livre nouveau (a new book)	une nouvelle idée (a new idea)
pauvre	une famille pauvre (a poor family)	un pauvre homme (a wretched man)
prochain	dimanche prochain (next Sunday)	le prochain jour (the day after)
propre	une maison propre (a clean house)	sa propre voiture (his own car)
sale	une maison sale (a dirty house)	une sale affaire (an ugly affair)
seul	un homme seul (a lonely man)	un seul homme (one man)

Note: When you want to use the expression make + adjective, "this makes me happy," the equivalent in French of the verb "to make" is not *faire*, but *rendre*.

ceci me rend heureux – this makes me happy

EXERCISES

I. Learn the different meanings of adjectives placed before or after the noun by covering the column in the table and giving the meaning of each word in the covered column.

II. Place the adjectives correctly, before or after the noun, and make them agree with the noun.

1. une maison (grand, blanc)
2. une conférence (ennuyeux, long)
3. une porte (petit, ouvert)
4. des garçons (gros, lourd)
5. des femmes (actif, intelligent)
6. une église (vieux, abandonné)
7. les exercices (deux, premier)
8. une figure (gentil, souriant)
9. un vin blanc (petit, bon)
10. des compositions (clair, intéressant)

III. Give the feminine form of the following adjectives.

1. ancien
2. cruel
3. gentil
4. pareil
5. muet
6. net
7. gras
8. plat
9. bon
10. épais
11. fondateur
12. premier
13. dernier
14. complet
15. blanc
16. frais
17. long
18. public
19. sec
20. roux
21. doux
22. faux
23. favori
24. mauvais
25. nul

LESSON TEN

DIALOGUE

Au Restaurant Le Soir

JEAN-PIERRE: Voici le restaurant, le Jardin d'Epicure. Cela vous plaît?

PAUL: Oui, mais cette fois, c'est nous qui t'invitons!

LOUISE: C'est très élégant, ces nappes roses, ces serviettes blanches, des fleurs à chaque table et une délicieuse odeur...

LE GARÇON: Par ici, s'il vous plaît. Est-ce que cette table vous convient?

JEAN-PIERRE: Vous en avez une autre plus loin de la porte? Pour ne pas sentir le courant d'air?

LE GARÇON: Mais certainement, monsieur. Et celle-ci?

JEAN-PIERRE: Qu'en pensez-vous, Louise?

LOUISE: Oui, c'est parfait.

LE GARÇON: Voici un menu, madame, monsieur, monsieur.

JEAN-PIERRE: Désirez-vous prendre un apéritif? Vous, Louise?

LOUISE: Non merci, Jean-Pierre.

JEAN-PIERRE: Pas un petit Kir? Non? Et toi Paul?

PAUL: Moi, oui, je veux bien. Qu'est-ce que c'est?

At the Restaurant at Night

JEAN-PIERRE: Here is the restaurant, Epicure's Garden. Do you like it?

PAUL: Yes, but this time we are inviting you!

LOUISE: It is very elegant, these pink tablecloths, these white napkins, flowers on each table and this delicious smell...

WAITER: This way, please. Do you like this table?

JEAN-PIERRE: Do you have another one not so close to the door? So we will not feel the draft?

WAITER: Certainly, sir. How about this one?

JEAN-PIERRE: What do you think, Louise?

LOUISE: Yes, it is perfect.

WAITER: Here is a menu, *madame, monsieur, monsieur.*

JEAN-PIERRE: Would you like an "aperitif" drink? You, Louise?

LOUISE: No, thank you, Jean-Pierre.

JEAN-PIERRE: Not a little *Kir*? No? And you Paul?

PAUL: Yes, I would like one. What is it?

LOUISE: Tu me feras goûter?

JEAN-PIERRE: Voici nos verres roses de Kir. C'est du vin blanc avec un peu de crème de cassis. C'est une spécialité de Dijon en Bourgogne. Kir est le nom de l'homme qui l'a rendu populaire. C'était le maire de Dijon. Vous aimez ça?

PAUL: C'est délicieux.

JEAN-PIERRE: Maintenant, choisissons notre menu. Les entrées, c'est pour commencer. Leur bisque de homard est exquise mais il y a beaucoup d'autres choses. Un petit fromage de chèvre sur salade frisée pour toi, Paul? Et pour moi la salade avec gésiers et lardons. La bisque pour vous, Louise? Ou six escargots avec de l'ail et du beurre?

LOUISE: Gésiers, c'est ce que je crois? Des estomacs de poulets?

JEAN-PIERRE: Exactement.

LOUISE: Et le ris de veau, qu'est-ce que c'est?

JEAN-PIERRE: C'est une partie très tendre du veau, préparée avec des champignons et de la crème. Et toi, Paul? Tu veux goûter une andouillette?

PAUL: Non merci. Je vais prendre le magret de canard, bien cuit.

JEAN-PIERRE: Pour moi aussi, saignant. Et pour Louise? Une patte de poularde à la crème aux truffes. Du vin rouge, un Brouilly, pour nous, et pour Louise un Muscadet.

LOUISE: Un verre seulement, s'il vous plaît.

LOUISE: You will let me taste yours?

JEAN-PIERRE: Here are our pink glasses of *Kir*. It is white wine with a little black currant liquor in it. It is a specialty of Dijon in Burgundy. Kir is the name of the man who made it popular. He was the mayor of Dijon. Do you like it?

PAUL: It is delicious.

JEAN-PIERRE: Now, let us choose our menu. The *entrées* are starters. Their lobster bisque is delicious but there are many other things. A little goat cheese on chicory salad for you, Paul? And for me, the salad with gizzards and bacon. The bisque for you, Louise? Or six snails with garlic and butter?

LOUISE: Gizzards, is it what I think? Chickens' stomachs?

JEAN-PIERRE: Exactly.

LOUISE: And the veal sweetbreads, what is that?

JEAN-PIERRE: A very tender part of veal, prepared with mushrooms and cream. And you, Paul? Do you want to try a tripe sausage?

PAUL: No, thank you. I will take the breast of duck, well done.

JEAN-PIERRE: The same for me, barely grilled. And for Louise? A chicken leg in truffle cream. Then a red wine, a Brouilly, for us and a Muscadet for Louise.

LOUISE: Only a glass, please.

Paul: Comme tout ceci est exquis! Merci, Jean-Pierre, de nous avoir amenés ici.

Jean-Pierre: Mais il faut prendre un dessert, maintenant. Pour toi Paul?

Paul: Un sorbet de pomme verte, sans vodka!

Jean-Pierre: Rien pour vous, Louise? Vous êtes trop sage! Une crème brulée pour moi, et trois express après.

Louise: En fait, je change d'avis, je vais essayer une île flottante!

PAUL: How delicious all of this is! Thank you, Jean-Pierre, for bringing us here.

JEAN-PIERRE: But we should have a dessert now. For you, Paul?

PAUL: A green apple sherbet, without vodka!

JEAN-PIERRE: Nothing for you, Louise? You are too good! A *crème brulée* for me, and three espresso coffees, afterwards.

LOUISE: Actually, I change my mind, I will try an *île flottante*!

VOCABULARY

ail, l' *m.*	garlic
amener	to bring
andouillette, l' *f.*	tripe sausage
apéritif, l' *m.*	drink
après	afterwards
autres choses	other things
beurre, le *m.*	butter
bien cuit	well done
bisque de homard, la *f.*	cream of lobster (bisque)
Bourgogne	Burgundy
canard, le *m.*	duck
cela (ça)	that
celle-ci	this one
cette fois	this time
champignon, le *m.*	mushroom
changer d'avis	to change one's mind
chaque	each
choisir	to choose
commencer	to start
convenir	to be satisfactory
courant d'air, le *m.*	draft
crème, la *f.*	cream
crème brulée, la *f.*	custard with caramel
crème de cassis, la *f.*	black currant liquor
délicieux	delicious
désirer	to like, to want
dessert, le *m.*	dessert
Dijon	(city in Burgundy)
en fait	actually
entrée, l' *f.*	first course
escargot, l' *m.*	snail

estomac, l' *m.*	stomach
exactement	exactly
exquis	exquisite
faire goûter	to let taste
fromage de chèvre, le *m.*	goat cheese
garçon, le *m.*	boy
gésier, le *m.*	gizzard
homme, l' *m.*	man
île flottante, l' *f.*	(a custard dessert with whipped egg whites on top: *lit.* floating island)
Kir	(name of a drink with white wine and black currant liquor)
lardon, le *m.*	bacon bit
magret, le *m.*	breast of duck
maire, le *m.*	mayor
Muscadet, le *m.*	(wine of the Loire Valley)
nappe, la *f.*	tablecloth
odeur, l' *f.*	smell
par ici	this way
parfait	perfect
partie, la *f.*	part
patte, la *f.*	leg
petit	small
plaire	to please
plus loin de	away from
pomme verte, la *f.*	green apple
porte, la *f.*	door
poularde, la *f.*	chicken (fattened)
pour	so that
rendre populaire	to popularize
ris de veau, le *m.*	veal sweetbreads
rouge	red
sage	wise, sensible
saignant	barely cooked
salade frisée, la *f.*	curly chicory

sans	without
sentir	to feel
serviette, la *f.*	napkin
seulement	only
sorbet, le *m.*	sherbet
spécialité, la *f.*	specialty
tout ceci	all of this
très tendre	very tender
trop sage	too restrained
truffe, la *f.*	truffle
verre, le *m.*	glass
vodka, la *f.*	vodka
vouloir bien	to be willing

GRAMMAR

Reflexive Verbs

Forms

Reflexive verbs are verbs of all conjugations recognizable because their infinitive is preceded by a reflexive pronoun, for example se *laver* (to wash oneself). In its conjugation, each subject pronoun–*je, tu, il, elle, nous, vous, ils, elles*–is accompanied by an object pronoun of the same person. These object pronouns are: *me, te, se, nous, vous, se.*

These object pronouns are direct or indirect objects and mean that the action carried out by the subject of the verb is reflected onto that subject.

Il se lève. – He gets (himself) up.
Il se lave les dents. – He brushes his teeth.

These verbs are very numerous in French, some of them with meanings that do not imply the "reflection" of the action.

s'en aller – to go away
Il s'en va. – He goes away.
Nous nous en allons. – We are leaving.

Note: When the infinitive of the reflexive verb depends on another verb, the pronoun used must be of the same person as that of the conjugated verb.

se promener – to walk
Nous allons nous promener. – We are going to take a walk.

[Note also that many verbs have a non-reflexive form as well, i.e. *laver* (to wash), *lever* (to raise), *promener* (to walk).]

Conjugation

Reflexive verbs generally follow regular conjugations; the only difference being that the reflexive pronoun is included.

In compound tenses, all reflexive verbs are conjugated with *être*.

Je me suis levé. (*se lever* – to get up)
I got up.

Elles se sont levées tôt.
They (*f.*) got up early.

Vous vous tenez bien. (*se tenir* – to behave)
You are behaving well.

Elles se vendent bien. (*se vendre* – to sell)
They sell well.

Constructions

- Place of the reflexive pronoun

  The rule given earlier on the place of object pronouns applies in this case. (See Lesson Three.)

  Normal order for several pronouns in front of the verb:

me	le	lui	y	en
te	la	leur		
se	les			
nous				
vous				
se				

Reflexive pronouns can be direct or indirect objects but they are always placed first.

Il se le prépare. (*se préparer* – to prepare oneself)
He prepares it for himself.
Je m'en prépare.
I prepare some of it for myself.

Nous nous y sommes bien amusés. (*s'amuser* – to amuse oneself)
We enjoyed ourselves there.

- Direct or indirect objects

When the verb has a direct object, the reflexive pronoun, without any change of form or place, becomes an indirect object.

Elle s'est lavé les cheveux. (*se laver* – to wash oneself)
She washed her hair. (*s'* = indirect object)

Ils se sont réjouis de la nouvelle. (*se réjouir* – to rejoice)
They rejoiced about the news. (*se* = direct object)

- Agreement of past participle

In compound tenses of verbs conjugated with *être* the past participle agrees with the subject, but if the reflexive verb has a direct object, there is no agreement.

Elle s'est lavé les cheveux.
She washed her hair (d.o).

Elles se sont remis des cadeaux.
They gave presents to one another.
> no agreement: *des cadeaux* = direct object/*se* = indirect object

But:
Elle s'est remise de sa maladie. (*se remettre* – to recover)
She recovered from her illness.
> agreement: *se* = direct object

Idiomatic Uses

A large number of verbs that have a reflexive form do not have a reflexive meaning. They are used "idiomatically" with a specific meaning.

se mettre à (to start doing something)
Elle s'est mise à pleurer. – She burst into tears.

s'en aller (to leave)
Maintenant, nous nous en allons. – Now we are leaving.
Allez-vous en. – Go away.

se souvenir de (to remember)
Elle se souvient de ses vacances. – She remembers her vacation.

se rendre à + name of place (to go to)
Je vais me rendre à Paris. – I am leaving for Paris.

se trouver (to be in a certain place or situation)
Elle se trouva seule. – She was alone.

se faire à (to become used to)
C'était dur mais il s'y est fait. – It was hard but he got used to it.

se passer de (to do without)
Il ne peut pas se passer de sucre. – He cannot live without sugar.

ne pas se dire (to speak incorrectly)
Cela ne se dit pas. – This is not the way to say that.

ne pas se faire (that should not be done – mostly about manners)
Cela ne se fait pas. – It is not polite to do that.

Reflexive Uses with a Passive Meaning

Ceci ne se fait pas comme ça.
This is not done that way.

Les pommes se vendent à six francs le kilo.
Apples sell (are sold) for six francs a kilo.

EXERCISES

I. Fill in the blank with the correct form of the verb given. For each phrase you will use three tenses.

1. Vous ______ très rapidement. (s'habiller)
2. Cette habitude ______ en travaillant. (se former)
3. Ce beau vase ______ en tombant. (se casser)
4. Tu ______ le doigt. (se couper)
5. Elle ______ (se brosser) les cheveux avant de ______ (se coucher).
6. Nous ______ (se laver) les mains avant le repas.

II. Answer the following questions with a short sentence using a reflexive verb.

1. Comment vous appelez-vous?
2. Comment s'appelle votre père? Votre mère?
3. Où se trouve votre maison?
4. Où se trouve votre travail?
5. Est-ce que vous vous intéressez à la politique?
6. Est-ce que vous vous dépêchez pour voir tous les monuments possible?
7. Est-ce que vous vous fatiguez de marcher à travers la ville?
8. Est-ce que vous vous reposez bien pendant la nuit?

III. First identify the infinitive of the verb, then write the form in the person indicated by the pronoun, keeping the same tense.

1. Il s'est amusé. (vous)
2. Elle ne s'ennuiera pas. (nous)
3. Nous nous étions trompés. (elles)
4. Ils se couchent. (tu)

5. Nous nous rencontrerons. (ils)
6. Vous ne vous ferez pas de mal. (je)
7. Elle s'est intéressée. (ils)
8. Nous nous fréquentons. (elles)
9. Il s'en est aperçu. (je)
10. Vous ne vous ressemblez pas. (ils)

LESSON ELEVEN

DIALOGUE

Après le Diner

JEAN-PIERRE: Merci, Paul et Louise, pour cette bonne soirée.

PAUL: Avec plaisir! Quel délicieux dîner! Mais maintenant, une bonne promenade à pied va me faire du bien, pour la digestion!

JEAN-PIERRE: Paul, tu vas faire ta digestion dans la voiture.

PAUL: Où est ta voiture?

JEAN-PIERRE: Elle est assez loin, tu auras ta petite promenade quand même!

LOUISE: Est-ce que c'est difficile de stationner à Paris?

JEAN-PIERRE: Tu penses! C'est impossible! Mais nous sommes des milliers de fous qui essaient chaque jour. Ah! Tu vois la voiture rouge, dans ce coin? C'est ma voiture. Est-ce qu'il y a un papier sur le pare-brise?

PAUL: Un papier? Le pare-brise?

JEAN-PIERRE: Oui, la brise, c'est le vent, l'air qui souffle... 'Pare' c'est...

PAUL: Je comprends! Et le papier, c'est de la police?

After Dinner

Jean-Pierre: Thank you for this good evening, Paul and Louise.

Paul: With pleasure! What a delicious dinner! But now a good walk will do me a lot of good, for my digestion!

Jean-Pierre: Paul, you are going to do your digesting in the car.

Paul: Where is your car?

Jean-Pierre: It is quite far, you will have your little walk all the same!

Louise: Is it hard to park in Paris?

Jean-Pierre: You bet! It is impossible! But we are thousands of crazy people who try to every day. Ah! You see the red car, in that corner? That's my car. Is there a slip of paper on my windshield?

Paul: A paper? The windshield?

Jean-Pierre: Yes, the "brise" is the wind, the air blowing around... "Pare" is...

Paul: I understand! And the paper is from the police?

JEAN-PIERRE: Bien sûr! Une contravention, ou, comme on dit, une 'contredanse'! Et les dames qui vérifient les voitures qui ont le droit, ou pas le droit, de stationner, celles qui contrôlent les parcmètres, on les appelle les 'pervenches'. Ce sont des fleurs bleues, mais on ne les aime pas. Avant, leur uniforme était de couleur rouge-violet, et on les appelait 'les aubergines', un bon légume, mais pas élégant! Alors elles ont protesté et on leur a donné des uniformes bleu clair, avec même un petit chapeau bleu clair. C'est plus joli, mais on ne les aime pas quand même!

LOUISE: Je crois que vous n'avez pas de 'contredanse', Jean-Pierre.

JEAN-PIERRE: Quelle chance! Mais cette autre voiture bloque ma sortie.

PAUL: Je vais rester dehors et te faire signe.

JEAN-PIERRE: Ah! Nous sommes libres! Je vais vous emmener voir la Tour Eiffel.

LOUISE: Mais... Nous l'avons déjà vue.

JEAN-PIERRE: La nuit? Illuminée?

LOUISE: Non, pas la nuit. Je ne sais pas quelle heure il est, mais la circulation est toujours très active! Et tous ces gens sur les trottoirs, Paris ne dort jamais! Quand le métro s'arrête-t-il?

JEAN-PIERRE: À une heure du matin et il reprend à cinq heures. Il est minuit maintenant.

PAUL: Ah! Regardez la Tour Eiffel toute en or! Et pas de projecteurs autour?

JEAN-PIERRE: Of course! A ticket or as we say, a *contradance*! And the ladies who check the cars, which are allowed, or not allowed, to be parked, who control the parking meters, they are called the "periwinkles." They are blue flowers, but they are not liked. Before, their uniforms were a purplish red and we called them the "eggplants," a good vegetable, but not elegant! So they protested and they gave them light blue uniforms, even with a small light blue hat. It looks nicer, but they are not liked anyways!

LOUISE: I think that you do not have a "contradance," Jean-Pierre.

JEAN-PIERRE: What luck! But this other car is blocking my exit.

PAUL: I will stay out to direct you.

JEAN-PIERRE: Ah! We are free! I am going to take you to see the Eiffel Tower.

LOUISE: But... We have already seen it.

JEAN-PIERRE: At night? All lit up?

LOUISE: No, not at night. I do not know what time it is, but traffic is still very active! And all these people on the sidewalks, Paris never sleeps! When does the subway stop running?

JEAN-PIERRE: At one o'clock in the morning and it starts again at five o'clock. It is midnight now.

PAUL: Ah! Look at the Eiffel Tower all in gold! And no projectors outside?

JEAN-PIERRE: Non, toute la lumière est intérieure, depuis quatre, cinq, peut-être dix ans.

LOUISE: C'est magnifique. Comme un bijou de filigrane d'or. Ah! Monsieur Eiffel peut être fier de son oeuvre.

JEAN-PIERRE: Et si nous allions voir tous les autres monuments illuminés?

PAUL: Merveilleux!

JEAN-PIERRE: No, all the lighting is on the inside, and has been so for four, five, maybe ten years.

LOUISE: It is magnificent. A jewel of gold filigree. Ah! Monsieur Eiffel can be proud of his work.

JEAN-PIERRE: And why not go see all the other monuments lit up?

PAUL: Marvelous!

VOCABULARY

active	active
assez loin	quite far
aubergine, l' *f.*	eggplant
autour	around
avec plaisir	with pleasure
bleu clair	light blue
bloquer	to block
chance, la *f.*	luck
contravention, la *f.*	ticket
contrôler	to control
dame, la *f.*	woman
dehors	outside
déjà	already
délicieux	delicious
depuis	since
difficile	difficile
digestion, la *f.*	digestion
dîner, le *m.*	dinner
dormir	to sleep
droit, le *m.*	right to do something
emmener	to take someone to
essayer	to try
faire du bien	to do someone good
faire signe	to signal
fier	proud
filigrane, la *f.*	filigree
fou, le *m.*	crazy person
illuminé	lit up
joli	pretty
légume, le *m.*	vegetable
libre	free

lumière, la *f.*	light
merveilleux	marvelous
milliers, des *m.*	thousands
minuit	midnight
nuit, la *f.*	night
oeuvre, l' *f.*	work
or, l' *m.*	gold
papier, le *m.*	paper
parcmètre, le *m.*	parking meter
pare-brise, le *m.*	windshield
pervenche, la *f.*	periwinkle
peut-être	perhaps
police, la *f.*	police
projecteur, le *m.*	projector
protester	to protest
quand même	all the same
quel...	what a...
reprendre	to start again
rester	to remain
rouge violet	purple red
s'arrêter	to stop running
soirée, la *f.*	evening
sortie, la *f.*	the way out
souffler	to blow
stationner	to park
Tu penses!	You bet!
uniforme, l' *m.*	uniform
vent, le *m.*	wind
vérifier	to check

GRAMMAR

The Passive Voice

There are two voices in French as in English: the active voice and the passive voice. In grammar, a voice is a complete conjugation with a fundamental meaning.

ACTIVE VOICE

The subject of the verb does the action indicated by the meaning of the verb.

J'ouvre la porte.
I open the door.

PASSIVE VOICE

The subject of the verb receives the action indicated by the verb.

La porte est ouverte par le garçon.
The door is opened by the boy.

The "agent" does the action: by the boy. The preposition *par* precedes the noun indicating the agent: *par le garçon.*

Forms

The passive voice is obtained by inserting the forms of the verb *être* (to be) in the appropriate persons and tenses, between the subject and the verb in the past participle form.

Il aime. Il est aimé.
He loves. He is loved.

Elle aimera. Elle sera aimée.
She will love. She will be loved.

Note:

I. Only verbs that have a direct object can be formed in the passive voice. The direct object becomes the subject of the passive verb. These verbs are called transitive (*tr.*).

Il a choisi ces cadeaux pour vous.
He chose these presents for you.

Ces cadeaux ont été choisis par lui pour vous.
These presents were chosen for you by him.

The construction of the verb will often be different in French and in English.

Ils ont regardé ces belles photos.
They looked at these beautiful photos.

Ces belles photos ont été regardées par eux.
These beautiful photos were "looked at" by them.

II. As the passive can be formed in English with verbs that are not transitive (that cannot have a direct object) some expressions cannot be translated directly from the English passive form to the French.

In English: to give something (d.o.) to someone (i.o.)
He was given a car for his birthday.
(i.o. becomes the subject)

In French: *donner quelque chose à quelqu'un*
direct object: *quelque chose*
Une voiture lui a été donnée pour son anniversaire.
A car was given to him for his birthday.
(In French, only the direct object can become the subject of the passive verb. *À quelqu'un,* an indirect object, cannot be the subject of the verb.)

III. When a personal subject is desired, the pronoun *on* (one) is used:

On lui a donné une voiture.
He was given a car.

The meaning is passive, but the French construction is active.

The same reasoning applies to expressions such as:

he was asked to... (*demander qq ch à qqn*)
he was ordered to... (*ordonner qq ch à qqn*)

And to the innumerable verbs constructed after this pattern:

direct object – a thing
indirect object – with *à* + a person

On a répondu <u>à</u> la question.
The question was answered.

EXERCISES

I. Change the following sentences into a passive form.

1. Un homme courageux a sauvé ce garçon.
2. Des ingénieurs habiles ont construit ce pont.
3. Un musicien célèbre a écrit cette chanson.
4. Cette entreprise a gagné beaucoup d'argent.
5. Son travail prend tout son temps.
6. Des personnes généreuses ont élevé cet enfant.

II. Translate the following sentences using the passive voice when possible, and the form *on* when not possible.

1. He was asked many questions.
2. We were ordered to stop the car.
3. He was loved by all his friends.
4. She was admired for her intelligence.
5. The group was led by a guide.
6. The tourist was given interesting information.

LESSON TWELVE

DIALOGUE

Promenade Autour de la Sorbonne

PAUL: Ce matin, quand je me réveillais, j'ai eu une bonne idée pour nos activités de la journée.

LOUISE: Très bien, moi aussi. Mais peut-être que ton idée est plus intéressante que la mienne.

PAUL: Nous n'avons pas encore vu le quartier des étudiants, la Sorbonne, le Panthéon, et la rue de la Huchette.

LOUISE: Je regarde ma carte. C'est presque à côté. Nous prenons l'autobus 38 et nous descendons au Val de Grâce. Ensuite, nous marchons.

PAUL: D'abord, nous nous arrêterons à notre café favori, avenue Jean Moulin, pour le café et le croissant du matin.

LOUISE: En route! Mais prenons notre parapluie. As-tu remarqué toutes ces femmes bien habillées qui passent? Et combien il y a de vestes rouges et de pantalons, ou jupes noires? Et puis des écharpes jaune vif. C'est joli, n'est-ce pas? Ça fait chic.

PAUL: Ah! Oui. Tu as ta carte pour l'autobus? Le voilà! Tu vois l'église avec le dôme au bout de la rue? C'est le Val de Grâce.

LOUISE: J'ai vu une belle sculpture, du bus, là-bas à gauche, dans un jardin avec une fontaine. Allons la voir! C'est merveilleux, cet énorme globe, avec cette grande allée d'arbres derrière. Elle nous invite à marcher.

A Stroll Around the Sorbonne

PAUL: This morning, as I was waking up, I had a good idea for our activities of the day.

LOUISE: Very good, me too. But perhaps your idea is better than mine.

PAUL: We have not yet seen the section of the students, the Sorbonne, the Pantheon, and the rue de la Huchette.

LOUISE: I'm looking at my map. It's almost next door. We take the 38 bus and we get off at Val de Grace. After that, we walk.

PAUL: First, we will stop at our favorite café, on avenue Jean Moulin, for the morning coffee and croissant.

LOUISE: Let's go! But let's take our umbrellas. Have you noticed all these well-dressed women who walk by? And how many red jackets with black pants, or black skirts, there are? And then bright yellow scarves. It is pretty, isn't it? It looks chic.

PAUL: Ah! Yes. You have your pass for the bus? There it is! You see the church with its dome at the end of the street? It is the Val de Grâce.

LOUISE: I saw a beautiful sculpture, from the bus, over there to the left, in a garden with a fountain. Let's go see it! It's marvelous, this enormous globe, with this long tree-lined alley behind. It invites us to walk.

PAUL: Et nous arrivons au jardin du Luxembourg!

LOUISE: Et cet autre grande église, à droite, avec un grand dôme?

PAUL: C'est... c'est le Panthéon! C'était une église, mais maintenant, c'est le monument où sont enterrés les plus grands hommes de ce pays. Tu vois l'inscription au dessus de l'entrée: 'A toutes les gloires de la France'. Tiens, Victor Hugo est enterré ici. Nous devons revenir voir l'intérieur.

LOUISE: Descendons la rue Soufflot. C'était l'architecte qui a construit le Panthéon au XVIIIème siècle. Et maintenant, nous tournons à droite. C'est bien le boulevard St. Michel. Des boutiques de vêtements, des blue-jeans comme aux Etats-Unis, et des vestes, des tricots, et partout, soldes! Rabais, prix extraordinaires!

PAUL: Si tu vois une de ces vestes rouges, tu pourrais l'essayer...

Louise essaie une veste.

LOUISE: Qu'est-ce que tu en penses, Paul? Tu l'aimes?

PAUL: Mais oui! Et cette écharpe jaune? Tu auras l'air tout à fait française, maintenant.

LOUISE: Et à droite, ici, encore un dôme. Lis la plaque au coin de la rue.

PAUL: Place de la Sorbonne. Fondée en 1220 par Robert de Sorbon. Mais ces bâtiments-ci ont seulement 300 ou 350 ans.

LOUISE: Seulement? Ah! J'ai tellement faim. Allons déjeuner!

PAUL: And we reach the Luxembourg Gardens!

LOUISE: And this other great church to the right, with a tall dome?

PAUL: That is... that is the Panthéon! It was a church but now it is the monument where the greatest men of the country are buried. You see the inscription above the entrance: "To all the glories of France." Well, Victor Hugo is buried here. We must come back to visit the inside.

LOUISE: Let's go down the rue Soufflot. He was the architect who built the Pantheon in the eighteenth century. And now, let's turn to the right. It is indeed the boulevard St. Michel. Clothes shops, blue jeans as in the States, and jackets, sweaters, and everywhere, sales! Markdowns, extraordinary prices!

PAUL: If you see one of those red jackets, you could try it...

Louise tries on a jacket.

LOUISE: What do you think of it, Paul? Do you like it?

PAUL: But of course! And this yellow scarf? You are going to look perfectly French now.

LOUISE: And to the right, here, another dome. Read the plaque at the corner of the street.

PAUL: Place de la Sorbonne. Founded in 1220 by Robert de Sorbon. But these buildings are only 300 or 350 years old.

LOUISE: Only? Ah! I am so hungry. Let's go have lunch!

VOCABULARY

activité, l' *f.*	activity
allée, l' *f.*	alley
arbre, l' *m.*	tree
au bout de	at the end of
au dessus de	above
avenue, l' *f.*	avenue
avoir faim	to be hungry
bien habillé	well dressed
boutique, la *f.*	shop
ça fait chic	it looks smart, chic
chez...	at...
combien	how many
derrière	behind
du bus	from the bus
écharpe, l' *f.*	scarf
encore un	another one
énorme	enormous
ensuite	after that
entrée, l' *f.*	entrance
espérer	to hope
essayer	to try on
être enterré	to be buried
étudiant, l' *m.*	student
extraordinaire	extraordinary
favori	favorite
fondé	founded
fontaine, la *f.*	fountain
globe, le *m.*	globe
gloire, la *f.*	glory
idée, l' *f.*	idea
inscription, l' *f.*	inscription

jaune vif	bright yellow
journée, la *f.*	day
jupe, la *f.*	skirt
là-bas	over there
lire	to read
ne ... pas encore	not yet
pantalon, le *m.*	pants
passer	to walk by
pays, le *m.*	country
presque à coté	almost next door
prix, le *m.*	price
quand	when
rabais, le *m.*	discount
revenir	to come back
sculpture, la *f.*	sculpture
se réveiller	to wake up
soldes, les *f.*	bargains
tellement	so much
tricot, le *m.*	sweater
vêtement, le *m.*	clothing
voir	to see

GRAMMAR

Demonstrative Adjectives and Pronouns

These adjectives and pronouns are used to attract attention to the word they precede.

Forms

Adjectives Placed Before a Noun

	masculine	*feminine*	*neuter*	
sg.	ce/cet	cette	ce	(this)
pl.	ces	ces		(these)
sg.	ce ... ci	cette ... ci	ceci	(this ... here)
	ce ... là	cette ... là	cela	(this ... there)
pl.	ces ... ci	ces ... ci		(these ... here)
	ces ... là	ces ... là		(these ... there)

Pronouns

	masculine	*feminine*	
sg.	celui + de	celle + de	(that of)
	celui + que	celle + que	(that which)
pl.	ceux + de	celles + de	(those of)
	ceux + que	celles + que	(those which)
sg.	celui-ci	celle-ci	(this one)
	celui-là	celle-là	(that one)
pl.	ceux-ci	celles-ci	(these ones)
	ceux-là	celles-là	(those ones)

Usage

- *ce* + singular noun

- *cet* before a noun starting with a vowel or a mute *h*

- *Ci* and *là* are placed after the noun for emphasis or opposition.

  J'aime cette photo-ci mais je n'aime pas cette photo-là.
  I like this photograph (here) but I don't like that photograph (there).

  On principle *ci* indicates what is nearer, *là* what is farther away.

- In conversation, *cela* becomes *ça*.

- Demonstrative adjectives can be used with a temporal sense:

  ce soir – tonight
  ce matin – this morning
  ces temps-ci... – these days...
  ces jours-ci... – these days...
  en ce temps-là... – in those days...

- Demonstrative pronouns: *Celui, celle,* and *ceux* are always used before a *de* or a *que*.

  celui de ma soeur – the one my sister has
  celle que je connais – the one I know

Note: The English "the one" is never translated directly in French because one is a number, not a pronoun. The demonstrative in the appropriate form is the only pronoun to use before *de* or *que*.

Uses of ce (c' in front of a vowel)

This form is neuter—neither masculine nor feminine—but used with the verb *être* it acts as masculine.

Regardez cette image (f.). C'est très beau.
Look at this image. It is very beautiful.

An antecedent of the relative pronoun must be used when there is no noun to serve as antecedent in the sentence: *ce qui, ce que, ce dont,* even when there is a preposition.

Je lui ai dit ce qui me fait plaisir.
I told him what I like.

Voici ce dont nous parlons. (*parler de* – to speak of)
This is what we talk about.

Voilà ce à quoi ils se sont résignés.
Here is what they resigned themselves to.

Voilà ce pour quoi il dépense son argent.
Here is what he uses his money for.

Ce replaces the English "he," "she," "it," and "they" in front of *être* followed by:

1. article
   possessive + noun
   demonstrative

   Voici Marie. C'est ma soeur.
   This is Mary. She is my sister.

   Ce sont des gens charmants.
   They are charming people.

II. a person's name

C'est Monsieur Dupont.
It's Mister Dupont.

III. a pronoun of any kind

C'est celle qui m'a parlé.
She is the one who talked to me.

C'est moi!
It is I.

IV. to sum up an idea

Ça, c'est merveilleux.
That is marvelous.

EXERCISES

I. Place the correct demonstrative adjective before the following nouns.

1. ________ beau jour (this fine day)
2. ________ belle journée
3. ________ belles journées
4. ________ beaux jours
5. ________ ami de la famille
6. ________ amis de la famille

II. Translate the expression in English using a demonstrative pronoun.

1. Je préfère ______ (this) à ______ (that).
2. Il préfère ______ (this one) et non ______ (that one).
3. J'aime cette photo-ci. Je n'aime pas ______ (that one).
4. ______ (the one) qu'il m'a montré est plus beau.
5. J'ai vu les photos de Paul mais non ______ de Marie.
6. De belles statues? J'ai vu ______ de la Place de la Concorde.
7. Avez-vous vu les grands tableaux de ce peintre?
   Oui, j'ai vu ______ (these), mais non ______ (those).
8. Des livres? ______ (the ones) que vous aimez sont ici.
9. Des pommes? ______ (the ones) que vous aimez sont sur la table.
10. Un employé? ______ (the one) à qui j'ai demandé cela.

III. In the following sentences use *ce* or *il/elle* as needed.

1. ______ (she is) une belle jeune fille.
2. Paul? ______ (he is) mon meilleur ami.
3. ______ (this) n'est pas beau.
4. Paul? ______ est très gentil.
5. ______ (it) est évident.

6. Etes-vous Marie? Oui, _______ (I am) moi.
7. Ces papiers? Oui, _______ (they are) les miens.
8. Cette maison? _______ est très chère.
9. _______ (who is it)?
10. (She is) _______ Madame C.
11. _______ (it is you)!

LESSON THIRTEEN

DIALOGUE

Promenade sur le Boulevard St. Michel

LOUISE: C'est ça, un sandwich jambon-beurre?

PAUL: Oui, une demi-baguette coupée en long, bien beurrée et des tranches de jambon cuit. Mmm! C'est délicieux!

LOUISE: Mais le jambon a du gras!

PAUL: C'est vrai, mais c'est bon. Tu peux l'enlever si tu veux. Tu tires, et le gras se détache.

LOUISE: C'est vrai que c'est bon! Le pain est si croustillant. Mais je ne vais jamais tout manger.

PAUL: Tu laisseras ce que tu ne voudras pas. Comme c'est agréable de manger dehors, à l'ombre des arbres de l'avenue!

LOUISE: Eh bien! Comment ça se fait? J'ai tout fini. Et maintenant, un bon café et nous continuons notre promenade. Tu as ton parapluie?

PAUL: Oui je l'ai, mais le soleil brille. Tant mieux, il n'est pas nécessaire.

LOUISE: Ce boulevard a toujours été la promenade des étudiants. Mais aujourd'hui, il y a douze autres universités dans Paris et beaucoup d'étudiants n'ont pas cette belle promenade.

PAUL: Voilà une grande librairie, de l'autre côté de la rue.

A Walk on St. Michel Boulevard

LOUISE: That's what a ham-and-butter sandwich is?

PAUL: Yes, half a *baguette,* split lengthwise, well buttered, and slices of cooked ham. Mmm! It's delicious!

LOUISE: But the ham has fat!

PAUL: That's true, but it tastes good. You can take it off if you want. You pull and the fat comes off.

LOUISE: It's true that it is good! The bread is so crusty. But I am never going to eat all of it.

PAUL: You will leave what you do not want. How pleasant to eat outside under the shade of the trees of the avenue!

LOUISE: Well, how about that? I have finished all of it. Now a good cup of coffee and we continue our stroll. You have your umbrella?

PAUL: Yes, I have it, but the sun is shining. So much the better, we don't need it.

LOUISE: This boulevard has always been the student's walk. But today there are twelve other universities in Paris and many students do not have this beautiful walk.

PAUL: There is a large bookstore, on the other side of the street.

Louise: Et tous ces étudiants, de types si différents vont et viennent. Ils portent des livres, des sacs. Les filles et les garçons sont habillés avec des T-shirts et des pantalons, beaucoup de jeans. Et ils ont l'air heureux, n'est-ce pas?

Paul: Mais qu'est-ce que c'est que ça? Des vieux murs décrépits en brique, tout détruits? Et une grande affiche avec une dame à la licorne?

Louise: Ces murs détruits, ce sont, dit mon guide, les restes de Thermes, un établissement de bains du temps des Romains, au 2ème siècle après J.C.

Paul: Au temps où Paris s'appelait Lutetia?

Louise: Oui, et la population locale les Parisii.

Paul: C'est eux qui ont gagné! Aujourd'hui, on a Paris et nous sommes des Parisiens!

Louise: Maintenant nous arrivons en bas du boulevard St. Michel. La Seine est proche. Traversons. Au feu vert, Paul!

Paul: Tu vois devant toi la grande fontaine St. Michel, construite au XVIIème siècle...

Louise: Elle est toute récente!

Paul: ...pour célébrer des travaux qui ont apporté les eaux d'une source loin dans la campagne aux Parisiens. Quand il fait chaud, beaucoup de gens sont assis sur le bord et trempent leurs pieds dans l'eau.

Louise: Il faut traverser de nouveau l'avenue! Qu'est-ce que tu lis sur la plaque?

LOUISE: And all these students, of so many different types, come and go. They carry books, bags. Girls and boys are dressed in T-shirts and pants, many wear jeans. And they look happy, don't they?

PAUL: But what is this? Old, decrepit walls of brick, all broken up? And a large sign with a woman and a unicorn?

LOUISE: Those broken-down walls are, my guidebook says, the remnants of Thermi, bathhouse buildings dating from the times of the Romans, in the 2nd century A.D.

PAUL: At the time Paris was called Lutetia?

LOUISE: Yes, and the local population the Parisii.

PAUL: And they are the ones who won! Today, we have Paris and we are Parisians!

LOUISE: Now we are coming to the lower end of St. Michel boulevard. The Seine is near. Let's cross the street. At the green light, Paul!

PAUL: You see in front of you the great St. Michel fountain, built in the seventeenth century…

LOUISE: It is quite recent!

PAUL: …to celebrate works that brought the waters from a spring far in the countryside to the Parisians. When it is hot, many people are seated on the rim and dip their feet in the water.

LOUISE: We cross the avenue again! What do you read on this sign?

PAUL: Rue de la Huchette! Il n'y a pas de voitures car c'est une rue piétonne, que c'est bien! Et je me rappelle, c'est dans cette rue qu'il y a un théâtre où ils jouent *La Cantatrice Chauve* depuis 1947! Allons voir si nous pourrions avoir des places pour ce soir!

PAUL: Rue de la Huchette! There are no cars as it is a pedestrian street, how nice! And I remember, it is in this street that there is a theater where they have been playing *The Bald Soprano* since 1947! Let's go and see if we could have seats for tonight!

VOCABULARY

affiche, l' *f.*	poster
apporter	to bring
après J.C.	A.D.
baguette, la *f.*	bread (long, thin loaf)
beurre, le *m.*	butter
beurrée	buttered
bord, le *m.*	edge
briller	to shine
brique, la *f.*	brick
campagne, la *f.*	in the countryside
célébrer	to celebrate
ce que	what
ce soir	tonight
c'est ceux qui	they are the ones who
chaud	hot
comment ça se fait?	how did it happen?
continuer	to continue
coupé	cut
croustillant	crusty
cuit	cooked
décrépits	run-down
de l'autre côté de	on the other side of
depuis	since
douze	twelve
en bas de	at the foot of
enlever	to cut off
en long	lengthwise
établissement de bains, l' *m.*	bathhouse
feu vert, le *m.*	green light
gagner	to win out
gras, le *m.*	fat

heureux	happy
jambon, le *m.*	ham
jouer	to play
La Cantatrice Chauve	The Bald Soprano (E. Ionesco play)
laisser	to leave
leur	their
librairie, la *f.*	bookstore
licorne, la *f.*	unicorn
locale	local
loin	far away
mur, le *m.*	wall
pieds, les *m.*	feet
piétonne, la *f.*	pedestrian
place, la *f.*	seat
population, la *f.*	population
proche	near
qu'est-ce que c'est que ça?	what is that?
restes, les *m.*	remains
Romains, les *m.*	Romans
sac, le *m.*	bag
se détacher	to come free
si différent	so different
soleil, le *m.*	sun
source, la *f.*	spring
tant mieux	so much the better
théâtre, le *m.*	theater
Thermes, les *m.*	Roman Baths
tirer	to pull
toute récente	quite recent
tranche, la *f.*	slice
travaux, les *m.*	works
tremper	to dip
type, le *m.*	type
voiture, la *f.*	car
vouloir	to want

GRAMMAR

Comparison of Adjectives, Nouns, and Adverbs

Comparison of Adjectives

There are three levels of comparison: equality, superiority, and inferiority. They are expressed with the use of an adverb + adjective + *que*.

Equality: *aussi* + adjective + *que*

Jean est aussi grand que son frère.
John is as tall as his brother.

Superiority: *plus* + adjective + *que*

Jean est plus grand que son frère.
John is taller than his brother.

Inferiority: *moins* + adjective + *que*

Jean est moins grand que son frère.
John is shorter than his brother.

Irregular Forms

bon (good)
- superiority: *meilleur que...* (better than)
- inferiority: *moins bon que...* (less good than)
- equality: *aussi bon que...* (as good as)

mauvais (bad)
- superiority: *pire* or *plus mauvais* (worse/more bad)

Comparison of Nouns

Equality: *autant de ... que ...* (as many as)

J'ai autant d'amis que Paul.
I have as many friends as Paul.

Superiority: *plus de ... que ...* (more than)

J'ai plus d'argent que lui.
I have more money than he has.

Inferiority: *moins de ... que ...* (less than)

J'ai moins d'amis que Paul.
I have fewer friends than Paul.

Constructions

- After a number: *de plus que...* (more than)
  de moins que... (less than)

  J'ai quatre livres de plus que vous.
  I have four books more than you have.

- Emphasis: the adverbs *bien, beaucoup, tellement,* etc. are placed before the expression of comparison.

  Louise est bien plus jolie que Marie.
  Louise is much prettier than Mary.

- *Beaucoup* should not be used before *meilleur.*

  Ce café est bien meilleur que l'autre.
  This coffee is much better than the other one.

- The comparative adverb should be repeated before each adjective.

  Il est plus aimable, plus poli, plus sérieux que les autres.
  He is kinder, more polite and more serious than the others.

- Equality is expressed with *même* + *que.*

  J'ai les mêmes idées que vous.
  I have the same ideas that you have.

Superlative Forms

- Adjectives

  Superiority: *le/la/les plus* + adjective + *de* (the most ... of)

  C'est l'histoire la plus triste de toutes.
  It is the saddest of all stories.

  Inferiority: *le/la/les moins* + adjective + *de* (the least ... of)

  Les pommes les moins belles de la récolte.
  The worst-looking apples of the harvest.

Irregular Forms:

An article is placed before the comparative.

la meilleure performance – the best performance
la pire performance – the worst performance

• Nouns

Superiority: *le plus de* + noun + *de* (the most ... of)

Il a le plus grand nombre de livres.
He has the highest number of books.

Inferiority: *le moins de* + noun + *de* (the least ... of)

Pas le moins du monde!
Not at all. (*lit.* not the least in the world)

Note: *Dans*, the translation of English "in," is not used in French.

Comparison of Adverbs

These forms are the same as those for adjectives, with *le* added before the adverb in the superlative form.

Je fais ceci le moins souvent possible.
I do this as seldom as possible.

Je fais ceci moins souvent que cela.
I do this less often than that.

Useful Expressions

- *valoir mieux* – it is better to...
- *plus ... plus* – more ... more
- *plus ... moins* – more ... less
- *plus ... mieux* – more ... better

You will notice that there is no article before the adverb.

Plus il voyage, plus il veut voyager.
The more he travels, the more he wants to travel.

Plus je travaille, moins j'aime travailler.
The more I work, the less I like to work.

- *de plus en plus* – more and more
- *de moins en moins* – less and less

Il pleut de plus en plus.
It is raining more and more.

Je te comprends de moins en moins.
I understand you less and less.

- *encore plus* – even more
- *encore moins* – even less
- *faire de son mieux* – make all possible effort/do one's best

Je suis sûr qu'il fait de son mieux.
I am sure that he does his best.

EXERCISES

I. Degrees of comparison: Fill in the blanks using the comparative expression needed to give the right meaning to the sentence.

1. Un melon est ______ un petit pois. (gros)
2. Un chien est ______ un cheval. (intelligent)
3. Il y a ______ de personnes ______ opinions.
4. Il y a ______ (jours) dans une semaine ______ dans un mois.
5. L'argent n'est pas ______ l'or. (cher)
6. J'ai dix dollars. Il a vingt dollars.
   Il a dix dollars ______ moi.
   J'ai dix dollars ______ lui.
7. Elle a trente ans. Il a quarante ans.
   Il a ______ elle.
   Elle a ______ lui.
8. Il a ______ (grand – superlative) maison du village.
9. C'est l'exercice ______ (difficile – superlative) du livre.
10. C'est l'action ______ (audacieuse) ______ siècle. (superlative)

II. Translate the following expressions.

1. The more he works, the more he earns.
2. The less he reads, the more he writes.
3. The more he works, the less we see him.
4. I have the same bag as you.
5. We have a better car than they have.
6. Our situation is worse than yours.
7. This flower is prettier than this one.
8. This flower is not as pretty as that one.
9. This cake is not better than this one.
10. There are as many chairs as guests.

LESSON FOURTEEN

DIALOGUE

Au Musée du Louvre

PAUL: J'ai envie d'aller au Louvre dire bonjour à la Mona Lisa et acheter des livres d'art pour emporter avec nous.

LOUISE: Dans quelle partie de Paris le Louvre se trouve-t-il?

PAUL: Au centre, près de la Seine. C'était la résidence des rois de France quand ils étaient en ville, avant la révolution de 1789.

LOUISE: Oui, je sais! Quel dommage de ne pas être ici pour les fêtes du 14 Juillet. Il y a des feux d'artifice magnifiques sur la Seine, sur la Tour Eiffel...

PAUL: C'est l'autobus 68 qui va au Louvre. Il s'arrête au même endroit que le 38. Nous allons voir un nouvel itinéraire! En passant en haut du boulevard Raspail, il faut faire attention à la statue de Balzac par Rodin. Et juste avant, nous traverserons le boulevard Montparnasse.

LOUISE: Montparnasse, c'était le quartier des artistes, non?

PAUL: Oui. Ce soir, nous irons diner à la Coupole, un restaurant célèbre de ce quartier.

LOUISE: Voilà l'autobus. On montre sa carte et, en route. Pardon, monsieur, pour descendre juste avant la Seine, c'est quel arrêt? Quai Voltaire! Merci bien. Nous y voilà. On descend, on traverse la rue. On prend le Pont Royal, et devant nous, c'est le Louvre, un immense palais, et à gauche, les jardins des Tuileries.

At the Louvre Museum

PAUL: I would like to go to the Louvre to say hello to the Mona Lisa and to buy some art books to take back with us.

LOUISE: In what part of Paris is the Louvre?

PAUL: In the center, close to the Seine. It was the residence of the French kings when they were in town, before the revolution of 1789.

LOUISE: Yes, I know! It's a pity not to be here for the festivities of July 14th. There are magnificent fireworks on the Seine, on the Eiffel Tower...

PAUL: It is the bus 68 that goes to the Louvre. It stops at the same place as bus 38. We are going to see a new itinerary! In coming to the boulevard Raspail we must look out for the statue of Balzac by Rodin. And just before, we will cross the boulevard Montparnasse.

LOUISE: Montparnasse, that was the artists' section, wasn't it?

PAUL: Yes. Tonight we will have dinner at La Coupole, a famous restaurant of this neighborhood.

LOUISE: Here comes the bus. We show our pass and off we go. Excuse me, *monsieur*, to get off just before the Seine, what is the stop? Quai Voltaire? Thank you. Here we are. We get off, cross the street and take the Royal Bridge, and in front of us, here is the Louvre, an immense palace, and to the left are the gardens of the Tuileries.

PAUL: Et là-bas, très loin, c'est l'Arc de Triomphe?

LOUISE: Oui, mais malheureusment, par derrière, on voit aussi la grande Arche de la Défense, un bâtiment très récent.

PAUL: Et ici aussi, il y a un arc de triomphe, tout en marbre rose, avec dessus un chariot et des chevaux dorés. Superbe!

LOUISE: Et voici la fameuse pyramide.

PAUL: C'est bizarre, ce verre qui brille au milieu de cette grande cour avec ses bâtiments tout ornés de sculptures et de statues, de l'âge classique.

LOUISE: On avait besoin d'une autre entrée, parce qu'il y avait trop de visiteurs à la porte d'entrée du bâtiment, et des files d'attente trop longues. Maintenant, on peut entrer tout de suite.

Plus tard.

PAUL: Nous avons passé deux heures à regarder des statues!

LOUISE: La Vénus de Milo, elle est belle. Et la Victoire de Samothrace, impressionante, et nous avons fait un petit salut de loin à la Joconde...

PAUL: Nous avons dix kilos de livres à rapporter chez nous! Très lourd!

LOUISE: J'ai aimé le portrait de ce roi avec le grand chapeau noir. C'était une belle journée!

PAUL: And way over there, that is the Arch of Triumph?

LOUISE: Yes, but unfortunately, in back of it, you see also the Great Arch of the Defense, a very recent building.

PAUL: And right here also, there is a triumphal arch, all of pink marble with a chariot and horses on top, all in gold. Magnificent!

LOUISE: And here is the famous pyramid.

PAUL: It looks odd, this shiny glass in this great courtyard with its buildings all decorated with sculptures and statues of the classical age.

LOUISE: There was the need for another entrance because there were too many visitors at the gate of the building and people stood in line for too long. Now, you can enter right away.

Later.

PAUL: We spent two hours looking at statues!

LOUISE: The Venus of Milo, beautiful. The Victory of Samothrace, astonishing, and we said a little hello from a distance, to the Mona Lisa...

PAUL: And now we have 20 pounds of books to take back home! Very heavy!

LOUISE: I liked the portrait of that king with the big black hat. It was a lovely day!

VOCABULARY

14 Juillet, le *m.*	July 14th
âge classique, l' *m.*	the classical period
Arc de Triomphe, l' *m.*	Arch of Triumph
Arche, l' *f.*	Arch
artiste, l' *m.*	artist
au milieu de	in the middle of
avoir envie	to feel like
Balzac	(a famous writer of the XIXth century)
bâtiment, le *m.*	building
bonjour	good morning
briller	to shine
centre, le *m.*	center
chariot, le *m.*	chariot
cheval, le *m.*	horse
cour, la *f.*	courtyard
Défense, la *f.*	a section of Paris
dix kilos	(about 20 pounds)
doré	gilded
en haut de	at the top of
faire attention	to pay attention
fameux	much talked about
fête, la *f.*	festivities
feux d'artifice, les *m.*	fireworks
file d'attente, la *f.*	waiting line
ici aussi	here too
itinéraire, l' *m.*	itinerary
long	long
lourd	heavy
magnifique	magnificent
malheureusement	unfortunately
marbre, le *m.*	marble

même, le *m.*	the same
Mona Lisa/La Joconde	(painting by Leonardo da Vinci)
nouvel	new
par	by
près de	near
Pyramide, la *f.*	Pyramid
quel dommage!	it's too bad!
résidence, la *f.*	residence
révolution, la *f.*	revolution
Rodin	(a famous sculptor of the XIXth century)
se trouver	to be placed
superbe	very beautiful, superb
tout de suite	right away
très	very
très loin	in the distance
trop de	too many
verre, le *m.*	glass
Vénus de Milo, la *f.*	(Venus of Milo, statue)
Victoire de Samothrace, la *f.*	(Victory of Samothrace, statue)
visiteur, le *m.*	visitor

GRAMMAR

The Infinitive

It is the basic mode of the verb and the one you find in the dictionary. It has two tenses, the present, for example *aimer* (to love) and the past perfect, for example *avoir aimé* (to have loved), *s'être levé* (to have gotten up), *être allé* (to have gone). The infinitive cannot have a subject but it can have direct and indirect objects.

Rule: When a verb comes immediately after another verb, the second one is always an infinitive, except when the first one is *avoir* or *être*.

Uses

The infinitive can be used as a noun.

un être humain – a human being
le lever du soleil – the rising of the sun
le coucher du soleil – the setting of the sun

It can be used as a sort of mild imperative.

Voir page 18.
See page 18. (in a book)

Ouvrir la boîte. Prendre les instruments avec précaution.
Open the box and take out the instruments cautiously.

The infinitive is used as the object of a verb: direct, indirect or prepositional.

Note: All prepositions are followed by the infinitive form of the verb with <u>one</u> exception: the preposition *en* (followed by a present participle). After the preposition *après* the tense of the infinitive is always past perfect.

Elle m'a invité à venir jouer au tennis avec elle.
She invited me to come and play tennis with her.

Elle m'a dit en partant 'adieu'.
She said (to me) as she left "good-bye."

Elle a fini par comprendre.
She finally understood. / She ended up understanding.

Après avoir réfléchi, elle a acheté le manteau.
After thinking it over, she bought the coat.

Constructions

Infinitive clause in English: "I expect you to be home before 12:00." In this sentence, the "you" is the subject of the verb "to be." In French, the infinitive cannot have a subject, so after the main verb the conjunction *que* is added and a normal sentence is written: *Je compte que tu seras rentré avant 12 heures.* If the second verb does not have a subject, the infinitive is used: *Je compte rentrer avant 12 heures.*

The impersonal constructions <u>*c'est* + adjective</u> and <u>*il est* + adjective</u> are used with the <u>infinitive</u> in expressions such as:

C'est facile à comprendre.
It is easy to understand.

Il est agréable de se promener.
It is pleasant to take walks.

Constructions respond to intricate rules. A simple "rule of thumb" can be established. If the expression is short, with no objects attached, *c'est* + adjective + *à* + infinitive is used.

C'est difficile à dire.
It is difficult to say.

If the expression is longer: "It is difficult to say this word," the form *il est* + adjective + *de* + infinitive must be used.

Il est difficile de dire ces mots.
It is difficult to say these words.

EXERCISES

I. Infinitive after prepositions: Translate the verb using an infinitive.

1. prêt à ______ (to cook)
2. avant de ______ (to come)
3. commencer par ______ (to announce)
4. insister pour ______ (to leave)
5. heureux de ______ (to have finished)
6. triste de ______ (not to have seen)
7. passer du temps à ______ (to work)
8. Il préfère ______ (to travel) tout seul.

II. Translate the following sentences, noting that a participle in *–ing* in English = the infinitive in French.

1. He likes working there.
2. She prefers waiting.
3. We spent our time playing.
4. sad to be seeing this
5. happy to be visiting this monument
6. Insist on not paying.
7. start by studying
8. before accepting

III. Translate the expressions in English.

1. (After seeing this) il est parti.
2. Elle m'a invité à (to come and have dinner).
3. Elle s'est arrêtée de (laughing).
4. Elle a dit de (to work hard).
5. Elle a fini par (to start singing).

6. Ils ont peur de (to be stopped).
7. Elle est contente (to have gone up the Eiffel Tower).
8. Elle regrette (not to have visited) ces jardins.

LESSON FIFTEEN

DIALOGUE

A la Poste

PAUL: Nous avons ces gros livres qui sont très lourds. Et nous n'aurons pas de place dans nos valises. Je vais faire un paquet et les envoyer par la poste. Ils ont probablement des boîtes pour les mettre, et un tarif special pour les livres. Je vais demander où est la poste... Voilà les renseignements. On va tout droit vers la rue d'Alesia. On tourne à gauche, sur le trottoir de droite et on arrive à la poste. La façade est jaune et bleu. Bien, nous y voilà. Un guichet libre. Je m'avance, je dis 'Bonjour Madame'. Et la dame me dit sèchement 'Vous avez un numéro?' en pointant son doigt vers l'entrée. Je vais voir. Il y avait une machine avec un bouton. Je presse le bouton, et la machine dit: 'attendez'. J'attends, et un billet sort qui m'indique que j'ai le numéro 97 et que j'attendrai onze minutes. Chaque guichet a un numéro qui s'allume en rouge et les numéros des billets paraissent en rouge sur un tableau avec le numéro du guichet où on doit aller. Il y a trois rangées de sièges pour attendre confortablement. Pas de dispute sur qui est arrivé le premier! Après 11 minutes et demie, mon numéro est en rouge sur le tableau. J'achète deux grandes boîtes jaunes et bleues. Au Monoprix en face, j'achète un rouleau de ruban collant.

LOUISE: Bien, mais nous allons garder les livres pendant quelques jours, pour les regarder, non?

PAUL: Oui, c'est une bonne idée. Et ce matin j'ai vu une charcuterie avec beaucoup de...

LOUISE: Qu'est-ce que c'est qu'une charcuterie?

At the Post Office

PAUL: We have these big books that are very heavy. And we will not have space in our suitcases. I am going to wrap them up and send them by mail. They probably have boxes to put them in and special rates for books. I am going to ask where the post office is... Here is the information. You go straight to the street Alésia. You turn left, onto the right-hand sidewalk and you come to the post office. It has a yellow and blue front. Fine, here we are. A window is free, I step forward and I say: *Bonjour Madame.* And the lady said stiffly "do you have a number?" pointing her finger towards the entrance. I go to see. There was a machine with a button. I push the button. The machine says: "Wait." I wait and a ticket comes out, indicating that I have number 97 and that I will wait for eleven minutes. Each window has a number that lights up in red and the ticket numbers appear in red on a display board with the number of the window that the person should go to. There are three rows of seats for a comfortable wait. No argument about who came first! After eleven and a half minutes my number comes up in red on the board. I buy two large yellow and blue boxes. Then I go to the Monoprix across the street to buy a roll of tape.

LOUISE: Good, but we are going to keep the books for a few days to look at them, aren't we?

PAUL: Yes, it is a good idea. And this morning I saw a *charcuterie* with lots of...

LOUISE: What's a *charcuterie?*

PAUL: C'est un magasin où l'on vend tous les produits faits avec du porc, différentes sortes de jambons, crus et cuits, des pâtés, des saucisses, des terrines, des pâtés en croûte. Et aussi des salades de carottes, de celeri rave, de pommes de terre, et même des tartes. Tout avait l'air très bon. J'ai rapporté du Monoprix des assiettes, des cuillères, des fourchettes, tout ce qu'il nous faut pour un pique-nique.

LOUISE: Ici, dans la chambre?

PAUL: Non, ma chère belle! Il y a un charmant petit jardin public presque sur la rue des Plantes.

LOUISE: Super! (J'ai entendu une jeune fille qui disait ça hier!) Merveilleux! Partons vite, j'ai très faim.

PAUL: It is a store where they sell products made with pork, all kinds of hams, raw and cooked, patés, sausages, *terrines*, patés in pastry crusts. And also salads; carrot, root celery, potato, and even pies. Everything looked very good. At the Monoprix store I bought plates, spoons and forks, everything we need for a picnic

LOUISE: Here, in the room?

PAUL: No, my dearest! There is a charming little public garden right off the rue des Plantes.

LOUISE: Super! (I heard a girl saying that yesterday!) Marvelous! Let's go at once. I am very hungry.

VOCABULARY

attendre	to wait
billet, le *m.*	ticket
bleu	blue
boîte, la *f.*	box
bouton, le *m.*	button
bureau, le *m.*	office
carotte, la *f.*	carrot
celeri rave, le *m.*	root celery
charcuterie, la *f.*	pork butcher
collant	adhesive
confortablement	comfortably
croûte, la *f.*	crust
cru	raw
cuillère, la *f.*	spoon
cuit	cooked
différentes sortes	various kinds
dispute, la *f.*	dispute
doigt, le *m.*	finger
en face	across the street
envoyer	to send
façade, la *f.*	front, facade
fourchette, la *f.*	fork
garder	to keep
gros	thick
hier	yesterday
jaune	yellow
jeune fille, la *f.*	girl
machine, la *f.*	machine
Monoprix	(a supermarket)
numéro, le *m.*	number
paquet, le *m.*	parcel

pas de place	no room
pâté, le *m.*	"paté"
pique-nique, le *m.*	picnic
pointer	to point
pomme de terre, la *f.*	potato
porc, le *m.*	pork
poste, la *f.*	post office
premier, le *m.*	the first
presque	almost
probablement	probably
produit, le *m.*	product
quelques	a certain number of
rangée, la *f.*	row
rapporter	to bring back
renseignement, le *m.*	information
rouge	red
rouleau, le *m.*	roll
ruban, le *m.*	tape
s'allumer	to light up
s'avancer	to step forward
saucisse, la *f.*	sausage
sèchement	dryly
siège, le *m.*	seat
special	special
tableau, le *m.*	display board
tarif, le *m.*	rate
tarte, la *f.*	pie
terrine, la *f.*	a type of paté
valise, la *f.*	suitcase

GRAMMAR

Possessive Adjectives and Pronouns

Possessive Adjectives

Possessive adjectives are placed before the noun and agree in gender and number with the noun they modify. In English, in the third person, the form of the adjective depends on the gender of the possessor: his mother, his daughter, her father, her son. In French, the agreement is strictly grammatical: *sa mère, sa fille, son père, son fils*. The possessor in every case cannot be ascertained.

Forms

- one possessor:

mon – my (sg. m.)	*ma* – my (sg. f.)	*mes* – my (pl. m./f.)
ton – your (sg. m.)	*ta* – your (sg. f.)	*tes* – your (pl. m./f.)
son – his (sg. m.)	*sa* – her (sg. f.)	*ses* – his/her (pl. m./f.)

- several possessors:

notre – our (sg. m./f.)	*nos* – our (pl. m./f.)
votre – your (sg. m./f.)	*vos* – your (pl. m./f.)
leur - their (sg. m./f.)	*leurs* – their (pl. m./f.)

mon livre, mes livres – my book, my books
ma table, mes tables – my table, my tables
notre maison, leur maison – our house, their house
leurs parents – their parents

Note: The forms *mon*, *ton*, and *son* are used instead of *ma*, *ta*, and *sa* when the word that follows starts with a vowel.

son amie, sa belle amie – his/her friend, his/her beautiful friend

The possessive adjective must be repeated before each noun in an enumeration.

Tu prendras ton manteau, ta veste, tes gros souliers.
You will take your coat, your jacket, your heavy shoes.

Use of the Article with the Meaning of a Possessive

A definite article—*le, la, les*—is used instead of a possessive adjective when someone mentions parts of his or her body, including the mind. The same articles are used when someone else speaks about a person.

Elle a le nez droit.
Her nose is straight.

Tu as l'esprit rapide.
Your mind works fast

J'ai mal au pied.
My foot hurts.

Levez la main droite.
Raise your right hand.

But the possessive adjective is used if the noun designating a part of the body is modified or if it is the subject of the verb.

Mes pieds sont froids. – My feet are cold.
Il a levé sa grande main. – He raised his large hand.

Ses longs cheveux flottaient dans le vent.
Her long hair was floating in the wind.

Other Ways of Expressing Possession

I. *être à* + noun + disjunctive pronouns (*moi, toi, lui, elle, nous, vous, eux, elles*)

Ce chien est à eux.
This is their dog.

Ceci est-il à vous? Non, c'est à eux.
Is this yours? No, it is theirs.

II. *appartenir à* – to belong to

A qui la maison appartient-elle?
To whom does the house belong?

III. The verb *avoir* is used in many expressions of possession.

J'ai faim. – I am hungry.
J'ai soif. – I am thirsty.
J'ai mal. – I feel a pain.
J'ai froid. – I am cold.

Note: In these expressions, the use of the verb "to be" in English is equivalent to the use of *avoir* in French.

Possessive Pronouns

The possessive pronoun is used to avoid repeating the noun with the possessive adjective. The pronoun must give the indication of the person of the possessor and the gender and number of the thing possessed.

person	*one object possessed* m. object/f. object	*several objects possessed* m. objects/f. objects	
one possessor:			
je	le mien/la mienne	les miens/les miennes	(mine)
tu	le tien/la tienne	les tiens/les tiennes	(yours)
il/elle	le sien/la sienne	les siens/les siennes	(his, theirs)
several possessors:			
nous	le nôtre/la nôtre	les nôtres/les nôtres	(ours)
vous	le vôtre/la vôtre	les vôtres/les vôtres	(yours)
ils/elles	le leur/la leur	les leurs/les leurs	(theirs)

Note: When the possessive pronoun is used after the expression *il/elle est...* the pronoun *il/elle* becomes *c'est.*

Voici mon sac. C'est le mien.
Here is my bag. It is mine.

Voilà son père. C'est le sien.
Here comes his father. He is his.

EXERCISES

I. Fill in the blanks with a possessive adjective.

1. Posez ______ affaires sur ______ table.
2. J'aime prendre ______ propres décisions mais j'écouterai ______ idées.
3. ______ maison et ______ maison sont près l'une de l'autre.
4. Les saisons de l'année ont ______ caractéristiques, mais chacune a ______ moments agréables et ______ moments désagréables.
5. Nous irons à la réunion. ______ opinions seront importantes.
6. Paul joue avec ______ trompette, Marie joue avec ______ tricycle.
7. Est-ce que tu te disputes avec ______ amis?
8. C'est une belle tour. J'admire ______ hauteur extraordinaire.
9. J'ai rencontré les voisins de Paul et de Marie. Ce sont ______ meilleurs amis.
10. Fido est le chien de Paul et de Marie. C'est ______ chien.

II. Replace the underlined expressions with a possessive pronoun. After each phrase, indicate the number of things possessed and possessors.

1. J'ai vu <u>mes amis</u>.
2. Ils ont fini <u>leur composition</u> (*f.*).
3. Je rapporte <u>vos livres</u>.
4. Je ne sais rien de <u>leurs opinions</u> (*f.*).
5. Vous irez avec <u>votre groupe</u> (*m.*).
6. Voici <u>les fleurs de ma mère</u>.
7. Nous irons à <u>la maison de nos parents</u>.
8. On admire <u>son courage</u>.

LESSON SIXTEEN

DIALOGUE

Une Visite

LOUISE: Oh là là, Paul, qu'est-ce que je trouve?

PAUL: Quoi, c'est grave?

LOUISE: J'avais complètement oublié!

PAUL: Mais quoi?

LOUISE: Je regarde dans mon agenda. Et voilà la feuille! La visite à Madame Irène Mignard!

PAUL: Qui est Madame Mignard? Je la connais?

LOUISE: Non, et moi non plus. C'est ça qui m'ennuie. Attends, attends, je vais t'expliquer. C'est une dame, une vieille dame que ma mère m'a demandé d'aller voir. Ne fais pas la grimace. Tu n'as pas besoin d'y aller, toi. Mais moi, il n'y a rien à faire puisque j'y ai pensé, et que j'ai retrouvé son adresse.

PAUL: Mais qui est-ce?

LOUISE: C'est une dame chez qui ma mère avait une chambre quand elle a passé un an à Paris, avant de se marier. Très gentille dame. Elle m'a même envoyé quelques cadeaux quand j'étais petite.

PAUL: Alors il faut lui téléphoner.

A Visit

LOUISE: Oh my, oh my, Paul, what do I find here?

PAUL: What? Is it serious?

LOUISE: I had completely forgotten!

PAUL: But what?

LOUISE: I look in my agenda, and here is the paper! The visit to Madame Irene Mignard!

PAUL: Who is Madame Mignard? Do I know her?

LOUISE: No, and I don't, either. That is what bothers me. Wait, wait, I will explain. She is a lady, an old lady that my mother asked me to go and see. Don't make a face. You don't have to go. But for me, there is nothing to be done since I thought about it, and I found her address.

PAUL: But who is she?

LOUISE: She is a lady in whose apartment my mother had a room when she was spending a year in Paris, before she got married. Very nice lady. She even sent me presents when I was small.

PAUL: Then you must call her.

LOUISE: Oui. 01.42.53.47.54. Allô, Madame Mignard? Je suis la fille de Elizabeth Cushman qui... Très bien. Je viens tout de suite. Il me faudra bien une heure. Oui, j'ai le plan. Merci beaucoup.

PAUL: Moi, je vais aller voir l'Arche de la Défense, un bâtiment très curieux.

LOUISE: Alors, nous prendrons le métro ensemble jusqu'à Trocadéro et tu iras jusqu'à Charles de Gaulle-Etoile.

Plusieurs heures plus tard.

LOUISE: Bonjour! Bonsoir! C'était beau ton Arche? Ah! Tu nous a apporté des fleurs. Comme elles sont jolies!

PAUL: Oui, trés impressionnant, comme architecture moderne, géometrique. Mais j'aime mieux l'Arc du Carousel au Louvre, avec ses décorations bien classiques. Et ta visite?

LOUISE: La dame était charmante, très gentille. Elle m'a dit qu'elle revoyait ma mère en me regardant, et que j'étais jolie comme 'un coeur'. Et l'appartement était si élégant, les fauteuils, les coussins, les tapis, les lampes, les miroirs, tout si bien choisi. Elle a servi le thé dans les tasses les plus raffinées et elle m'a fait raconter ce que nous faisions. Il y avait une autre dame là, et elle m'a proposé d'aller avec elle au Printemps, demain. Alors tu n'as pas besoin de venir. J'ai rendez-vous avec elle à 9h30 demain. Je commence à bien me débrouiller dans le métro.

LOUISE: Yes. 01.42 53.47.54. *Allô Madame Mignard?* I am the daughter of Elizabeth Cushman who... Wonderful. I will be coming right away. But it will take me an hour. Yes, I have a map. Thank you very much.

PAUL: For my part, I am going to see the Arch of La Defense, a very strange building.

LOUISE: Then we will take the subway together as far as Trocadéro, and you will go to Charles de Gaulle-Etoile.

A few hours later.

LOUISE: Good afternoon, good evening! Was it beautiful, your Arch? Ah! You brought back some flowers. How pretty they are!

PAUL: Yes, very impressive as architecture, modern, geometric. But I prefer the Arch of the Carousel at the Louvre with its classical decorations. And your visit?

LOUISE: The lady was charming, very kind. She told me she could see my mother when looking at me, that I was as pretty as a "sweetheart." And the apartment was so elegant, with armchairs, cushions, rugs, lamps, mirrors, everything so well chosen. She served tea in the most delicate and pretty cups, and she had me tell what we were doing. There was another lady there and she offered me to go with her tomorrow to the Printemps department store. So you don't have to go. I will meet her tomorrow at 9:30. I am getting to be pretty good at finding my way in the métro.

VOCABULARY

adresse, l' *f.*	address
agenda, l' *m.*	agenda
aimer mieux	to prefer
Arche de la Défense, l' *m.*	(monument)
attendre	to wait
cadeaux, les *m.*	presents
Charles de Gaulle-Etoile	(a subway station)
charmante	charming
chez qui	at whose house
connaître	to know
coussin, le *m.*	cushion
curieux	strange
décoration, la *f.*	decoration
ennuyer	to bother
ensemble	together
expliquer	to explain
faire la grimace	to make a face
faire raconter	to ask to tell
fauteuil, le *m.*	armchair
feuille, la *f.*	sheet of paper
fleurs, les *f.*	flowers
gentil	nice
géométrique	geometric
grave	serious
il me faudra bien	it will certainly take me
il n'y a rien à faire	there is nothing to do
jolie comme un coeur	*lit.* pretty as a heart
jusqu'à	up to
lampe, la *f.*	lamp
mère, une *f.*	mother
miroir, le *m.*	mirror

moderne	modern
(tu) n'as pas besoin	(you) don't need to
oublier	to forget
plusieurs	several
proposer	to offer
puisque	since
raffiné	refined
rendez-vous, le *m.*	appointment
revoir	to meet again
se débrouiller	to find one's way
se marier	to get married
tapis, le *m.*	rug
tasse, la *f.*	cup
tout de suite	right away
Trocadéro	(a subway station)
visite, la *f.*	visit

GRAMMAR

Negative Expressions and Constructions

The basic negative word in French is *ne*, placed before the verb, which is followed by a second negative word *pas. Ne ... pas* is the most frequently used negative.

Il ne comprend pas.
He does not understand.

Constructions: Place of ne ... pas

subject + *ne* + verb + *pas* + noun objects

Il n'aime pas les épinards.
He does not like spinach.

- With compound tenses:

  subject + *ne* + *être* / *avoir* + *pas* + past participle + object

  Il n'a pas aimé les photos.
  He did not like the photos.

- With object pronouns:

  Il ne le leur a pas raconté.
  He did not tell it to them.

  Note: See place of object pronouns in Lesson Three.

- In interrogative sentences:

  Il ne me l'a pas donné.
  He did not give it to me.

  Ne me l'a-t-il pas donné?
  Did he not give it to me?

- In front of an infinitive: *ne pas*

  Il préfère ne pas venir.
  He prefers not to come.

- When there is no verb in the sentence, only *pas* is used.

  Qui veut ce livre? Pas moi!
  Who wants this book? Not I!

- *Pas* is used before an adjective or an adverb to give it a negative meaning.

  pas joli, pas souvent – not nice, not often

- After a negative verb or expression, the partitive article *des* becomes *de*.

  J'ai acheté des pommes. Je n'ai pas acheté de pommes.
  I bought apples. I did not buy apples.

  Note: This rule is strictly observed even in casual conversation.

Expressions of Restriction: ne ... que, seulement

- Construction: *ne ... que*

  ne + verb + *que* + noun object
  ne + object pronouns + verb + *que*

Il n'a qu'une pomme.
He has only one apple.

Il ne le leur a dit qu'hier.
He told them about it only yesterday.

Note: *Ne ... que* is not a negative. So the partitive article does not change.

Il n'a que des pommes vertes.
He has only green apples.

- *Seulement* can be used in all constructions.

J'ai seulement une pomme.
I have only one apple.

Seulement must be used instead of *ne ... que*:

I. when there is no verb

Qu'as-tu acheté? Seulement des pommes.
What did you buy? Only some apples.

II. when the word *que* is used in the sentence

Il m'a écrit qu'il ne venait pas.
Il m'a seulement écrit qu'il ne venait pas.
He only wrote that he was not coming.

III. when the restriction is on the subject of the verb

Marie viendra dimanche.
Seule Marie viendra dimanche.
Seulement Marie viendra dimanche.
Only Mary will come on Sunday.

IV. when the restriction is on the verb

Je n'ai pas parlé, j'ai seulement écouté.
I did not speak, I only listened.

Note: After a negative question, the affirmative answer is not *oui* but *si.*

Il n'est pas en bonne santé? Mais si.
He is not in good health? Yes, he is.

Negative Adverbs

If a negative word other than *pas* is used in the sentence, *pas* must be deleted. But several negative words other than *pas* can be used together in the sentence and *ne* is always required before the verb.

Jamais personne ne me dit rien.
No one ever tells me anything.

Negative Adjectives

- *aucun, nul* – not one, none, no one
- *pas un* – not one
- *personne* – no one

Aucun and *nul* agree in gender and number with the noun they qualify.

Personne is invariable and masculine.

Personne n'est bon, ici.
No one is good, here

Note: This use of *personne* is the opposite of *une personne* (a person).

When the pronoun *personne* is used with an adjective, a *de* is added between the pronoun and the adjective.

Je n'ai rencontré personne d'intéressant.
I did not meet anyone who was interesting.

- *rien* – nothing

  It takes the place of *pas* beside the verb.

  Add *de* when it is modified by an adjective.

  Je n'ai rien vu de beau.
  I did not see anything beautiful.

  Rien d'intéressant.
  Nothing interesting.

Negative Conjunctions

- *ni ... ni* – neither ... nor

  Ne must be used with the negative verb.

  Il a vu Paris mais ni Lyon ni Marseille.
  He saw Paris but neither Lyons nor Marseilles.

  Ni Jean ni Paul ne savaient rien.
  Neither John nor Paul knew anything.

EXERCISES

I. Change the following sentences into the negative.

1. Jeanette veut ce document.
2. Nous aimons manger des gâteaux.
3. Apportez-moi des oranges.
4. Ils ont pu voir cela.
5. Son ami le lui a donné.
6. On lui en fera beaucoup.
7. Entendez-vous tous les mots?
8. Peut-être faudrait-il le lui écrire?
9. Vous l'avez probablement oublié.
10. Je vous prie de venir à mon bureau. (infinitive in the negative)

II. Place the negative expression in the given sentences and translate into English. Compare in each case the French and the English construction.

1. Paul va souvent au musée. (ne ... jamais)
2. J'ai entendu. (ne ... pas ... bien)
3. Nous l'avons trouvé. (ne ... nulle part)
4. Appelez-moi. (ne ... plus)
5. Elle a envie de travailler. (ne ... guère)
6. Nous avons froid. (ne ... pas du tout)
7. Ils ont voulu ceci. (ne ... rien)
8. Des nouvelles sont arrivées. (ne ... pas encore)

III. Turn each phrase into a negative sentence using *ne* + *ni ... ni*.

1. Nous irons au restaurant et au théâtre.
2. Je prends du pain, du beurre et du café le matin.
3. Il va nous dire où et comment ceci est arrivé.

4. Elle et lui savent toute l'histoire.
5. J'ai beaucoup de papiers et de crayons.
6. Il sait cuisiner et jardiner.
7. Vous lui donnerez du lait et des biscuits.
8. J'ai confiance et amitié pour lui.

LESSON SEVENTEEN

DIALOGUE

Les Champs Elysées

PAUL: Tu sais qu'on peut visiter les égoûts de Paris?

LOUISE: Les égoûts? Tu veux dire les égoûts, les galeries sous la terre où les eaux des toilettes et des baignoires coulent? Et on est dans le noir quand le soleil brille dehors?

PAUL: Exactement! En rentrant par l'autobus, j'ai vu une file d'attente sur le trottoir. C'était Place Denfert-Rochereau, où il y a le lion de bronze, devant une porte marquée: Egoûts de Paris. Il y avait beaucoup de monde.

LOUISE: Eh bien! Pas pour moi!

PAUL: Ça doit être très curieux. Et puis, quand on rentre aux Etats-Unis, on peut dire: 'Moi...'

LOUISE: Si tu veux, vas-y, vas-y. Moi, je vais au Printemps avec Jeanine. Donne-moi la liste de ce que tu veux que j'achète pour toi. Merci.

PAUL: Si on se retrouvait au Rond Point des Champs Elysées.

LOUISE: C'est vrai! Nous n'y sommes pas encore allés.

PAUL: A l'arrêt de l'autobus 68 venant d'ici. Marque-le sur ta carte. A quatre heures? Parfait! Au revoir!

A quatre heures.

LOUISE: Alors, tu es descendu dans les égoûts?

The Champs Elysées

PAUL: Do you know that you can visit the sewers of Paris?

LOUISE: Sewers? You mean sewers, underground galleries where the waters from toilets and bathtubs are running? And you are in the dark when the sun is shining outside?

PAUL: Exactly! On the bus coming back, I saw people lined up on the sidewalk. That was Place Denfert-Rochereau, where there is the bronze lion, before a door marked: Paris Sewers. There were lots of people.

LOUISE: Well, not for me!

PAUL: It must be very curious. And then, when we return to the United States you can say "I..."

LOUISE: If you want to, go see it! For my part, I am going to the Printemps with Jeanine. Give me the list of what you want me to buy for you. Thanks.

PAUL: How about meeting at the Rond Point of the Champs Elysées.

LOUISE: That's right! We have not been there yet.

PAUL: At the stop of bus 68 coming from here. Mark it on your map. At four? Fine. See you later!

At four o'clock.

LOUISE: Well, did you go down to the sewers?

PAUL: Non, après tout, je suis allé me promener dans le quartier des peintres, par là-bas, près du Parc Montsouris, pas loin de notre hôtel. Et tu as fait de nombreux achats?

LOUISE: Oui, des écharpes, des châles, des C.D. de chansons françaises, des articles de cuisine épatants... Trop de choses! Trop difficile de choisir.

PAUL: Je vais porter tes paquets. Regarde comme le soleil fait briller toutes les feuilles des arbres! Nous remontons les Champs Elysées, nous allons vers le soleil. Et il y a tant de monde, qui monte et qui descend. Mais ici, attention, il y a beaucoup de pickpockets. Ils ont les doigts qui prennent un portefeuille dans un sac, ou une poche de veste, et on n'a rien senti!

LOUISE: Si on entrait dans une de ces galeries? Quels beaux bijoux! Regarde ces bracelets.

PAUL: Viens, tu vas en choisir un, comme souvenir de cette promenade.

LOUISE: Il est magnifique, je suis si contente! Et qu'est-ce que c'est que ça?

PAUL: C'est une horloge. Une construction en verre avec des petits pots qui reçoivent de l'eau pour chaque minute, et ici pour les heures. C'est très ingénieux et beau.

LOUISE: Le soleil baisse et l'Arc de Triomphe devient de plus en plus massif.

PAUL: Qui l'a construit?

PAUL: No, after all, I went for a walk in the section of the painters, close to the Park Montsouris, not far from our hotel. And you brought many things?

LOUISE: Yes, scarves, shawls, CDs of French songs, marvelous kitchen articles... Too many things! So hard to choose.

PAUL: I will carry your bags. Look how the sun is shining on every leaf of the trees! We are walking up the Champs Elysées, toward the sun. There are so many people, who go up and down. But here, let's be careful. There are many pickpockets. They have fingers that take a wallet out of a bag or a pocket, and you feel nothing at all!

LOUISE: How about going into one of these commercial galleries? What beautiful jewelry! Look at those bracelets.

PAUL: Let's go in. You will choose one, as a souvenir of this stroll.

LOUISE: It is magnificent, I am so pleased! And what is this?

PAUL: It is a clock. A construction of glass tubes with little pots that receive water for each minute and here for the hours. It is very ingenious and beautiful.

LOUISE: The sun is getting lower and the Arch of Triumph more and more massive.

PAUL: Who built it?

LOUISE: Napoléon a fait dessiner la place, avec une étoile de douze avenues, mais l'arc a été construit entre 1806 et 1836. Aujourd'hui, la place s'appelle Charles de Gaulle-Etoile. Et le tombeau du Soldat Inconnu est sous l'arche, marqué par une flamme qui brûle toujours.

PAUL: Traversons! Il y a un policier qui nous protège.

LOUISE: Et là sur la face qui regarde les Champs Elysées tu vois cette statue qui a la bouche grande ouverte. Elle chante la Marseillaise pour appeler tout le monde à défendre la liberté.

PAUL: Voilà beaucoup de choses importantes et émouvantes, auxquelles il faut penser.

LOUISE: Napoleon had the square designed with a star of twelve avenues but the arch was built between 1806 and 1836. Today this is called Place Charles de Gaulle-Etoile and the tomb of the Unknown Soldier is under the arch, marked by a flame that burns constantly.

PAUL: Let's go across! There is a policeman here to protect us.

LOUISE: And there on the side that looks toward the Champs Elysées, you see this statue who has its mouth wide open. It sings the Marseillaise to call everyone to defend liberty.

PAUL: Those are many important and moving things about which we must think.

VOCABULARY

achat, l' *m.*	purchase
article de cuisine, l' *m.*	kitchen utensil
au revoir	good-bye
auxquelles	to which
baignoire, la *f.*	bathtub
baisser	to lower
bijou, le *m.*	jewel
bouche, la *f.*	mouth
bracelet, le *m.*	bracelet
bronze, le *m.*	bronze
brûler	to burn
châle, le *m.*	shawl
comme	as
construire	to build
couler	to run
dehors	outside
de plus en plus	more and more
doigt, le *m.*	finger
eau, l' *f.*	water
écharpe, l' *f.*	scarf
égoût, l' *m.*	sewer
émouvant	moving
épatant	wonderful
étoile, l' *f.*	star
faire briller	to make shine
faire dessiner	to have someone draw
feuille, la *f.*	leaf
flamme, la *f.*	flame
galerie, la *f.*	gallery
grande ouverte	wide open
horloge, l' *f.*	clock
inconnu	unknown

ingénieux	clever
je vais porter	I am going to carry
liberté, la *f.*	liberty
lion, le *m.*	lion
marqué	marked
massif	massive
monde, le *m.*	people
noir, le *m.*	darkness
nombreux	many
paquet, le *m.*	package
parfait	perfect
pas loin de	not far from
pickpocket, le *m.*	thief
poche, la *f.*	pocket
policier, le *m.*	policeman
portefeuille, le *m.*	wallet
pot, le *m.*	pot
pouvoir	to be able to
protéger	to protect
quels	what
recevoir	to receive
rien	nothing
Rond-point	rotary, traffic circle
savoir	to know
sentir	to feel
se retrouver	to meet
soldat, le *m.*	soldier
souvenir, le *m.*	souvenir
tant de	so many
toilette, la *f.*	toilet
tombeau, le *m.*	tomb
traverser	to cross the street
trop de	too many
verre, le *m.*	glass
veste, la *f.*	jacket

GRAMMAR

How To Express Anteriority

Verb Tenses: Past Perfect, Pluperfect, Compound Past Perfect, Future Perfect

The French language uses the tenses of the verbs to place events on the line of time, indicating which one came before or after another, from the present to the past or from the present to the future.

From the present, the past perfect places a fact in the past. Another action taking place before this last one will be expressed in the pluperfect.

Time:	pluperfect	past perfect	present
	C	B	A

Quand j'ai fini mon travail, je vais me promener.
When I have finished my work, I am taking a walk.
[past perfect] [present]

J'avais fini mon travail, et je suis allé me promener.
I had finished my work, and I took a walk.
[pluperfect] [past perfect]

If the verb for action C is introduced with a conjunction of time such as *quand* (when), *aussitôt que* or *dès que* (as soon as), the verb tense becomes the compound past perfect.

Quand j'ai eu fini mon travail, je suis allé me promener.
When I had finished my work, I took a walk.
[compound past perfect] [past perfect]

The same system applies to the expression of anteriority in the future.

Time:	present	anterior future	future
	A	B	C

All these verb tenses are compound forms made up with the auxiliary in the necessary form + past participle.

Forms

I. Pluperfect / *Plus-que-parfait*

This tense is a compound tense: auxiliary verb in the imperfect form (*avoir* or *être*) + past participle.

aimer (to love) – *j'avais aimé* (I had loved), etc.
tomber (to fall) – *j'étais tombé* (I had fallen), etc.
se lever (to get up) – *je m'étais levé* (I had gotten up), etc.

1. This tense can be used by itself.

   J'avais toujours pensé à cela.
   I had thought about it all the time.

2. Or to indicate an action having taken place before another one in the past:

   Il avait déja compris quand j'ai fini ma phrase.
   He had already understood when I finished my sentence.

3. When the verb of the main clause is in the imperfect, the pluperfect has the meaning of habitual action.

   Quand il avait pris son dîner, il allait se promener.
   When he had eaten his dinner, he would go for a walk.

Note: The pluperfect and the imperfect contain the idea that it was his habit and the use of these tenses is necessary to express this idea.

4. With a negative verb, the pluperfect is used in the main clause, followed by:

   depuis + past perfect tense of the verb to express the idea that something has not been done until the moment indicated, or by *depuis* + imperfect tense to express a habitual action.

   Il n'avait pas fait d'exercice depuis 6 mois quand il s'est mis au régime.
   He had not done any exercise for six months when he went on a diet.

   Il n'avait pas fait d'exercice depuis qu'il écrivait son roman.
   He had not done any exercise since he started writing his novel.

   Note: Observe the vocabulary used in these constructions.

II. Compound Past Perfect / *Passé Surcomposé*

This tense consists of: past perfect auxiliary + past participle. It is not used for reflexive verbs, or verbs with *être* as auxiliary.

aimer (to love) – *j'ai eu aimé* (I had loved), etc.

This tense is used to express the anteriority of an action when the main verb is in the past perfect. It is never used by itself but only after a conjunction of time: *quand* (when), *aussitôt que* (as soon as), *dès que* (as soon as). Note that in English this tense does not exist, and can be approximately translated as the pluperfect (I had loved, etc.).

Dès qu'il a eu compris la situation, il est parti.
As soon as he had understood the situation, he left.

III. Future Perfect / *Futur Antérieur*

This tense indicates that an action in the future will take place before another action is realized.

Time:	present	future perfect	future
	A	B	C

This is a compound tense: future auxiliary + past participle.

aimer (to love) – *j'aurai aimé* (I will have loved), etc.
tomber (to fall) – *je serai tombé* (I will have fallen), etc.
se lever (to get up) – *je me serai levé* (I will have risen), etc.

The idea to be expressed is that one action (B) will take place before a second action (C) takes place too. A conjunction is often used after the verb expressing the anterior action, the first one on the timeline.

J'aurai fini ce travail avant ton retour.
I will have finished this work before your return.

J'aurai fini ce travail quand vous reviendrez.
I will have finished this work when you return.

Note: In English the present tense is used after "when," but in French, after *quand* the future is necessary to express the idea of a future action.

Dès que vous serez revenu, je vous expliquerai la situation.
As soon as you return, I will explain the situation.

Note: It is necessary to use the tenses expressing anteriority every time sentences contain two verbs expressing actions done one before the other. No other constructions make clear the idea you want to convey in such cases.

EXERCISES

I. In the following sentences, change the verb of the main clause to the past and the verb of the subordinate clause to the pluperfect to indicate that the second action took place before the first.

Pattern: Imperfect & Pluperfect
Past Perfect & Compound Past Perfect/Pluperfect

1. Je vous dis qu'il a fini son travail.
2. Il oublie ce qu'il a promis.
3. Je sais qu'elle est arrivée.
4. Sais-tu si elle est arrivée?
5. Ne sais-tu pas si ils sont arrivés?
6. L'erreur que tu as faite est considérable.
7. Quand tu fais une erreur, le sais-tu?
8. Dès que je fais une erreur, elle le sait.
9. Aussitôt que je dis cela, je le regrette.

II. Complete the following sentences using the pluperfect form of the verb given, observing the tense used in the first part of the sentence.

1. J'aurais été content si elle ______ (venir me voir).
2. Je n'aurais pas été content s'il ______ (ne pas être là).
3. L'herbe était toute jaune parce qu'il ______ (ne pas pleuvoir).
4. L'herbe était très verte parce qu'il ______ (pleuvoir).
5. Elle se reposait l'après-midi quand ______ (faire une promenade).
6. Elle ne dormait pas bien quand ______ (ne pas faire une promenade).
7. Nous avons acheté la maison que ______ (visiter).
8. Elle rentrait à la maison dès que ______ (finir ses achats).

III. Use the future and the future perfect as needed in the following sentences.

1. Je te verrai quand tu ______ (finir).
2. Tu me le diras dès que ce ______ (arriver).
3. Je ______ (se réjouir) quand cela aura été fait.
4. Nous irons vous voir aussitôt que vous ______ (s'installer).
5. Je ______ (croire) cela quand je l'aurai vu.
6. Je te le donnerai dès que tu ______ (le demander poliment).

LESSON EIGHTEEN

DIALOGUE

A Montmartre

PAUL: Tu as écrit des cartes postales à tous tes parents et tes amis?

LOUISE: Presque. Voilà ma liste.

PAUL: La tienne est mieux remplie que la mienne.

LOUISE: Je vais écrire un message plus court pour celles qui me restent. Et des timbres? Tu as ceux qu'il te faut?

PAUL: Oui, j'en ai beaucoup. Et il y a une boîte aux lettres, jaune et bleue, dans la petite rue tout près. Ou le bureau de l'hôtel.

LOUISE: Et puis, nous allons à Montmartre?

PAUL: Il y a beaucoup de nuages dans le ciel mais aussi du soleil. Voilà mon parapluie, voilà le tien. Nous sommes prêts. Je n'ai plus de film dans mon appareil de photo. Et dans le tien?

LOUISE: Je suis à la moitié de ma pellicule. Est-ce qu'il y a toujours des peintres à photographier à Montmartre?

PAUL: Je suppose! Nous allons prendre l'autobus jusqu'à la Gare de l'Est, et là le métro jusqu'à Barbès-Rochechouart. Puis nous monterons jusqu'au sommet de la butte.

LOUISE: La butte?

At Montmartre

PAUL: Did you write postcards to all your relatives and friends?

LOUISE: Almost. Here is my list.

PAUL: Yours is filled up more than mine.

LOUISE: I am going to write shorter messages on those I have left. And stamps? Do you have those that you need?

PAUL: Yes. I have many. And there is a mailbox, yellow and blue, in that small street near by. Or the hotel desk.

LOUISE: And then, we go to Montmartre?

PAUL: There are many clouds in the sky, but also sunshine. Here is my umbrella, and here is yours. We are ready. I don't have any more film in my camera, and in yours?

LOUISE: I have about half of my roll left. Are there still painters to photograph, in Montmartre?

PAUL: I suppose so! We are going to take the bus up to the Gare de l'Est and the subway up to Barbès-Rochechouart. Then we will walk up to the top of the mound.

LOUISE: The mound?

PAUL: Oui, une petite colline. Montmartre vient de 'mons martyrum' les martyrs du commencement de l'ère chrétienne. Il y a une grande église en haut, avec des coupoles blanches très hautes. Elle a été construite de 1876 à 1910. Il parait qu'elle est très critiquée par les Français.

LOUISE: Comme la Tour Eiffel?

PAUL: Exactement. Et le plus grand dôme a 80 mètres de hauteur. 240 pieds!

LOUISE: Pas possible!

PAUL: Donc nous sommes de l'autre côté de Paris! Tiens, qu'est-ce qu'il m'a donné cet homme, à la sortie du métro? 'Monsieur Cadabra protège votre avenir. Résultats guarantis. Tous problèmes résolus.' Et une liste...

LOUISE: Bien! Mais nous n'avons pas de problèmes, n'est-ce pas? Montons cette rue, et voilà la basilique.

PAUL: Toute blanche, et énorme. Ses pierres ne prennent pas la pollution.

LOUISE: C'est très beau, ces coupoles, sur le ciel bleu avec ces gros nuages.

PAUL: Nous tournons à gauche et nous trouvons le quartier, le village avec ses petites maisons, et des arbres.

LOUISE: Regarde cette rue, on dirait un tableau de... De qui? Ah! d'Utrillo, Maurice Utrillo. Est-ce qu'on pourrait trouver un tableau comme ça?

PAUL: Yes, a small hill. "Montmartre" comes from "mons martyrum," the martyrs of the beginning of the Christian era. There is a big church at the top, with several very high white cupolas. It was built from 1876 to 1910. It seems that it is very much criticized by the French.

LOUISE: Like the Eiffel Tower?

PAUL: Exactly. The biggest dome is eighty meters tall. 240 feet!

LOUISE: Incredible!

PAUL: So, we are on the other side of Paris! Well what did he give me, this man, at the entrance to the métro? "Monsieur Cadabra protects your future. Guaranteed results. All problems solved." And a list...

LOUISE: Well, we don't have any problems, have we? Let's go up this street and here is the basilica.

PAUL: All white and enormous. Its stone does not take pollution.

LOUISE: They are very beautiful, these cupolas on the blue sky with those big clouds.

PAUL: We turn left and we find the neighborhood, the village with its small houses, and trees.

LOUISE: Look at this street. It looks like a picture of... Who is it? Ah! Of Utrillo. Maurice Utrillo. Could we find a picture like that?

PAUL: Allons voirs sur la place et choisissons quelque chose qui nous plaît.

LOUISE: Ah! Voilà. J'aime celui-là. C'est bien dessiné, très calme. Ça coûte trop cher?

PAUL: Allons en voir d'autres. Il n'y a pas trop de monde. On peut flâner. C'est agréable...

LOUISE: Bonjour, monsieur. J'aime vos tableaux. Nous allons prendre celui-là.

PAUL: Je crois qu'il va pleuvoir! Descendons vite avec notre Utrillo! Cet homme avait l'air d'un vrai peintre avec son chapeau et sa barbe.

Paul: Let's go to the square and choose one that we like.

Louise: Ah! Here is one. I like that one. It is well drawn, very calm. Is it too expensive?

Paul: Let's see some other ones. There are not too many people. One can walk leisurely. It feels good...

Louise: Good morning, *monsieur*. I like your pictures. We are going to take that one.

Paul: I think it is going to rain! Let's go down quickly with our Utrillo! This man looked like a real painter with his hat and beard.

VOCABULARY

ami, l' *m.*	friend
appareil de photo, l' *m.*	camera
barbe, la *f.*	beard
boîte aux lettres, la *f.*	mailbox
bureau, le *m.*	desk
butte, la *f.*	hill
carte postale, la *f.*	postcard
celles qui	those that (*f.*)
ceux qui	those that (*m.*)
chapeau, le *m.*	hat
chrétien	christian
colline, la *f.*	hill
court	short
critiquer	criticize
d'autres	others
ère, l' *m.*	era
est, l' *m.*	east*
flâner	to stroll
hauteur, la *f.*	height
jusqu'à	up to
liste, la *f.*	list
martyr, le *m.*	martyr
message, le *m.*	message
mienne, la *f.*	mine
mieux	better
moitié, la *f.*	half
ne ... plus	no longer
on dirait	one would say

*With the meaning "east" each letter is pronounced in "est," e-s-t, as opposed to "est," ê, the third person singular of the verb *être*.

parapluie, le *m.*	umbrella
peintre, le *m.*	painter
pellicule, la *f.*	roll of film
pollution, la *f.*	pollution
presque	almost
prêt	ready
quelque chose	something
rempli	filled
résolu	solved
rester	to remain
sommet, le *m.*	top
sortie, la *f.*	exit
tien, le *m.*	yours
tienne, la *f.*	yours
timbre, le *m.*	stamp
tout près	near by

GRAMMAR

The Conditional

The conditional is a mode of the verb that expresses the idea of a possibility, affirmative or negative, of something taking place, provided some conditions are met. A conditional sentence is composed of two parts: one stating the condition starting with the conjunction *si* (if), and one stating the consequence.

Forms

The present conditional is formed with the future construction of the verb, substituting the endings of the imperfect for those of the future.

endings	*aimer* (to love)	*se lever* (to get up)
-ais	j'aimerais	je me lèverais
-ais	tu aimerais	tu te lèverais
-ait	il/elle aimerait	il/elle se lèverait
-ions	nous aimerions	nous nous lèverions
-iez	vous aimeriez	vous vous lèveriez
-aient	ils/elles aimeraient	ils/elles se lèveraient

The past conditional consists of the auxiliary in the conditional + past participle.

aimer	*tomber*
j'aurais aimé	je serais tombé(e)
tu aurais aimé	tu serais tombé(e)
il/elle aurait aimé	il/elle serait tombé(e)
nous aurions aimé	nous serions tombés/ées
vous auriez aimé	vous seriez tombés/ées
ils/elles auraient aimé	ils/elles seraient tombés/ées

se lever

je me serais levé(e)
tu te serais levé(e)
il se serait levé/elle se serait levée
nous nous serions levés/ées
vous vous seriez levés/ées
ils/elles se seraient levés/ées

Uses

The conditional expresses a possibility.

J'aimerais venir vous voir.
I would like to come and see you.

It is used as a polite way of asking something.

Pourriez-vous me prêter un stylo?
Could you lend me a pen?

It is used after verbs such as *se demander* (to wonder) in a past tense, followed by a *si* (if, whether), which indicates a question and not a conditional.

Je me demandais si elle finirait tôt.
I was wondering whether she would finish early.

Je me demandais si vous auriez aimé venir avec nous.
I was wondering if you would have liked to come with us.

Expressing a Condition and its Results

These are sentences made of two parts:

One in which the verb is either in the future or in the conditional present or past tenses. It expresses the results of the condition contained in the second part of the sentence.

One beginning with *si* + a verb in one of the tenses of the indicative mood: present, imperfect, past perfect, pluperfect.

Si je viens, je vas téléphonerai.
If I come, I will call you.

Si je venais, je vous téléphonerais.
If I came, I would call you.

Si j'étais venu, je vous aurais téléphoné.
If I had come, I would have called you.

Note: The future tense or the conditional present or past tenses are never used after *si*, contrary to English usage.

Use of Tenses to Obtain Specific Meanings

A rigorous sequence of tenses is used to obtain the following meanings.

I. Action still possible in the present or in the future.

1. *si* + present 2. imperative, present or future

Si le temps est beau, sors.
If the weather is nice, go out!

Si le temps est beau, je sors.
If the weather is nice, I go out.

Si le temps est beau, je sortirai.
If the weather is nice, I will go out.

II. Action not possible, but desired.

1. *si* + imperfect — 2. conditional present

Si le temps était beau, je sortirais.
If the weather was nice, I would go out.

III. Action imagined in the past, but no longer possible.

1. *si* + pluperfect — 2. past tense of the conditional

Si le temps avait été beau, nous serions sortis.
If the weather had been nice, we would have gone out.

S'il était venu tôt, je serais parti avec lui.
If he had come early, we would have gone there together.

Note: In these sentences the use of tenses is the same in English and in French. However many English expressions use a conditional after "if," a construction that is absolutely incorrect in French.

IV. Action perhaps realized in the past, and the result of the action.

1. *si* + past perfect — 2. past perfect, present or future

S'il a lu cette lettre, il ne l'a pas comprise.
If he read this letter, he did not understand it.

In this construction the meaning of the *si* + past perfect phrase must be "if it is true that..."

TABLE OF CONSTRUCTION OF CONDITIONAL SENTENCES

Action possible	*Result*
si + present indic.	imperative/present indicative/future/future perfect
Action not possible in the present	*Result*
si + imperfect	present conditional/past conditional
Action not realized in the past	*Result*
si + pluperfect	present conditional/past conditional
Realized action in the past	*Result*
si + past perfect	present/future/past perfect/future perfect

Note: The correspondence of tenses shown in this table must be strictly observed as necessary to obtain the desired meaning.

EXERCISES

While doing these exercises, check the tenses in the table.

I. Give the conditional and the past conditional forms of the following verbs given in the present indicative tense.

1. j'ai
2. elle veut
3. ils vont
4. tu tombes
5. nous faisons
6. il perd
7. elles espèrent
8. tu te lèves
9. vous écrivez
10. on peut
11. nous courons
12. vous verrez
13. elles savent
14. vous connaissez
15. il appelle

II. Write conditional sentences using the alternating constructions given in the table and using a variety of subject pronouns. The *si* clause is not always first.

1. avoir de l'argent – acheter une maison
2. avoir plus d'énergie – aller faire une promenade
3. arriver en retard – ne pas pouvoir entrer dans la salle
4. donner un conseil – connaître le problème
5. aller plus vite – ne pas regarder le paysage
6. être prêt – venir plus tôt
7. se lever tôt – voir le lever du soleil
8. servir un bon dîner – faire le marché
9. envoyer un cadeau – avoir l'adresse de ces personnes
10. savoir toutes ces choses – ne pas écrire cet article

III. Fill in the blanks with a form of the verbs given so that the sentences are correct.

1. Si vous ne ______ (pouvoir) pas venir, ______ (téléphoner) moi!

2. S'il ______ (comprendre) le problème, il ______ (ne pas dire) cela.
3. Si elle ______ (vouloir) l'aider, elle ______ (faire) une bonne action.
4. Si nous ______ (entendre) ces paroles, cela nous ______ (faire) plaisir.
5. Si vous ______ (ne pas acheter) cette maison, vous le ______ (regretter).
6. Elle ______ (venir) nous voir si elle ______ (connaître) la route.
7. Vous ______ (réussir) mieux si vous ______ (travailler) plus sérieusement.
8. Nous ______ (ne pas perdre) notre temps si nous ______ (aller) la voir.

LESSON NINETEEN

DIALOGUE

Courses Au Bon Marché

PAUL: Il faudrait penser à faire nos bagages. Tu ne crois pas?

LOUISE: Pas encore, pas encore!

PAUL: Nous partons lundi, et demain c'est dimanche, donc nous ne pourrons pas faire des courses.

LOUISE: Non?

PAUL: Tous les magasins seront fermés pour le dimanche.

LOUISE: Mais qu'est-ce tu voudrais acheter?

PAUL: Nos valises ne sont pas assez grandes pour mettre tous les objets que nous avons achetés, ici et là: tes jupes, ton manteau, mon costume...

LOUISE: Il faut aller jusqu'au Printemps?

PAUL: Non, je viens de remarquer un autre grand magasin, sur la route de l'autobus 68. Ça s'appelle Le Bon Marché.

LOUISE: Ça veut dire pas cher, n'est-ce pas? Est-ce vraiment bon marché?

PAUL: Probablement que non. Peut-être que le nom veut dire simplement que c'est un marché où les produits sont bons et les prix honnêtes.

Shopping at the Bon Marché

PAUL: We should think about packing, don't you think?

LOUISE: Not yet! Not yet!

PAUL: We are leaving on Monday and tomorrow is Sunday, so we will not be able to go and buy things.

LOUISE: No?

PAUL: All stores will be closed for Sunday.

LOUISE: But what would you like to buy?

PAUL: Our suitcases are not large enough to hold all the objects that we have bought here and there: your skirts, your coat, my suit...

LOUISE: We have to go all the way to the Printemps?

PAUL: No, I have just noticed another department store on the route of bus 68. It is called the Bon Marché.

LOUISE: That means cheap, doesn't it? Is it really cheap?

PAUL: Probably not. Perhaps the name means simply that it is a market where products are good and prices fair.

LOUISE: Allons-y. Où faut-il descendre?

PAUL: A Sèvres-Babylone.

LOUISE: Quels drôles de noms! Hier Barbès-Rochechouart, aujourd'hui...

PAUL: Les arrêts prennent le nom de rues, et de rues qui se croisent. Et les rues, dans cette ville, ont des noms historiques: des personnes, des évènements, des endroits...

LOUISE: C'est ça, le Bon Marché. Ça a l'air ancien...

PAUL: Mais dedans, c'est très moderne. C'était le premier Grand Magasin de Paris, établi ici en 1852 par un Monsieur Boucicaut qui a eu l'idée brillante que les clients aimeraient avoir tous les objets qu'ils voulaient dans un seul grand bâtiment. Il a donné des droits et des avantages à ses employés, surtout des femmes, pour rendre leur travail moins pénible, comme des périodes de repos, des journées de dix heures et le droit de protester contre certaines situations de travail. En dix ans, il avait dix fois plus de capital!

LOUISE: Oh! Regarde les jolis chapeaux. Il me va bien?

PAUL: Tu n'aimerais pas mieux le rouge?

LOUISE: Et l'étiquette dit qu'on peut le rouler pour le mettre dans sa valise.

PAUL: Juste ce dont nous avons besoin.

LOUISE: Prenons ce joli chapeau et allons voir les valises.

LOUISE: Let's go there. Where do we get off?

PAUL: At Sèvres-Babylone.

LOUISE: What strange names! Yesterday Barbès-Rochechouart, today...

PAUL: Bus and subway stops take the names of streets and of street crossings. And streets, in this city, have names related to history, people, events, places...

LOUISE: This is the Bon Marché. It looks old...

PAUL: But inside it is very modern. It was the first department store in Paris, established here in 1852 by a man called Monsieur Boucicaut, who had the brilliant idea that customers would like to have all the items they wanted in one single large building. He gave his employees, mostly women, rights and advantages to make their work less difficult, like rest periods, ten-hour work days and the right to protest against certain work conditions. In ten years he had ten times more capital!

LOUISE: Oh! Look at the pretty hats. Does it look good on me?

PAUL: You would not like the red one better?

LOUISE: And the label says that you can roll it up and put it in your suitcase.

PAUL: Exactly what we need.

LOUISE: Let's take this nice hat and let's go see the suitcases.

PAUL: Et une de ces belles chemises roses pour moi. On aura la place!

LOUISE: Et un presse-ail!

PAUL: Un presse-ail? Pourquoi pas la Pierre de Rosetta, dans la reproduction du Louvre?

LOUISE: Allons voir les valises!

PAUL: And one of those elegant pink shirts for me. We will have space for it!

LOUISE: And a garlic press!

PAUL: A garlic press? Why not the Louvre reproduction of the Rosetta Stone?

LOUISE: Let's go see the suitcases!

VOCABULARY

aller bien	to be becoming (clothing)
arrêt, l' *m.*	stop
assez ... pour	enough to
avantage, l' *m.*	advantage
bon marché	cheap
brillant	brilliant
capital, le *m.*	capital
ce dont	that which
chapeaux, les *m.*	hats
chemise, la *f.*	shirt
client, le *m.*	client
costume, le *m.*	suit
dimanche	Sunday
dix fois	ten times
droits, les *m.*	rights
employé, l' *m.*	employee
endroit, l' *m.*	place
étiquette, l' *f.*	price tag
faire des courses	to go shopping
faire les bagages	to pack (luggage)
il faudrait	we should
honnête	fair
lundi	Monday
manteau, le *m.*	coat
pas encore	not yet
pénible	tiring
Pierre de Rosetta, la *f.*	Rosetta Stone
presse-ail, le *m.*	garlic press
prix, le *m.*	price
produit, le *m.*	product
quels drôles de...	what strange...

remarquer	to notice
rose	pink
se croiser	to meet, to cross
valise, la *f.*	suitcase
venir de	to have just

GRAMMAR

The Subjunctive

The subjunctive is a mood used in subordinate clauses, after another verb + *que*. Verbs that require a construction with the subjunctive must be learned.

Forms

I. regular verbs

The ending *-ent* of the 3rd person plural of the present indicative is replaced by the endings:

	singular	*plural*
1st	-e	-ions
2nd	-es	-iez
3rd	-e	-ent

aimer – que j'aime
finir – que je finisse
vendre – que je vende

II. irregular verbs

- *avoir* and *être*

avoir

que j'aie	que nous ayons
que tu aies	que vous ayez
qu'il ait	qu'ils aient

être

que je sois que nous soyons
que tu sois que vous soyez
qu'il soit qu'ils soient

- Five verbs with one radical for all forms

faire (to do) – *que je fasse*
pouvoir (to be able to) – *que je puisse*
falloir (to be necessary) – *qu'il faille* (3rd pers. sg. only)
pleuvoir (to rain) – *qu'il pleuve* (3rd pers. sg. only)
savoir (to know) – *que je sache*

- *aller* and *vouloir*

aller (to go) – *que j'aille, que nous allions, que vous alliez, qu'ils aillent*
vouloir (to want) – *que je veuille, que nous voulions, que vous vouliez, qu'ils veuillent*

For other irregular forms see Appendix.

Past Subjunctive

The past subjunctive is a compound tense:

auxiliary verb in the subjunctive + past participle

Je suis contente qu'il ait apporté ces fleurs.
I am happy that he brought these flowers.

The past subjunctive always indicates an action that takes place before the action indicated by the verb of the main clause, and must be used to provide this meaning.

Uses

I. independent clause

As a form of the 3rd person imperative:

Qu'il entre!
Let him come in.

To express a wish:

Vive la France.
Long live France.

Que Dieu vous bénisse.
May God bless you. (when someone sneezes)

II. dependent clause

The verb of the main clause makes it necessary to use a subjunctive form after the *que* of the main clause.

- After a verb expressing doubt, improbability:

  douter – to doubt
  il semble – it seems
  il n'est pas probable – it is not probable

- After a verb expressing will, desire, order:

  vouloir – to want
  demander – to order
  exiger – to require
  refuser – to prevent

défendre – to forbid
dire – to give an order, to tell
Etc.

- After verbs expressing sentiments, emotion:

être heureux, triste, etc. – to be happy, sad, etc.
craindre – to fear
aimer, etc. – to like

- After impersonal expressions:

il faut – it is necessary
il est nécéssaire – it is necessary
il est possible – it is possible
il est impossible – it is impossible
il est regrettable – it is too bad
il vaut mieux – it is better
il est bon, juste, utile – it is good, just, useful
il est important – it is important
Etc.

Many of these verbs and expressions are constructed differently in English but in French you have to put *que* at the end of the main clause and the following verb in the subjunctive.

Il est important que vous lui parliez.
It is important for you to talk to him.

Je veux que vous veniez avec nous.
I want you to come with us.

- Verbs expressing ideas of thinking or declaring are followed by an indicative if the verb is in the affirmative form but the subjunctive if the form is negative.

Je pense qu'il vient.
I think he is coming.

Je pense qu'il viendra.
I think he will come.

Je ne pense pas qu'il vienne.
I do not think he will come.

III. In dependent clauses after some conjunctions:

pour que – so that
afin que – so that
de peur que – for fear that
de façon que – in such a way that
de sorte que – in such a manner that
à moins que – unless
sans que – without (+ verb)
pourvu que – provided (+ verb)
avant que – before
jusqu'à ce que – until
en attendant que – until
bien que – although
soit que ... soit que – either ... or

Je vous donne ceci pour que vous le lisiez.
I give you this so that you read it.

J'arriverai à 3 heures à moins que le train soit en retard.
I will arrive at 3:00 unless the train is late.

Vous ferez ceci avant que la secrétaire parte.
You will do this before the secretary leaves.

Tenses

The main verb can be in the present, the past or the future. The verb in the *que* clause will be a present subjunctive if the action indicated takes place at the same time or will take place in the future.

The past tense of the subjunctive will be used only if the action it indicates has taken place before the action of the main verb.

Je suis heureux qu'il vienne.
I am happy that he is coming. (at some later time)

Il sera heureux qu'elle vienne.
He will be happy that she is coming. (at some later date)

Nous étions heureux qu'elle vienne.
We were happy that she was coming. (at a later date)

Il était heureux qu'elle soit venue.
He was happy that she had come. (at an earlier date)

Elle a été heureuse qu'il soit venu.
She had been happy that he had come. (at an earlier date)

EXERCISES

I. In the following list of verb forms, you will underline those that are in the subjunctive and write the infinitive.

1. je crois qu'il dort
2. je ne crois pas qu'il vienne
3. je veux qu'il le sache
4. il ne désire pas qu'elle le prenne
5. il pense qu'il le sait
6. elle est triste qu'il soit parti
7. il est nécéssaire que tu le fasses
8. il est important que tu le dises
9. il est sûr qu'il est parti
10. je le fais pour que tu dormes bien
11. je resterai jusqu'à ce qu'il parte
12. je rentrerai quand il partira
13. elle le lui dit de peur qu'il n'ait pas compris
14. j'irai à condition que tu y ailles
15. écris-lui à moins que tu ne le veuilles pas
16. la loi ordonne que vous payiez vos impôts

II. Make one sentence with the pairs of sentences given, using the subjunctive when necessary. Identify the various verb tenses. The pronouns in ( ) are not used when there is a dependent clause.

1. Elle a oublié de venir / je (le) regrette
2. Marie voyagera avec lui / il (le) désire
3. Nous allons au cinéma / je (le) propose
4. C'est très important? / je ne (le) pense pas
5. C'est terrible / elle a perdu son porte-monnaie
6. Je vous enverrai des nouvelles / attendez!
7. Vous (le) souhaitez / ils ne viendront pas

8. Elle est étonnée / il n'est pas encore arrivé
9. Il est obligatoire / on lit ces documents
10. Elle préfère / il ne (le) sait pas

III. Complete the following sentences with the correct form of the verb.

1. Il demande que je ______ (venir) le voir.
2. C'est dommage que vous ne ______ (pouvoir) pas être présent.
3. Elle veut qu'on ______ (faire) le marché tout de suite.
4. Nous sommes heureux que vous ______ (recevoir – past subj.) de ses nouvelles.
5. Nous pensons qu'il ______ (oublier) de venir.
6. Il faut que vous ______ (apprendre) beaucoup de mots.
7. J'arriverai avant qu'il ______ (partir).
8. Je ne crois pas que vous ______ (avoir) raison.

LESSON TWENTY

DIALOGUE

Avant le Départ

PAUL: Comme le temps a passé vite! Et il faut que nous partions demain?

LOUISE: Oui. Je suis content que nous soyons restés dans cet hotel. Les gens sont aimables et il est bien placé.

PAUL: Alors tout était parfait?

LOUISE: Absolument.

PAUL: C'est extraordinaire que nous ayons fait tant de choses.

LOUISE: Et j'ai inscrit presque tout dans mon journal pour que nous nous rappelions tous ces bons moments. Même la visite au Bon Marché et la promenade jusqu'à St. Germain des Prés, et le délicieux dîner au Petit St. Benoît.

PAUL: Vite! On bourre les valises et on va faire une dernière promenade.

LOUISE: Ah! Celle-ci est difficile à fermer. Mais... Bon, ça y est!

PAUL: Il y a encore beaucoup de choses dans la chambre, mais on verra ça demain.

LOUISE: Tu veux te promener dans le parc Montsouris?

PAUL: Montsouris! Le mont de souris!

Before the Departure

PAUL: How fast time went! And we must leave tomorrow?

LOUISE: Yes. I am glad we stayed in this hotel. People are pleasant and it is well situated.

PAUL: So everything was perfect?

LOUISE: Absolutely.

PAUL: It is extraordinary that we did so many things.

LOUISE: And I wrote down almost everything in my journal so that we can remember all these good moments. Even the visit to the Bon Marché and the walk to St. Germain des Près, and the delicious dinner at the Petit St. Benoît.

PAUL: Quick! Let's stuff the suitcases and go for a last walk.

LOUISE: Ah! This one is hard to close. But... Good! It's done!

PAUL: There are still many things in the room but we will see about those tomorrow.

LOUISE: Do you want to go for a walk in the Montsouris Park?

PAUL: Montsouris! The hill of a mouse!

LOUISE: Pourquoi pas? Ce n'est pas loin. Tu l'as découvert l'autre jour. C'était un quartier de peintres et d'écrivains au commencement du XXème siècle. Braque a vecu là, et Henry Miller.

PAUL: Ah! Quel joli jardin, avec ces roses et toutes ces autres fleurs, des dahlias jaunes et rouges, des sauges bleues... Et puis il y a un petit lac, avec des canards et des cygnes qui nagent dessus.

LOUISE: Pourquoi ne pas jeter le reste de ton sandwich aux canards?

PAUL: Mon sandwich est très bon et je veux le finir. J'ai toujours faim. J'ai plus faim que ces canards. Tout le monde leur jette du pain. Ce n'est peut-être même pas bon pour leurs estomacs.

LOUISE: Juste un petit morceau, pour les voir venir! Ah! Les voilà tous!

PAUL: C'est un petit caillou que j'ai jeté!

LOUISE: Oh! Le méchant! Mais le soleil se couche. Nous allons dîner dans le même restaurant où nous avons si bien mangé notre premier soir. Tu es d'accord?

PAUL: Tu as les meilleures idées. Je crois que je vais prendre une sole, normande, comme toi la première fois. Ah! Je me sens si bien dans ce pays. Je suis si triste de partir. Mais nous reviendrons bientôt, n'est-ce pas?

LOUISE: Je l'espère bien!

LOUISE: Why not? It is not far. You discovered it the other day. It was a district of painters and writers at the beginning of the XXth century. Braque lived there, and Henry Miller.

PAUL: Ah! What a pretty garden, with these roses and so many other flowers, red and yellow dahlias, blue sage... And there is a small lake, with ducks and swans swimming in it.

LOUISE: Why don't you throw to the ducks what is left of your sandwich?

PAUL: My sandwich is very good and I want to finish it. I am still hungry. I am hungrier than those ducks. Everyone throws bread to them. It may not even be good for their stomachs.

LOUISE: Just a small piece, to see them come! Ah! Here they all come!

PAUL: It was a pebble I threw in!

LOUISE: How mean of you! But the sun is setting. We are going to have dinner in the same restaurant where we ate so well the first night. Is that all right with you?

PAUL: You have the best ideas. I think I am going to have a *sole normande* as you did the first time. Ah! I feel so good in this country. I am so sad to leave. But we will soon come back, won't we?

LOUISE: I certainly hope so!

VOCABULARY

absolument	absolutely
autre jour, l' *m.*	the other day
bourrer	to stuff
caillou, le *m.*	pebble
canard, le *m.*	duck
ça y est	it's done
Comme...!	how
cygne, le *m.*	swan
être d'accord	to agree
fermer	to close
inscrire	to write, to inscribe
jeter	to throw
journal, le *m.*	journal, diary
lac, le *m.*	lake
méchant	mean
même, le *m.*	the same one
morceau, un *m.*	a piece
nager	to swim
parc Montsouris, le *m.*	(a park in Paris)
pays, le *m.*	country
presque	almost
sauf que	except that
sauge, la *f.*	sage
si triste	so sad
souris, la *f.*	mouse
tant de...	so many
vite	quickly
vivre	to live

GRAMMAR

Adverbs

Adverbs are invariable words that modify the meaning of the word they precede or follow. They modify verbs, adjectives or other adverbs.

Il parle vite.
He speaks fast.

Il parle très vite.
He speaks very fast.

Ceci est extrêmement beau.
This is extremely beautiful.

There are numerous adverbs indicating:

manner: *bien* (well), *mal* (badly), *ensemble* (together), etc.

time: *aujourd'hui* (today), *hier* (yesterday), *souvent* (often), *toujours* (always), etc.

place: *devant* (in front), *derrière* (behind), *loin* (far), *près* (near), etc.

quantity: *beaucoup* (many), *trop* (too much), *peu* (little), *aussi* (as much as), etc.

affirmation or negation: *oui* (yes), *peut-être* (maybe), *ne ... pas* (to not), etc.

adverbial expressions, made of several words: *à peu près* (almost), *en même temps* (at the same time), *quelque part* (somewhere), etc.

Forms

Many adverbs are formed by adding the ending *-ment* to the feminine form of adjectives, or directly to the adjective when it ends in *e* or another vowel.

doux, douce, doucement – sweet, sweetly
précis, précisément – precisely
facile, facilement – easy, easily

For adjectives that end in *-ant* the ending becomes *-amment*, and endings in *-ent* become *-emment.*

savant, savamment – learned, in a learned way
eminent, eminemment – eminent, eminently

Irregular Forms

bon, bien – good, well
meilleur, mieux – better, better
mauvais, mal – bad, badly
petit, peu – small, little

Place of the Adverb

In front of the adjective or adverb it modifies:

Ceci est particulièrement bon.
This is particularly good.

After the verb it modifies, and never between the subject and the verb as in English:

Il vient souvent nous voir.
He often comes to see us.

When the verb is a compound tense the adverb is placed between the verb and the past participle if it has no more than three syllables:

Je l'ai vite fini.
I finished it quickly.

Il l'a rarement vu.
He rarely saw him

Il lui a parlé raisonnablement.
He spoke to him reasonably.

Adverbs of manner or time are often placed at the beginning of a sentence:

Silencieusement, elle est entrée dans la chambre.
Silently, she entered the bedroom.

Note: An adverb should never be placed at the end of a sentence, several words away from the word it modifies.

EXERCISES

I. Write the adverb corresponding to the following adjectives.

1. rapide
2. patient
3. faux
4. long
5. sec
6. élégant
7. absolu
8. grand
9. petit

II. Place the adverb in the sentence.

1. Ils lui ont donné des cadeaux. (encore)
2. Ils sont revenus de leur travail. (très tard)
3. N'oubliez pas de compter votre argent. (bien)
4. Ils ont aimé ce tableau. (toujours)
5. Ce travail était plus difficile. (autrefois)
6. Ce sera possible. (heureusement)

III. Translate the words between ( ) and observe the place of the adverb, while writing the whole sentence.

1. Ils pourront _______ le faire. (soon)
2. Elle la rencontrait _______ quand elles étaient voisines. (many times)
3. Vous avez l'air _______ heureux. (particularly)
4. Nous partirons _______ demain soir. (late)
5. Il a couru _______ qu'il est fatigué. (so fast)
6. _______, on a tout vendu. (unfortunately)

APPENDIX

VERB CONJUGATIONS

Synopsis of Verb Tenses

This synopsis of verb tenses contains only the tenses used in conversational style and not those that are used almost exclusively in literary works.* In the indicative, the present, imperfect, past perfect, future, pluperfect, compound past perfect, and anterior future are given. In the conditional and the subjunctive, the present and past tenses are provided, and in the participle and the infinitive forms, the present and past tenses. This synopsis also includes the imperative.

Indicative / *Indicatif*

Present / *Présent*: je donne (I give)
Imperfect / *Imparfait*: je donnais (I gave)
Past perfect / *Passé composé*: j'ai donné (I gave)
Future / *Futur*: je donnerai (I will give)
Pluperfect / *Plus-que-parfait*: j'avais donné (I had given)
Compound past perfect / *Passé surcomposé*: j'ai eu donné (I had given)
Anterior future / *Futur antérieur*: j'aurai donné (I will have given)

Conditional / *Conditionnel*

Present / *Présent*: je donnerais (I would give)
Past / *Passé*: *j'aurais* donné (I would have given)

Subjunctive / *Subjonctif***

Present / *Présent*: que je donne (I give)
Past / *Passé*: que j'aie donné (I gave)

Participle / *Participe*

Present / *Présent*: donnant (giving)

Past / *Passé*: donné (given)

Compound present / *Passé du présent*: ayant donné

Infinitive / *Infinitif*

Present / *Présent*: donner (to give)
Past / *Passé*: avoir donné (to have given)

Imperative / *Impératif*

Donne! (give!)

*Note that the example used, *donner* (to give), represents *er* verbs only.
**Translation varies as this form is used differently in English and in French.

Conjugations

Regular Verbs

ER VERBS

Infinitive

donner – to give / *avoir donné* – to have given

Indicative

Present	Imperfect	Past Perfect
donne	donnais	ai donné
donnes	donnais	as donné
donne	donnait	a donné
donnons	donnions	avons donné
donnez	donniez	avez donné
donnent	donnaient	ont donné

Pluperfect	Compound Past Perfect
avais donné	ai eu donné
avais donné	as eu donné
avait donné	a eu donné
avions donné	avons eu donné
aviez donné	avez eu donné
avaient donné	ont eu donné

Future	Anterior Future
donnerai	aurai donné
donneras	auras donné
donnera	aura donné
donnerons	aurons donné
donnerez	aurez donné
donneront	auront donné

Conditional

Present	Past
donnerais	aurais donné
donnerais	aurais donné
donnerait	aurait donné
donnerions	aurions donné
donneriez	auriez donné
donneraient	auraient donné

Subjunctive

Present	Past
donne	aie donné
donnes	aies donné
donne	ait donné
donnions	ayons donné
donniez	ayez donné
donnent	aient donné

Participle

Present	Past
donnant	donné

Imperative: donne, donnons, donnez

IR VERBS

Infinitive

finir – to finish / *avoir fini* – to have finished

Indicative

Present	Imperfect	Past Perfect
finis	finissais	ai fini
finis	finissais	as fini
finit	finissait	a fini
finissons	finissions	avons fini
finissez	finissiez	avez fini
finissent	finissaient	ont fini

Pluperfect	Compound Past Perfect
avais fini	ai eu fini
avais fini	as eu fini
avait fini	a eu fini
avions fini	avons eu fini
aviez fini	avez eu fini
avaient fini	ont eu fini

Future	Anterior Future
finirai	aurai fini
finiras	auras fini
finira	aura fini
finirons	aurons fini
finirez	aurez fini
finiront	auront fini

Conditional

Present	Past
finirais	aurais fini
finirais	aurais fini
finirait	aurait fini
finirions	aurions fini
finiriez	auriez fini
finiraient	auraient fini

Subjunctive

Present	Past
finisse	aie fini
finisses	aies fini
finisse	ait fini
finissions	ayons fini
finissiez	ayez fini
finissent	aient fini

Participle

Present	Past
finissant	fini

Imperative: finis, finissons, finissez

RE VERBS

Infinitive

vendre – to sell / *avoir vendu* – to have sold

Indicative

Present	Imperfect	Past Perfect
vends	vendais	ai vendu
vends	vendais	as vendu
vend	vendait	a vendu
vendons	vendions	avons vendu
vendez	vendiez	avez vendu
vendent	vendaient	ont vendu

Pluperfect	Compound Past Perfect
avais vendu	ai eu vendu
avais vendu	as eu vendu
avait vendu	a eu vendu
avions vendu	avons eu vendu
aviez vendu	avez eu vendu
avaient vendu	ont eu vendu

Future	Anterior Future
vendrai	aurai vendu
vendras	auras vendu
vendra	aura vendu
vendrons	aurons vendu
vendrez	aurez vendu
vendront	auront vendu

Conditional

Present	Past
vendrais	aurais vendu
vendrais	aurais vendu
vendrait	aurait vendu
vendrions	aurions vendu
vendriez	auriez vendu
vendraient	auraient vendu

Subjunctive

Present	Past
vende	aie vendu
vendes	aies vendu
vende	ait vendu
vendions	ayons vendu
vendiez	ayez vendu
vendent	aient vendu

Participle

Present	Past
vendant	vendu

Imperative: vends, vendons, vendez

Irregular Verbs

AVOIR

Infinitive

avoir – to have / *avoir eu* – to have had

Indicative

Present	Imperfect	Past Perfect
ai	avais	ai eu
as	avais	as eu
a	avait	a eu
avons	avions	avons eu
avez	aviez	avez eu
ont	avaient	ont eu

Pluperfect	Compound Past Perfect
avais eu	ai eu eu
avais eu	as eu eu
avait eu	a eu eu
avions eu	avons eu eu
aviez eu	avez eu eu
avaient eu	ont eu eu

Future	Anterior Future
aurai	aurai eu
auras	auras eu
aura	aura eu
aurons	aurons eu
aurez	aurez eu
auront	auront eu

Conditional

Present	Past
aurais	aurais eu
aurais	aurais eu
aurait	aurait eu
aurions	aurions eu
auriez	auriez eu
auraient	auraient eu

Subjunctive

Present	Past
aie	aie eu
aies	aies eu
ait	ait eu
ayons	ayons eu
ayez	ayez eu
aient	aient eu

Participle

Present	Past
ayant	eu

Imperative: aie, ayons, ayez

ETRE

être – to be / *avoir été* – to have been

Indicative

Present	Imperfect	Past Perfect
suis	étais	ai été
es	étais	as été
est	était	a été
sommes	étions	avons été
êtes	étiez	avez été
sont	étaient	ont été

Pluperfect	Compound Past Perfect
avais été	ai eu été
avais été	as eu été
avait été	a eu été
avions été	avons eu été
aviez été	avez eu été
avaient été	ont eu été

Future	Anterior Future
serai	aurai été
seras	auras été
sera	aura été
serons	aurons été
serez	aurez été
seront	auront été

Conditional

Present	Past
serais	aurais été
serais	aurais été
serait	aurait été
serions	aurions été
seriez	auriez été
seraient	auraient été

Subjunctive

Present	Past
sois	aie été
sois	aies été
soit	ait été
soyons	ayons été
soyez	ayez été
soient	aient été

Participle

Present	Past
étant	été

Imperative: sois, soyons, soyez

OTHER IRREGULAR VERBS

- ***aller* – to go / *être allé* – to have gone**

Present participle: allant
Past participle: allé

Present: vais, vas, va, allons, allez, vont

Imperfect: allais
Past Perfect: suis allé(e)
Pluperfect: étais allé(e)
Compound Past Perfect: ai été allé(e)
Future: irai
Anterior Future: serai allé(e)

Conditional Present: irais
Conditional Past: serais allé(e)

Subjunctive Present: aille, ailles, aille, allions, alliez, aillent
Subjunctive Past: sois allé(e)

Imperative: va, allons, allez

- ***s'asseoir* – to sit (oneself) / *s'être assis* – to have sat (oneself)**

Present participle: asseyant
Past participle: assis

Present: m'assieds, t'assieds, s'assied, nous asseyons, vous asseyez, s'asseyent

Imperfect: m'asseyais
Past Perfect: me suis assis(e)
Pluperfect: m'étais assis(e)

Compound Past Perfect: m'ai été assis(e)
Future: m'assiérai
Anterior Future: me serai assis(e)

Conditional Present: m'assiérais
Conditional Past: me serais assis(e)

Subjunctive Present: m'asseye, t'asseyes, s'asseye, nous asseyions, vous asseyiez, s'asseyent
Subjunctive Past: me sois assis(e)

Imperative: assieds-toi, asseyons-nous, asseyez-vous

- ***battre* – to beat / *avoir battu* – to have beaten**

Present participle: battant
Past participle: battu

Present: bats, bats, bat, battons, battez, battent

Imperfect: battais
Past Perfect: ai battu
Pluperfect: avais battu
Compound Past Perfect: ai eu battu
Future: battrai
Anterior Future: aurai battu

Conditional Present: battrais
Conditional Past: aurais battu

Subjunctive Present: batte, battes, batte, battions, battiez, battent
Subjunctive Past: aie battu

Imperative: bats, battons, battez

- ***boire* – to drink / *avoir bu* – to have drunk**

Present participle: buvant
Past participle: bu

Present: bois, bois, boit, buvons, buvez, boivent

Imperfect: buvais
Past Perfect: ai bu
Pluperfect: avais bu
Compound Past Perfect: ai eu bu
Future: boirai
Anterior Future: aurai bu

Conditional Present: boirais
Conditional Past: aurais bu

Subjunctive Present: boive, boives, boive, buvions, buviez, boivent
Subjunctive Past: aie bu

Imperative: bois, buvons, buvez

- ***conclure* – to conclude / *avoir conclu* – to have concluded**

Present participle: concluant
Past participle: conclu

Present: conclus, conclus, conclut, concluons, concluez, concluent

Imperfect: concluais
Past Perfect: ai conclu
Pluperfect: avais conclu
Compound Past Perfect: ai eu conclu
Future: conclurai
Anterior Future: aurai conclu

Conditional Present: conclurais
Conditional Past: aurais conclu

Subjunctive Present: conclue, conclues, conclue, concluions, concluiez, concluent
Subjunctive Past: aie conclu

Imperative: conclus, concluons, concluez

- ***conduire* – to drive / *avoir conduit* – to have driven**

Present participle: conduisant
Past participle: conduit

Present: conduis, conduis, conduit, conduisons, conduisez, conduisent

Imperfect: conduisais
Past Perfect: ai conduit
Pluperfect: avais conduit
Compound Past Perfect: ai eu conduit
Future: conduirai
Anterior Future: aurai conduit

Conditional Present: conduirais
Conditional Past: aurais conduit

Subjunctive Present: conduise, conduises, conduise, conduisions, conduisiez, conduisent
Subjunctive Past: aie conduit

Imperative: conduis, conduisons, conduisez

- ***connaître* – to know / *avoir connu* – to have known**

Present participle: connaissant
Past participle: connu

Present: connais, connais, connaît, connaissons, connaissez, connaissent

Imperfect: connaissais
Past Perfect: ai connu
Pluperfect: avais connu
Compound Past Perfect: ai eu connu
Future: connaîtrai
Anterior Future: aurai connu

Conditional Present: connaîtrais
Conditional Past: aurais connu

Subjunctive Present: connaisse, connaisses, connaisse, connaissions, connaissiez, connaissent
Subjunctive Past: aie connu

Imperative: connais, connaissons, connaissez

- ***courir* – to run / *avoir couru* – to have run**

Present participle: courant
Past participle: couru

Present: cours, cours, court, courons, courez, courent

Imperfect: courais
Past Perfect: ai couru
Pluperfect: avais couru

Compound Past Perfect: ai eu couru
Future: courrai
Anterior Future: aurai couru

Conditional Present: courrais
Conditional Past: aurais couru

Subjunctive Present: coure, coures, coure, courions, couriez, courent
Subjunctive Past: aie couru

Imperative: cours, courons, courez

- ***craindre* – to fear / *avoir craint* – to have feared**

Present participle: craignant
Past participle: craint

Present: crains, crains, craint, craignons, craignez, craignent

Imperfect: craignais
Past Perfect: ai craint
Pluperfect: avais craint
Compound Past Perfect: ai eu craint
Future: craindrai
Anterior Future: aurai craint

Conditional Present: craindrais
Conditional Past: aurais craint

Subjunctive Present: craigne, craignes, craigne, craignions, craigniez, craignent
Subjunctive Past: aie craint

Imperative: crains, craignons, craignez

• ***croire*** **– to believe /** ***avoir cru*** **– to have believed**

Present participle: croyant
Past participle: cru

Present: crois, crois, croit, croyons, croyez, croient

Imperfect: croyais
Past Perfect: ai cru
Pluperfect: avais cru
Compound Past Perfect: ai eu cru
Future: croirai
Anterior Future: aurai cru

Conditional Present: croirais
Conditional Past: aurais cru

Subjunctive Present: croie, croies, croie, croyions, croyiez, croient
Subjunctive Past: aie cru

Imperative: crois, croyons, croyez

• ***cueillir*** **– to pick /** ***avoir cueilli*** **– to have picked**

Present participle: cueillant
Past participle: cueilli

Present: cueille, cueilles, cueille, cueillons, cueillez, cueillent

Imperfect: cueillais
Past Perfect: ai cueilli
Pluperfect: avais cueilli
Compound Past Perfect: ai eu cueilli
Future: cueillerai
Anterior Future: aurai cueilli

Conditional Present: cueillerais
Conditional Past: aurais cueilli

Subjunctive Present: cueille, cueilles, cueille, cueillions, cueilliez, cueillent
Subjunctive Past: aie cueilli

Imperative: cueille, cueillons, cueillez

- ***devoir* – to have to, must / *avoir dû* – to have had to**

Present participle: devant
Past participle: dû, due

Present: dois, dois, doit, devons, devez, doivent

Imperfect: devais
Past Perfect: ai dû
Pluperfect: avais dû
Compound Past Perfect: ai eu dû
Future: devrai
Anterior Future: aurai dû

Conditional Present: devrais
Conditional Past: aurais dû

Subjunctive Present: doive, doives, doive, devions, deviez, doivent
Subjunctive Past: aie dû

Imperative: dois, devons, devez

- ***dire* – to say / *avoir dit* – to have said**

Present participle: disant
Past participle: dit

Present: dis, dis, dit, disons, dites, disent

Imperfect: disais
Past Perfect: ai dit
Pluperfect: avais dit
Compound Past Perfect: ai eu dit
Future: dirai
Anterior Future: aurai dit

Conditional Present: dirais
Conditional Past: aurais dit

Subjunctive Present: dise, dises, dise, disions, disiez, disent
Subjunctive Past: aie dit

Imperative: dis, disons, dites

- ***écrire* – to write / *avoir écrit* – to have written**

Present participle: écrivant
Past participle: écrit

Present: écris, écris, écrit, écrivons, écrivez, écrivent

Imperfect: écrivais
Past Perfect: ai écrit
Pluperfect: avais écrit
Compound Past Perfect: ai eu écrit
Future: écrirai
Anterior Future: aurai écrit

Conditional Present: écrirais
Conditional Past: aurais écrit

Subjunctive Present: écrive, écrives, écrive, écrivions, écriviez, écrivent
Subjunctive Past: aie écrit

Imperative: écris, écrivons, écrivez

- ***envoyer* – to send / *avoir envoyé* – to have sent**

Present participle: envoyant
Past participle: envoyé

Present: envoie, envoies, envoie, envoyons, envoyez, envoient

Imperfect: envoyais
Past Perfect: ai envoyé
Pluperfect: avais envoyé
Compound Past Perfect: ai eu envoyé
Future: enverrai
Anterior Future: aurai envoyé

Conditional Present: enverrais
Conditional Past: aurais envoyé

Subjunctive Present: envoie, envoies, envoie, envoyions, envoyiez, envoient
Subjunctive Past: aie envoyé

Imperative: envoie, envoyons, envoyez

- ***faire* – to do / *avoir fait* – to have done**

Present participle: faisant
Past participle: fait

Present: fais, fais, fait, faisons, faites, font

Imperfect: faisais
Past Perfect: ai fait
Pluperfect: avais fait
Compound Past Perfect: ai eu fait
Future: ferai
Anterior Future: aurai fait

Conditional Present: ferais
Conditional Past: aurais fait

Subjunctive Present: fasse, fasses, fasse, fassions, fassiez, fassent
Subjunctive Past: aie fait

Imperative: fais, faisons, faites

- ***falloir* – to have to, must / *avoir fallu* – to have had to**

Present participle: —
Past participle: fallu

Present: il faut

Imperfect: il fallait
Past Perfect: il a fallu
Pluperfect: il avait fallu
Compound Past Perfect: il a eu fallu
Future: il faudra
Anterior Future: il aura fallu

Conditional Present: il faudrait
Conditional Past: il aurait fallu

Subjunctive Present: il faille
Subjunctive Past: il ait fallu

Imperative: —

- ***lire* – to read / *avoir lu* – to have read**

Present participle: lisant
Past participle: lu

Present: lis, lis, lit, lisons, lisez, lisent

Imperfect: lisais
Past Perfect: ai lu
Pluperfect: avais lu
Compound Past Perfect: ai eu lu
Future: lirai
Anterior Future: aurai lu

Conditional Present: lirais
Conditional Past: aurais lu

Subjunctive Present: lise, lises, lise, lisions, lisiez, lisent
Subjunctive Past: aie lu

Imperative: lis, lisons, lisez

- ***mettre* – to put / *avoir mis* – to have put**

Present participle: mettant
Past participle: mis

Present: mets, mets, met, mettons, mettez, mettent

Imperfect: mettais
Past Perfect: ai mis
Pluperfect: avais mis
Compound Past Perfect: ai eu mis
Future: mettrai
Anterior Future: aurai mis

Conditional Present: mettrais
Conditional Past: aurais mis

Subjunctive Present: mette, mettes, mette, mettions, mettiez, mettent
Subjunctive Past: aie mis

Imperative: mets, mettons, mettez

- ***mourir* – to die / *avoir été mort* – to have been dead**

Present participle: mourant
Past participle: mort

Present: meurs, meurs, meurt, mourons, mourez, meurent

Imperfect: mourais
Past Perfect: suis mort(e)
Pluperfect: étais mort(e)
Compound Past Perfect: ai été mort(e)
Future: mourrai
Anterior Future: serai mort(e)

Conditional Present: mourrais
Conditional Past: serais mort(e)

Subjunctive Present: meure, meures, meure, mourions, mouriez, meurent
Subjunctive Past: sois mort(e)

Imperative: meurs, mourons, mourez

- ***naître* – to be born / *avoir été né* – to have been born**

Present participle: naissant
Past participle: né

Present: nais, nais, naît, naissons, naissez, naissent

Imperfect: naissais
Past Perfect: suis né(e)
Pluperfect: étais né(e)
Compound Past Perfect: ai été né(e)
Future: naîtrai
Anterior Future: serai né(e)

Conditional Present: naîtrais
Conditional Past: serais né(e)

Subjunctive Present: naisse, naisses, naisse, naissions, naissiez, naissent
Subjunctive Past: sois né(e)

Imperative: nais, naissons, naissez

- ***ouvrir* – to open / *avoir ouvert* – to have opened**

Present participle: ouvrant
Past participle: ouvert

Present: ouvre, ouvres, ouvre, ouvrons, ouvrez, ouvrent

Imperfect: ouvrais
Past Perfect: ai ouvert
Pluperfect: avais ouvert
Compound Past Perfect: ai eu ouvert
Future: ouvrirai
Anterior Future: aurai ouvert

Conditional Present: ouvrirais
Conditional Past: aurais ouvert

Subjunctive Present: ouvre, ouvres, ouvre, ouvrions, ouvriez, ouvrent
Subjunctive Past: aie ouvert

Imperative: ouvre, ouvrons, ouvrez

- ***peindre* – to paint / *avoir peint* – to have painted**

Present participle: peignant
Past participle: peint

Present: peins, peins, peint, peignons, peignez, peignent

Imperfect: peignais
Past Perfect: ai peint
Pluperfect: avais peint
Compound Past Perfect: ai eu peint
Future: peindrai
Anterior Future: aurai peint

Conditional Present: peindrais
Conditional Past: aurais peint

Subjunctive Present: peigne, peignes, peigne, peignions, peigniez, peignent
Subjunctive Past: aie peint

Imperative: peins, peignons, peignez

- ***plaire* – to please / *avoir plu* – to have pleased**

Present participle: plaisant
Past participle: plu

Present: plais, plais, plaît, plaisons, plaisez, plaisent

Imperfect: plaisais
Past Perfect: ai plu
Pluperfect: avais plu
Compound Past Perfect: ai eu plu
Future: plairai
Anterior Future: aurai plu

Conditional Present: plairais
Conditional Past: aurais plu

Subjunctive Present: plaise, plaises, plaise, plaisions, plaisiez, plaisent
Subjunctive Past: aie plu

Imperative: plais, plaisons, plaisez

- ***pleuvoir* – to rain / *avoir plu* – to have rained**

Present participle: pleuvant
Past participle: plu

Present: il pleut

Imperfect: il pleuvait
Past Perfect: il a plu
Pluperfect: il avait plu
Compound Past Perfect: il a eu plu
Future: il pleuvra*
Anterior Future: il aura plu

Conditional Present: il pleuvrait
Conditional Past: il aurait plu

Subjunctive Present: il pleuve
Subjunctive Past: il ait plu

Imperative: —

*often used: *il va pleuvoir* = it is going to rain

- ***pouvoir* – to be able to / *avoir pu* – to have been able to**

Present participle: pouvant
Past participle: pu

Present: peux / puis, peux, peut, pouvons, pouvez, peuvent

Imperfect: pouvais
Past Perfect: ai pu
Pluperfect: avais pu
Compound Past Perfect: ai eu pu
Future: pourrai
Anterior Future: aurai pu

Conditional Present: pourrais
Conditional Past: aurais pu

Subjunctive Present: puisse, puisses, puisse, puissions, puissiez, puissent
Subjunctive Past: aie pu

Imperative: —

- ***prendre* – to take / *avoir pris* – to have taken**

Present participle: prenant
Past participle: pris

Present: prends, prends, prend, prenons, prenez, prennent

Imperfect: prenais
Past Perfect: ai pris
Pluperfect: avais pris
Compound Past Perfect: ai eu pris
Future: prendrai
Anterior Future: aurai pris

Conditional Present: prendrais
Conditional Past: aurais pris

Subjunctive Present: prenne, prennes, prenne, prenions, preniez, prennent
Subjunctive Past: aie pris

Imperative: prends, prenons, prenez

• ***recevoir* – to receive / *avoir reçu* – to have received**

Present participle: recevant
Past participle: reçu

Present: reçois, reçois, reçoit, recevons, recevez, reçoivent

Imperfect: recevais
Past Perfect: ai reçu
Pluperfect: avais reçu
Compound Past Perfect: ai eu reçu
Future: recevrai
Anterior Future: aurai reçu

Conditional Present: recevrais
Conditional Past: aurais reçu

Subjunctive Present: reçoive, reçoives, reçoive, recevions, receviez, reçoivent
Subjunctive Past: aie reçu

Imperative: reçois, recevons, recevez

• ***rendre* – to return, give back / *avoir rendu* – to have returned**

Present participle: rendant
Past participle: rendu

Present: rends, rends, rend, rendons, rendez, rendent

Imperfect: rendais
Past Perfect: ai rendu
Pluperfect: avais rendu
Compound Past Perfect: ai eu rendu
Future: rendrai
Anterior Future: aurai rendu

Conditional Present: rendrais
Conditional Past: aurais rendu

Subjunctive Present: rende, rendes, rende, rendions, rendiez, rendent
Subjunctive Past: aie rendu

Imperative: rends, rendons, rendez

- ***résoudre* – to resolve / *avoir résolu* – to have resolved**

Present participle: résolvant
Past participle: résolu

Present: résous, résous, résout, résolvons, résolvez, résolvent

Imperfect: résolvais
Past Perfect: ai résolu
Pluperfect: avais résolu
Compound Past Perfect: ai eu résolu
Future: résoudrai
Anterior Future: aurai résolu

Conditional Present: résoudrais
Conditional Past: aurais résolu

Subjunctive Present: résolve, résolves, résolve, résolvions, résolviez, résolvent
Subjunctive Past: aie résolu

Imperative: résous, résolvons, résolvez

- ***rire* – to laugh / *avoir ri* – to have laughed**

Present participle: riant
Past participle: ri

Present: ris, ris, rit, rions, riez, rient

Imperfect: riais
Past Perfect: ai ri
Pluperfect: avais ri
Compound Past Perfect: ai eu ri
Future: rirai
Anterior Future: aurai ri

Conditional Present: rirais
Conditional Past: aurais ri

Subjunctive Present: rie, ries, rie, riions, riiez, rient
Subjunctive Past: aie ri

Imperative: ris, rions, riez

- ***savoir* – to know / *avoir su* – to have known**

Present participle: sachant
Past participle: su

Present: sais, sais, sait, savons, savez, savent

Imperfect: savais
Past Perfect: ai su
Pluperfect: avais su
Compound Past Perfect: ai eu su
Future: saurai
Anterior Future: aurai su

Conditional Present: saurais
Conditional Past: aurais su

Subjunctive Present: sache, saches, sache, sachions, sachiez, sachent
Subjunctive Past: aie su

Imperative: sache, sachons, sachez

- ***suffire* – to suffice, to be enough / *avoir suffi* – to have sufficed**

Present participle: suffisant
Past participle: suffi

Present: suffis, suffis, suffit, suffisons, suffisez, suffisent

Imperfect: suffisais
Past Perfect: ai suffi
Pluperfect: avais suffi
Compound Past Perfect: ai eu suffi
Future: suffirai
Anterior Future: aurai suffi

Conditional Present: suffirais
Conditional Past: aurais suffi

Subjunctive Present: suffise, suffises, suffise, suffisions, suffisiez, suffisent
Subjunctive Past: aie suffi

Imperative: suffis, suffisons, suffisez

- ***suivre* – to follow / *avoir suivi* – to have followed**

Present participle: suivant
Past participle: suivi

Present: suis, suis, suit, suivons, suivez, suivent

Imperfect: suivais
Past Perfect: ai suivi
Pluperfect: avais suivi
Compound Past Perfect: ai eu suivi
Future: suivrai
Anterior Future: aurai suivi

Conditional Present: suivrais
Conditional Past: aurais suivi

Subjunctive Present: suive, suives, suive, suivions, suiviez, suivent
Subjunctive Past: aie suivi

Imperative: suis, suivons, suivez

- ***tenir* – to hold / *avoir tenu* – to have held**

Present participle: tenant
Past participle: tenu

Present: tiens, tiens, tient, tenons, tenez, tiennent

Imperfect: tenais
Past Perfect: ai tenu
Pluperfect: avais tenu
Compound Past Perfect: ai eu tenu
Future: tiendrai
Anterior Future: aurai tenu

Conditional Present: tiendrais
Conditional Past: aurais tenu

Subjunctive Present: tienne, tiennes, tienne, tenions, teniez, tiennent
Subjunctive Past: aie tenu

Imperative: tiens, tenons, tenez

- ***valoir* – to be worth / *avoir valu* – to have been worth**

Present participle: valant
Past participle: valu

Present: vaux, vaux, vaut, valons, valez, valent

Imperfect: valais
Past Perfect: ai valu
Pluperfect: avais valu
Compound Past Perfect: ai eu valu
Future: vaudrai
Anterior Future: aurai valu

Conditional Present: vaudrais
Conditional Past: aurais valu

Subjunctive Present: vaille, vailles, vaille, valions, valiez, vaillent
Subjunctive Past: aie valu

Imperative: vaux, valons, valez

- ***venir* – to come / *être venu* – to have come**

Present participle: venant
Past participle: venu

Present: viens, viens, vient, venons, venez, viennent

Imperfect: venais
Past Perfect: suis venu(e)
Pluperfect: étais venu(e)
Compound Past Perfect: ai été venu(e)
Future: viendrai
Anterior Future: serai venu(e)

Conditional Present: viendrais
Conditional Past: serais venu(e)

Subjunctive Present: vienne, viennes, vienne, venions, veniez, viennent
Subjunctive Past: sois venu(e)

Imperative: viens, venons, venez

- ***vivre* – to live / *avoir vécu* – to have lived**

Present participle: vivant
Past participle: vécu

Present: vis, vis, vit, vivons, vivez, vivent

Imperfect: vivais
Past Perfect: ai vécu
Pluperfect: avais vécu
Compound Past Perfect: ai eu vécu
Future: vivrai
Anterior Future: aurai vécu

Conditional Present: vivrais
Conditional Past: aurais vécu

Subjunctive Present: vive, vives, vive, vivions, viviez, vivent
Subjunctive Past: aie vécu

Imperative: vis, vivons, vivez

- ***voir* – to see / *avoir vu* – to have seen**

Present participle: voyant
Past participle: vu

Present: vois, vois, voit, voyons, voyez, voient

Imperfect: voyais
Past Perfect: ai vu
Pluperfect: avais vu
Compound Past Perfect: ai eu vu
Future: verrai
Anterior Future: aurai vu

Conditional Present: verrais
Conditional Past: aurais vu

Subjunctive Present: voie, voies, voie, voyions, voyiez, voient
Subjunctive Past: aie vu

Imperative: vois, voyons, voyez

- ***vouloir* – to want / *avoir voulu* – to have wanted**

Present participle: voulant
Past participle: voulu

Present: veux, veux, veut, voulons, voulez, veulent

Imperfect: voulais
Past Perfect: ai voulu
Pluperfect: avais voulu
Compound Past Perfect: ai eu voulu
Future: voudrai
Anterior Future: aurai voulu

Conditional Present: voudrais
Conditional Past: aurais voulu

Subjunctive Present: veuille, veuilles, veuille, voulions, vouliez, veuillent
Subjunctive Past: aie voulu

Imperative: veuille, veuillons, veuillez

KEY TO EXERCISES

Lesson I: The Present Tense and the Imperative

I.

1. nous arrivons
2. vous changez
3. elle achète
4. ils étudient
5. tu appelles
6. j'espère
7. vous finissez
8. elle dort
9. vous partez
10. nous bâtissons
11. il vient
12. elles peuvent
13. tu veux
14. il reçoit
15. nous perdons

II.

1. il chante
2. étudie-t-elle?
3. je ne dors pas
4. il ne peut pas
5. ne vient-elle pas?
6. elle perd
7. ils ne bâtissent pas
8. nous partons
9. arrive-t-elle?
10. il naît

III.

1. How long has she been sleeping?
2. She has been sleeping for 3 hours.
3. How long have they been traveling in France?
4. They have been traveling for four weeks.
5. For how many years have you known him?
6. I have known him for ten years.
7. How many days has he been working here?
8. He has been working here for 5 days.
9. I have been calling you for half an hour.

IV.

1. Je lis depuis ... heures.
2. Elle travaille depuis ... heures.
3. Elles jouent depuis ... heures.
   Voilà ... heures qu'elles jouent.
4. Je voyage depuis dix ans.

V.

1. chante; chantons; chantez
   ne chante pas; ne chantons pas; ne chantez pas
2. dors; dormons; dormez
   ne dors pas; ne dormons pas; ne dormez pas
3. mange; mangeons; mangez
   ne mange pas; ne mangeons pas; ne mangez pas
4. va; allons; allez
   ne va pas; n'allons pas; n'allez pas
5. sois; soyons; soyez
   ne sois pas; ne soyons pas; ne soyez pas
6. vois; voyons; voyez
   ne vois pas; ne voyons pas; ne voyez pas
7. attends; attendons; attendez
   n'attends pas; n'attendons pas; n'attendez pas
8. cours; courons; courez
   ne cours pas; ne courons pas; ne courez pas
9. crains; craignons; craignez
   ne crains pas; ne craignons pas; ne craignez pas
10. défends; défendons; défendez
    ne défends pas; ne défendons pas; ne défendez pas
11. fais; faisons; faites
    ne fais pas; ne faisons pas; ne faites pas
12. dis; disons; dites
    ne dis pas; ne disons pas; ne dites pas

Lesson II: Tenses Expressing Past Actions: The Imperfect and the Past Perfect

I.

1. finir - tu as finis
2. sourire – je souriais
3. connaître – j'ai connu

4. faire – ils faisaient
5. comprendre – il a compris
6. s'arrêter – ils se sont arrêtés
7. voir – nous voyions
8. entrer – je suis entré
9. engager – vous engagiez
10. partir – nous sommes partis
11. appeler – ils appelaient
12. être – tu as été
13. avoir – elle avait
14. apercevoir – elle a aperçu
15. boire – vous buviez

II.

1. je finissais
2. le voyage n'était pas
3. il y avait
4. nous marchions
5. c'était
6. nous nous reposions/nous mangions
7. ils portaient
8. un garçon faisait
9. les jours passaient
10. il arrivait/il fallait

III.

1. je suis revenu(e)/mon ami est venu
2. j'ai dit/le voyage n'a pas été
3. il y a eu
4. nous avons marché
5. Ça a été
6. nous nous reposions/nous mangions
7. les jours ont passé
8. le dernier jour est arrivé/il a fallu

Lesson III: Personal Pronouns

I.

1. je le veux
2. je ne les veux pas
3. en veux-tu?
4. donne lui
5. lui as-tu parlé?
6. ne lui as-tu pas parlé?
7. il va le dire
8. il ne va pas les dire
9. je la lui prends
10. je ne la lui prends pas
11. ils l'y ont vu
12. ils ne l'y ont pas vu
13. parlez moi
14. mettez m'en
15. elle y en a pris
16. elle n'y en a pas pris

II.

1. Je les lui donne.
2. Je ne les lui donne pas.
3. Je leur en donne.
4. Donne lui en.
5. Il nous en donne.
6. Il ne leur en donne pas.
7. Vous en donne-t-il?
8. Il ne m'en donne pas.

III.

1. J'y suis./Je n'y suis pas.
2. Elle l'aime./Elle ne l'aime pas.
3. Je vais lui parler./Je ne vais pas lui parler.
4. Elle leur en a parlé./Elle ne leur en a pas parlé.
5. Je vais vous le présenter.
6. Oui, j'en veux un.
7. Non, je n'en veux pas un.
8. Vas-tu y aller avec eux?/Ne vas-tu pas y aller avec eux?
9. La croyons-nous?/Ne la croyons-nous pas?
10. J'en ai dix.

IV.

1. Donne-le-lui.
2. Donne-le-lui.
3. Venez la leur raconter.
4. Dites-le-moi.
5. Chantez-nous-en.
6. Allons en chercher.
7. Venez-y.
8. Envoyez-m'en.
9. Ne lui en donnez pas.
10. Ecris-la-leur.

V.

1. Allez-vous-en.
2. Envoyez-nous-y.
3. Disons-la-lui.
4. Faisons-lui-en.
5. Demande-la-nous.
6. Occupez-vous-en.
7. Donne-m'en une.
8. Prends-les-lui.
9. Laissez-les-moi.
10. Prenez-leur-en.

Lesson IV: Articles

I.

definite articles

1. le livre (*m.*)
2. l'autobus (*m.*)
3. les trains (*m.*)
4. la composition (*f.*)
5. l'activité (*f.*)
6. le chapeau (*m.*)
7. les cousines (*f.*)
8. la vie (*f.*)
9. l'homme (*m.*)
10. l'eau (*f.*)

indefinite articles

1. des livres (*m.*)
2. des chapeaux (*m.*)
3. du soleil (*m.*)
4. de l'action (*f.*)
5. du bonheur (*m.*)
6. du temps (*m.*)
7. de la bonté (*f.*)
8. des sourires (*m.*)
9. de la confiance (*f.*)
10. des amitiés (*f.*)

II.

1. une pomme
2. le livre
3. des légumes
4. les tomates/l'été
5. le français/une langue
6. les Français/le bon vin
7. de lait ni de café
8. le samedi/une longue promenade
9. les promenades/le temps
10. de tomates
11. de fruits divers
12. de lapins/de la salade/le jardin

III.

1. Prends/Prenez une pomme.
2. N'achète/N'achètez pas de tomates.
3. Le samedi, nous ne travaillons pas.
4. Aimez-vous/Aimes-tu les légumes?
5. Mangez-vous/Manges-tu des légumes?
6. Le temps est beau pour une promenade.
7. En été nous faisons des promenades.
8. Aimez-vous le vin?

Lesson V: Interrogative Words and Constructions

I.

1. Invente-t-il...?
2. La jeune fille a-t-elle ouvert...? *or* Qui a ouvert la fenêtre?
3. N'as-tu pas compris...?
4. Ne pourra-t-il pas...?
5. Ne le recommencera-t-elle pas?

6. N'y pensez-vous plus...?
7. L'exercice est-il...?
8. Mes amis vont-ils acheter...?

II.

1. Où seras-tu? Où serez-vous?
2. Où partirez-vous?
3. A quelle heure va-t-il sortir?
4. Comment cette jeune fille par-elle?
5. Combien cet homme a-t-il gagné?
6. Quand ton camarade rentre-t-il?
7. Pourquoi pleure-t-elle?
8. Comment va son père? Comment son père va-t-il?

III.

1. Qui...?
2. Qu'...?
3. A qui...?
4. Pour qui...?
5. Avec quoi...?
6. Dans quoi...?
7. En quoi...?
8. Sans quoi...?

Lesson VI: Relative Pronouns

I.

1. qui
2. que
3. que
4. qui
5. qui
6. que

II.

1. dont elle avait envie
2. dont nous avons parlé ensemble
3. dont j'ignorais l'existence
4. dont il fait une étude
5. dont il vient
6. dont il s'occupe
7. dont vous avez besoin
8. dont elle se souvient
9. dont je peux me servir
10. dont tu as entendu la voix

III.

1. La personne chez qui nous sommes allés était aimable.
2. Ce garçon avec qui il s'est disputé est un brute.
3. Mon ami à qui nous avons rendu visite habite à Versailles.
4. Le patron pour qui je travaille est d'un caractère difficile.
5. Mon père, auprès de qui je suis restée, est malade.
6. Le juge, devant qui il va se présenter, est sévère.
7. La femme derrière qui je me tenais parlait sans arrêt.
8. Mon oncle, sur qui je compte, me prêtera de l'argent.

Lesson VII: The Future Tense

I.

1. j'aurai
2. nous serons
3. tu iras
4. vous courrez
5. il enverra
6. elles sauront
7. je ferai
8. nous devrons
9. tu croiras
10. il faudra
11. ils mourront
12. il pleuvra
13. elles pourront
14. je m'assiérai
15. nous tiendrons
16. tu viendras
17. vous verrez
18. il vaudra

II.

1. Comme il ne le verra pas, il ne le saura pas.
2. Si vous ne vous levez pas, vous serez en retard.
3. Si elle est vraiment gentille, nous irons avec elle au cinéma.
4. Nous nous demandons si elle saura résoudre ce problème.
5. Vous donnerez de vos nouvelles dès que vous le pourrez.
6. Si tu te perds, que feras-tu?
7. Crois-tu qu'il viendra demain?
8. Elle vous verra quand elle aura le temps.
9. Nous nous en irons quand nous aurons fini.
10. Vous vous coucherez dès que vous aurez envie de dormir.

III.

1. quand vous voudrez.
2. si vous êtes prêt.
3. quand vous rentrerez.
4. si vous revenez ici.
5. si vous donnez votre adresse.
6. quand nous aurons le temps.
7. quand ils auront etudié la question.
8. si nous avons le temps.

Lesson VIII: Nouns

I.

1. le
2. la
3. les (*m.*)
4. la
5. le
6. la
7. la
8. les (*f.*)
9. les (*m.*)
10. le
11. les (*f.*)
12. la
13. le
14. la
15. les (*m.*)
16. la
17. les (*m.*)
18. le
19. la
20. le
21. les (*m.*)
22. la
23. la
24. l' (*m.*)
25. le
26. l' (*f.*)
27. le
28. la
29. les (*f.*)
30. l' (*m.*)

II.

1. Regardez ces eaux bleues.
2. Ils ont les oreilles fines.
3. Les chats sont des animaux rusés.
4. Ce sont de beaux hommes.
5. Ce sont des garçons courageux.
6. Ces moteurs sont usés.
7. Ce sont de vieux amis.
8. Elle a les yeux alertes.

III.

1. Il sort avec son cousin.
2. Cette enfant a de bonnes maîtresses.
3. Elles engageront un avocat.
4. Ma tante ne va pas venir demain.
5. Les acteurs jouent une comédie ce soir.
6. Les lectrices sont nombreuses.
7. Je n'ai pas confiance dans cette conductrice.
8. Avez-vous un médecin habile?
9. J'ai entendu le loup cette nuit.
10. J'ai vu une jument dans le pré.

Lesson IX: Adjectives

I.
Use the table.

II.

1. une grande maison blanche
2. une longue conférence ennuyeuse
   une conférence longue et ennuyeuse
3. une petite porte ouverte
4. de gros garçons lourds
   des garçons gros et lourds

5. des femmes actives et intelligentes
6. une vieille église abandonnée
7. les deux premiers exercices
8. une gentille figure souriante
9. un bon petit vin blanc
10. des compositions claires et intéressantes

III.

1. ancienne
2. cruelle
3. gentille
4. pareille
5. muette
6. nette
7. grasse
8. plate
9. bonne
10. épaisse
11. fondatrice
12. première
13. dernière
14. complète
15. blanche
16. fraîche
17. longue
18. publique
19. sèche
20. rousse
21. douce
22. fausse
23. favorite
24. mauvaise
25. nulle

Lesson X: Reflexive Verbs

I.

Present

1. vous vous habillez
2. se forme
3. se casse
4. tu te coupes
5. elle se brosse ... avant de se coucher
6. nous nous lavons les mains

Future

1. vous vous habillerez
2. se formera
3. se cassera

4. tu te couperas
5. elle se brossera
6. nous nous laverons

Past Perfect

1. vous vous êtes habillé
2. s'est formée
3. s'est cassé
4. tu t'es coupé
5. elle s'est brossé
6. nous nous sommes lavé

II.

1. Je m'appelle...
2. Mon père s'appelle ... ma mère s'appelle
3. elle se trouve...
4. il se trouve...
5. oui, je m'intéresse à...
   non, je ne m'intéresse pas à...
6. oui, je me dépêche pour...
   non, je ne me dépêche pas pour...
7. oui, je me fatigue de...
   non, je ne me fatigue pas de...
8. oui, je me repose bien...
   non, je ne me repose pas bien...

III.

1. vous vous êtes amusé (one person)
   vous vous êtes amusés (several persons)
2. nous ne nous ennuierons pas
3. elles s'étaient trompées
4. tu te couches
5. ils se recontreront
6. je ne me ferai pas de mal
7. ils se sont intéressés
8. elles se fréquentent

9. je m'en suis aperçu
10. ils ne se ressemblent pas

Lesson XI: The Passive Voice

I.

1. Ce garçon a été sauvé par un homme courageux.
2. Ce pont a été construit par des ingénieurs habiles.
3. Cette chanson a été écrite par un musicien célèbre.
4. Beaucoup d'argent a été gagné par cette entreprise.
5. Tout son temps est pris par son travail.
6. Cet enfant a été élevé par des personnes généreuses.

II.

1. (poser des questions à quelqu'un)
   On lui a posé beaucoup de questions.
2. (ordonner à quelqu'un)
   On nous a ordonné d'arrêter la voiture.
3. Il était aimé par tous ses amis.
4. Elle était admirée pour son intelligence.
5. Le groupe était conduit par un guide.
6. (donner à)
   On a donné des renseignements intéressants au touriste.

Lesson XII: Demonstrative Adjectives and Pronouns

I.

1. ce beau jour
2. cette belle journée
3. ces belles journées
4. ces beaux jours
5. cet ami
6. ces amis

II.

1. ceci à cela
2. celle-ci et non celle-là
3. celle-là
4. celui...
5. celles de Marie
6. celles de...
7. ceux-ci mais non ceux-là
8. ceux que...
9. celles que
10. celui à qui

III.

1. C'est
2. C'est
3. Ce
4. Il
5. C'
6. c'est
7. ce sont
8. Elle
9. Qui est-ce?
10. C'est
11. C'est vous!

Lesson XIII: Comparison of Adjectives, Nouns, and Adverbs

I.

1. plus gros qu'
2. plus intelligent qu'
3. autant/que d'
4. moins de jours/que
5. aussi cher que

6. de plus que
   de moins que
7. dix ans de plus qu'
   dix ans de moins que
8. la plus grande
9. le plus difficile
10. la plus audacieuse du

II.

1. Plus il travaille, plus il gagne.
2. Moins il lit, plus il écrit.
3. Plus il travaille, moins nous le voyons.
4. J'ai le même sac que vous.
5. Nous avons une meilleure voiture que la leur.
6. Notre situation est plus mauvaise que la vôtre.
7. Cette fleur est plus jolie que celle-ci.
8. Cette fleur n'est pas aussi jolie que celle-là.
9. Ce gâteau n'est pas meilleur que celui-ci.
10. Il y a autant de chaises que d'invités.

Lesson XIV: The Infinitive

I.

1. à cuire
2. de venir
3. par annoncer
4. pour partir
5. d'avoir fini
6. de ne pas avoir vu
7. à travailler
8. voyager tout seul

II.

1. Il aime travailler là.
2. Elle préfère attendre.

3. Nous avons passé notre temps à jouer.
4. triste de voir cela
5. heureux de visiter ce monument
6. insister de ne pas payer
7. Commence par étudier.
8. avant d'accepter

III.

1. Après avoir vu ça
2. venir diner
3. rire
4. travailler dur
5. commencer à chanter
6. d'être arrêtés
7. d'être montée à la Tour Eiffel
8. de ne pas avoir visité

Lesson XV: Possessive Adjectives and Pronouns

I.

1. vos affaires/votre table
2. mes/vos (tes)
3. Ma/sa
4. leurs/ses/ses
5. nos
6. sa/son
7. tes
8. sa
9. leurs
10. leur

II.

1. les miens – one possessor, several objects
2. la leur – several possessors, one object
3. les vôtres – several possessors, several objects

4. des leurs – several possessors, several objects
5. le vôtre – one (or several) possessors, one object
6. les siennes – one possessor, several objects
7. la leur – several possessors, one object
8. le sien – one possessor, one object

Lesson XVI: Negative Expressions and Constructions

I.

1. Jeanette ne veut pas ce document.
2. Nous n'aimons pas manger de gâteaux.
3. Ne m'apportez pas d'oranges.
4. Ils n'ont pas pu voir cela.
5. Son ami ne le lui a pas donné.
6. On ne lui en fera pas beaucoup.
7. N'entendez-vous pas tous les mots?
8. Peut-être ne faudrait-il pas le lui écrire?
9. Vous ne l'avez probablement pas oublié.
10. Je vous prie de ne pas venir à mon bureau.

II.

1. Paul ne va jamais au musée. – Paul never goes to the museum.
2. Je ne l'ai pas bien entendu. – I did not hear it well.
3. Nous ne l'avons trouvé nulle part. – We did not find it anywhere.
4. Ne m'appelez plus. – Don't call me any longer.
5. Elle n'a guère envie de travailler. – She hardly feels like working.
6. Nous n'avons pas du tout froid. – We are not cold at all.
7. Ils n'ont rien voulu de ceci. – They did not want anything like that.
8. Des nouvelles ne sont pas encore arrivées. – No news have come yet.

III.

1. Nous n'irons ni au restaurant ni au théâtre.
2. Je ne prends ni pain, ni beurre, ni café le matin.

3. Il ne va nous dire ni où ni comment ceci est arrivé.
4. Ni elle ni lui ne savent toute l'histoire.
5. Je n'ai ni papiers ni crayons.
6. Elle ne sait ni cuisiner ni jardiner.
7. Vous ne lui donnerez ni lait ni biscuits.
8. Je n'ai ni confiance ni amitié pour lui.

Lesson XVII: How To Express Anteriority

I.

1. Je vous disais qu'il avait fini son travail.
2. Il a oublié ce qu'il avait promis.
3. Je savais qu'elle était arrivée.
4. Savais-tu si elle était arrivée?
5. Ne savais-tu pas s'ils étaient arrivés?
6. L'erreur que tu avais faite était considérable.
7. Quand tu avais fait une erreur, le savais-tu?
8. Dès que j'ai eu fait une erreur, elle l'a su.
9. Aussitôt que j'ai eu dit cela, je l'ai regretté.

II.

1. était venue me voir
2. n'avait pas été là
3. n'avait pas plu
4. avait plu
5. elle avait fait une promenade
6. elle n'avait pas fait une promenade
7. nous avions visitée
8. qu'elle avait fini ses achats

III.

1. auras fini
2. sera arrivé
3. me réjouirai
4. vous serez installés

5. croirai ce
6. l'auras demandé poliment

Lesson XVIII: The Conditional

I.

1. j'aurais/j'aurais eu
2. elle voudrait/elle aurait voulu
3. ils iraient/ils seraient allés
4. tu tomberais/tu serais tombé
5. nous ferions/nous aurions fait
6. il perdrait/il aurait perdu
7. elles espèreraient/elles auraient espéré
8. tu te lèverais/tu te serais levé
9. vous écririez/vous auriez écrit
10. on pourrait/on aurait pu
11. nous courrions/nous aurions couru
12. vous verriez/vous auriez vu
13. elles sauraient/elles auraient su
14. vous connaîtriez/vous auriez connu
15. il appellerait/il aurait appelé

II.

1. S'il a de l'argent, il achètera une maison.
2. Si j'avais plus d'énergie, j'irais faire une promenade.
3. Si nous étions arrivés en retard, nous n'aurions pas pu...
4. Tu nous donneras un conseil, si tu connais le problème.
5. Si nous allons plus vite, nous ne regarderons pas le paysage.
6. Si vous êtes prêt, il viendra plus tôt.
7. Si je me levais tôt, je verrais le lever du soleil.
8. Si elle servait un bon dîner, nous ferions le marché.
9. J'aurais envoyé un cadeau si j'avais eu l'adresse.
10. S'il avait su toutes ces choses, il n'aurait pas écrit cet article.

III.

1. pouvez/téléphonez
2. comprend/ne dira pas
   avait compris/n'aurait pas dit
   comprenait/ne dirait pas
3. veut l'aider/fera
   voulait l'aider/ferait
   avait voulu/aurait fait
4. entendions/ferait
   entendons/fera
   avions entendu/aurait fait
5. n'achetez pas/regretterez
   n'achetiez pas/regretteriez
   n'aviez pas acheté/l'auriez regretté
6. viendrait/connaissait
   serait venue/avait connu
7. auriez mieux réussi/aviez travaillé
   réussirez/travaillez
8. ne perdrons pas/allons
   ne perdrions pas/allions
   n'aurions pas perdu/étions allés

Lesson XIX: The Subjunctive

I.

1. —
2. vienne (venir)
3. sache (savoir)
4. prenne (prendre)
5. —
6. soit (être)
7. fasses (faire)
8. dises (dire)
9. —
10. dormes (dormir)
11. partes (partir)
12. —
13. ait compris (comprendre)
14. ailles (aller)
15. veuilles (vouloir)
16. payiez (payer)

II.

1. Je regrette qu'elle ait oublié de venir.
2. Il désire que Marie voyage avec lui.
3. Je propose que nous allions au cinéma.
4. Je ne pense pas que ce soit très important.
5. Il est terrible qu'elle ait perdu son porte-monnaie.
6. Attendez que je vous envoie des nouvelles.
7. Vous souhaitez qu'ils ne viennent pas.
8. Elle est étonnée qu'il ne soit pas encore arrivé.
9. Il est obligatoire qu'on lise ces documents.
10. Elle préfère qu'il ne le sache pas.

III.

1. vienne
2. puissiez
3. fasse
4. ayez reçu
5. a oublié
6. appreniez
7. parte
8. ayez

Lesson XX: Adverbs

I.

1. rapidement
2. patiemment
3. faussement
4. longuement
5. sèchement
6. élégamment
7. absolument
8. grandement
9. petitement

II.

1. Ils lui ont encore donné des cadeaux.
2. Ils sont revenus très tard de leur travail.
3. N'oubliez pas de bien compter votre argent.
4. Ils ont toujours aimé ce tableau.
5. Autrefois, ce travail était plus difficile.
6. Heureusement, ce sera possible.

III.

1. Ils pourront bientôt le faire.
2. Elle la rencontrait souvent...
3. Vous avez l'air particulièrement heureux.
4. Nous partirons tard demain soir.
5. Il a couru si vite qu'il est fatigué.
6. Malheureusement, on a tout vendu.

VOCABULARY

FRENCH-ENGLISH VOCABULARY

The words included in this glossary are those from the vocabulary lists and the dialogues. Therefore, a word may have additional meanings that are not presented here, and for which a dictionary can be consulted. Nouns are indicated here with gender and article. A semi-colon between words is used to show different meanings, and a comma is used to separate synonyms.

à	at; to
absolument	absolutely
achat, l' *m.*	purchase
acheter	to buy
à coté de	beside; close to
active *f.*	active
activité, l' *f.*	activity
admirer	to admire
adresse, l' *f.*	address
adresser	to speak to, to address
aéroport, l' *m.*	airport
affiche, l' *f.*	poster
âge classique, l' *m.*	the classical period
agenda, l' *m.*	agenda
agréable	pleasant
ail, l' *m.*	garlic
aimer	to like
aimer mieux	to prefer
air, l' *m.*	air
ajouter	to add
à la découverte	discovering
à l'esprit moderne	with a modern mind
à l'heure	on time
allée, l' *f.*	alley
aller	to go

aller à	to go to
aller bien	to be becoming (clothing)
allumer (s') *refl.*	to light up
alors	then
amener	to bring
ami, l' *m.*	friend
amuser (s') *refl.*	to amuse oneself
an, l' *m.*	year
andouillette, l' *f.*	tripe sausage
anglais	English
année, l' *f.*	year
annoncer	to announce
apercevoir	to catch a glimpse of
apéritif, l' *m.*	drink
à pied	on foot
appareil de photo, l' *m.*	camera
appartement, l' *m.*	apartment
appeler (s') *refl.*	to be called
apporter	to bring
apprendre	to learn
apprise *f.*	learned
appuyer	to push
après	after; afterwards
après J.C.	A.D.
à quelqu'un	to someone
à qui	to whom
à quoi pensons-nous?	what are we thinking about?
arbre, l' *m.*	tree
Arc de Triomphe, l' *m.*	Arch of Triumph
arche, l' *f.*	arch
arrêt, l' *m.*	stop
arrêter (s') *refl.*	to stop running
arrondissement, l' *m.*	section (neighborhood)
article, l' *m.*	article
article de cuisine, l' *m.*	kitchen utensil

artiste, l' *m.*	artist
à son époque	in his time
assécher	to drain
asseoir (s') *refl.*	to sit down
assez	quite enough
assez ... pour	enough to
à travers	across
attendre	to wait
attérir	to land
au	at the; with; in
aubergine, l' *f.*	eggplant
au bout de	at the end of
au-dessus de	above
Auguste Comte	(XIXth century philosopher; name of a street)
aujourd'hui	today
au milieu de	in the middle of
au revoir	good-bye
aussi	also
auteur, l' *m.*	author
autobus, l' *m.*	bus
autour	around
autre	other
autre, un *m.*	another
auxquelles	to which *f. pl.*
avancer (s') *refl.*	to step forward
avant	before
avantage, l' *m.*	advantage
avec	with
avec plaisir	with pleasure
avenue, l' *f.*	avenue
avion, l' *m.*	airplane
avoir	to have
avoir besoin (de)	to need
avoir envie (de)	to feel like

avoir faim	to be hungry
bagages, les *m.*	luggage
baguette, la *f.*	French baguette (bread)
baignoire, la *f.*	bathtub
baisser	to lower
Balzac	(a famous writer of the XIXth century)
bar, le *m.*	bar
barbe, la *f.*	beard
bassin, le *m.*	basin
bateau, le *m.*	boat
bâtiment, le *m.*	building
beau	beautiful
beaucoup	many
beurre, le *m.*	butter
beurrée *f.*	buttered
bien	well, good
bien cuit	well done (food)
bien habillé	well dressed
bien sûr	of course
bijou, le *m.*	jewel
billet, le *m.*	ticket
bisque de homard, la *f.*	cream of lobster (bisque)
bizarre	bizarre, strange
bleu	blue
bloquer	to block
boîte, la *f.*	box
boîte aux lettres, la *f.*	mailbox
bon	good *m.*
bonjour	good morning, hello
bon marché	cheap, affordable
bonne *f.*	good
bon nom, un *m.*	(a) good name
bord, le *m.*	edge
bouche, la *f.*	mouth
bouillir	to boil

Bourgogne	Burgundy
bourrer	to stuff
boutique, la *f.*	shop
bouton, le *m.*	button
bracelet, le *m.*	bracelet
brillant	brilliant; shiny
briller	to shine
brique, la *f.*	brick
bronze, le *m.*	bronze
brûler	to burn
bureau, le *m.*	desk
bus, le *m.*	bus
butte, la *f.*	hill
ça	that
cabine, la *f.*	cabin
cadeau, le *m.*	present
ça fait chic	it looks smart (chic)
café, le *m.*	coffee; café
café au lait, le *m.*	coffee with milk
campagne, la *f.*	countryside
canal, le *m.*	canal
canard, le *m.*	duck
capital, le *m.*	capital
carnet, le *m.*	notebook
carotte, la *f.*	carrot
carte, la *f.*	map; card
carte d'abonnement, la *f.*	membership card/ticket
carte postale, la *f.*	postcard
cassette, la *f.*	cassette tape
ça y est	it's done, that's it
ce	this; that
ceci	this
ce dont	that which
cela (ça)	that
célèbre	famous

célébrer	to celebrate
celeri rave, le *m.*	root celery
celle-ci	this one *f.*
celles	those *f.*
centaine, la *f.*	hundred
centigrade	centigrade
centre, le *m.*	center
ce que	what
certain	some; certain
certainement	certainly
ces	these *m./f.*
ce soir	tonight
cet	this *m.*
cette	this *f.*
ceux	those *m.*
chaise, la *f.*	chair
châle, le *m.*	shawl
chambre, la *f.*	room
champignon, le *m.*	mushroom
chance, la *f.*	luck
changer	to change
changer à	to change to
chanson, la *f.*	song
chapeau, le *m.*	hat
chaque	every; each
charcuterie, la *f.*	pork butcher
chariot, le *m.*	cart (luggage); chariot
Charles de Gaulle-Etoile	(a subway station)
château, le *m.*	castle
chaud	hot; warm
chaussure, la *f.*	shoe
chemise, la *f.*	shirt
cheval, le *m.*	horse
chez	at the house of
choisir	to choose

chose, la *f.*	thing
chrétien	Christian
ciel, le *m.*	sky
cinq	five
circuler	to ride
clair	clear; light
client, le *m.*	client
classe, la *f.*	class
cloche, la *f.*	bell
coin, le *m.*	corner
collant	adhesive
colline, la *f.*	hill
combien	how many
comme	as; just as; how
commencement, le *m.*	beginning
commencer	to begin
comment	how
comment ça se fait?	how did it happen?
commerçant, le *m.*	businessman, merchant
comprendre	to understand
conducteur, le *m.*	driver
confortablement	comfortably
connaître	to know
construire	to build
continuer	to continue
contraire, le *m.*	opposite
contrat, le *m.*	contract
contravention, la *f.*	ticket (fine)
contrôle des passeports, le *m.*	passport control
contrôler	to control
convenir	to be satisfactory
conversion, la *f.*	conversion
corridor, le *m.*	corridor
costume, le *m.*	suit (clothing)
côté	side

couler	to flow, to run
couleur, la *f.*	color
coup, le *m.*	stroke
coupé	cut
cour, la *f.*	courtyard
courant d'air, le *m.*	draft
courses, les *f.*	errands
court	short
cousin, le *m.*	cousin
coussin, le *m.*	cushion
couvert de	covered in
crème, la *f.*	cream
crème brulée, la *f.*	custard with caramel
crème de cassis, la *f.*	black currant liquor
critiquer	to criticize
croire	to believe
croiser (se) *refl.*	to meet, to cross paths
croissant, le *m.*	croissant
croustillant	crusty
croûte, la *f.*	crust
cru	raw
cuillère, la *f.*	spoon
cuit	cooked
curieux	strange
cygne, le *m.*	swan
d'accord	all right
dame, une *f.*	woman
dans	in
date d'entrée, la *f.*	date of entry
de	of; from
débrouiller (se) *refl.*	to find one's way
décalage horaire, le *m.*	jet lag
décoration, la *f.*	decoration
découverte, la *f.*	discovery
décrépit	run-down

Défense, la *f.*	(a section of Paris)
dehors	outside
déjà	already
déjeuner, le *m.*	lunch
délicieux	delicious
demain	tomorrow
demi-litre, le *m.*	half-liter
de plus en plus	more and more
depuis	for; from; since
derrière	behind
des	some; of
des Plantes	of the Plants
descendre	to step out; to go down, descend
désirer	to like, to want
dessert, le *m.*	dessert
détacher (se) *refl.*	to come free/off
détruire	to destroy
deux	two
devant	before; in front of
devoir	must
dictionnaire, le *m.*	dictionary
différent	different
différentes sortes	various kinds
difficile	difficult
digestion, la *f.*	digestion
Dijon	(a city in Burgundy)
dimanche	Sunday
dire	to say
dispute, la *f.*	dispute
dix	ten
doigt, le *m.*	finger
donc	so
donner	to give
dont	of which
doré	gilded

dormir	to sleep
douzaine, une *f.*	dozen
douze	twelve
droit, le *m.*	right (legal)
droite, la *f.*	right (direction)
du	some
eau, l' *f.*	water
écharpe, l' *f.*	scarf
écouter	to listen
écran, l' *m.*	screen
église, l' *f.*	church
égoût, l' *m.*	sewer
élégante *f.*	elegant
elle	she
emmener	to take someone to
émouvant	moving
employé, l' *m.*	employee
employer	to use
en	in; of them
en allant à	going to
en avion	by airplane
en bas	down there
en bas de	at the foot of
en ce moment	right now
en centigrades	in centigrades
en face	across the street
en face de	in front of
en Fahrenheit	into Fahrenheit
en haut de	at the top of
en long	lengthwise
en retard pour	late for
en route	let's go
en route pour	on the way to
en sauce tomate	in tomato sauce
encore un	another one

endroit, l' *m.*	place
enfance, l' *m.*	early years/childhood
enfant, l' *m.*	child
enlever	to remove
ennuyer	to bother; to bore
énorme	enormous
ensemble	together
ensuite	after that
entendre	to hear
entre	between
entrée, l' *f.*	entrance; first course
envoyer	to send
épatant	wonderful
époque	time period, era
épouser	to marry
ère, l' *m.*	era
escalier, l' *m.*	stairs
escargot, l' *m.*	snail
espace, l' *m.*	space
espérer	to hope
essayer	to try on
est, l' *m.*	east
est-ce que...	is (question)
est-ce que ceci...	is this
estomac, l' *m.*	stomach
et	and
et après?	and then?
établissement de bains, l' *m.*	bathhouse
étage, l' *m.*	floor, story
et demi	and a half
étiquette, l' *f.*	price tag
étoile, l' *f.*	star
être	to be
être d'accord	to agree
être enterré	to be buried

être fatigué	to be tired
être réveillé	to be awake
étudiant, l' *m.*	student
étudier	to study
Europe	Europe
exact	exact
exactement	exactly
expliquer	to explain
exposition universelle, l' *f.*	world fair
exquis	exquisite
extraordinaire	extraordinary
faire	to do
faire attention	to pay attention
faire bon (beau)	nice weather (*lit.* to do good)
faire briller	to make shine
faire des courses (achats)	to go shopping
faire dessiner	to have someone draw
faire du bien	to do someone good
faire goûter	to let taste
faire la grimace	to make a face
faire raconter	to ask to tell
faire signe	to signal
falloir	to have to
fameux	much talked about
famille, la *f.*	family
fauteuil, le *m.*	armchair
favori	favorite
féminin	feminine
femme, la *f.*	woman; wife
fenêtre, la *f.*	window
fête, la *f.*	party, festivities
feu, le *m.*	fire; traffic light
feu vert, le *m.*	green light
feuille, la *f.*	leaf; sheet of paper
feux d'artifice, les *m.*	fireworks

fier	proud
file d'attente, la *f.*	waiting line
filigrane, la *f.*	filigree
fille, la *f.*	girl
flamme, la *f.*	flame
flâner	to stroll
flèche, la *f.*	arrow
fleur, la *f.*	flower
flotter	to float
fois, la *f.*	instance, time
fondé	founded
fontaine, la *f.*	fountain
formel	formal
fou, le *m.*	crazy person
fourchette, la *f.*	fork
fraîche *f.*	fresh
français	French
Français, un *m.*	(a) Frenchman
fromage, le *m.*	cheese
fromage de chèvre, le *m.*	goat cheese
gagner	to win out
galerie, la *f.*	gallery
garçon, le *m.*	boy
garder	to keep
gare, la *f.*	train station
garnir	to garnish, to decorate
gazeuse *f.*	bubbly
geler	to freeze
gens, les *m. pl.*	people
gentil	nice
géométrique	geometric
gésier, le *m.*	gizzard
globe, le *m.*	globe
gloire, la *f.*	glory
grand	large

grande ouverte *f.*	wide open
Grand Magasin, le *m.*	department store
gras, le *m.*	fat
grave	serious
grenouille, la *f.*	frog
grille, la *f.*	grillwork fence
gros	thick
guichet, le *m.*	window (ticket counter), booth
guide Michelin, le *m.*	Michelin guidebook
habiter	to live, to inhabit
haut	tall
hauteur, la *f.*	height
heures, des *f.*	hours
heureux	happy
hier	yesterday
historique	historical
homme, l' *m.*	man
honnête	honest; fair
horaire, l' *m.*	schedule
horloge, l' *f.*	clock
horrible	horrible
hôtel, l' *m.*	hotel
hôtel de ville, l' *m.*	town hall
huit	eight
ici	here
idée, l' *f.*	idea
il	he; she; it; there
il fait beau	the weather is fine
il fait du soleil	the sun is shining
il faut	it is necessary
il n'y a rien à faire	there is nothing to do
il y a	...ago; there is
illuminé	lit up
imperméable	raincoat
impressionant	impressive

inconnu	unknown
ingénieur, l' *m.*	engineer
ingénieux	clever
inscription, l' *f.*	inscription
inscrire	to write down
interessant	interesting
intérieure *f.*	interior
intime	close; close friend
inviter	to invite
itinéraire, l' *m.*	itinerary
jambon, le *m.*	ham
jardin public, le *m.*	public garden
jardins, les *m.*	gardens
jaune vif	bright yellow
je	I
jeter	to throw
jeudi	Thursday
jeune	young
je vous présente...	let me introduce you to...
joli	pretty
jolie comme un coeur *f.*	*lit.* pretty as a heart
jouer	to play
jour, le *m.*	day
journal, le *m.*	newspaper; diary
journée, la *f.*	day
juin	June
jupe, la *f.*	skirt
jusqu'à	up to
jusqu'en haut	up to the top
justement	precisely
kilo	(about 2 pounds)
kilomètre, le *m.*	kilometer
Kir	(name of a drink with white wine and liquor of cassis)
l'(a)	the; it; her *f. sg.*

l'(e)	the; it; him *m. sg.*
La Cantatrice Chauve	The Bald Soprano (E. Ionesco play)
la	the; it; her *f. sg.*
là	there
là-bas	over there
lac, le *m.*	lake
laisser	to leave
lampe, la *f.*	lamp
langue, la *f.*	language; tongue
lardon, le *m.*	bacon bit
lecture, la *f.*	reading
légume, le *m.*	vegetable
le	the; it; him *m. sg.*
les	the; them *m./f. pl.*
leur	their; to them
lever (se) *refl.*	to get up
liberté, la *f.*	liberty
librairie, la *f.*	bookstore
libre	free
licorne, la *f.*	unicorn
lion, le *m.*	lion
lire	to read
liste, la *f.*	list
litre, le *m.*	liter
locale	local
loin	far away
long	long
long de, le	along
longtemps	for a long time
lourd	heavy
lumière, la *f.*	light
lundi	Monday
ma	my
macaroni, le *m.*	macaroni
machine, la *f.*	machine

madame	"madam"
mademoiselle	"miss"
magasin, le *m.*	store
magnifique	magnificent
magret, le *m.*	breast of duck
maintenant	now; right now
maire, le *m.*	mayor
mairie, la *f.*	town hall
mais	but
maison, la *f.*	house
malheureusement	unfortunately
manteau, le *m.*	coat
Marais, le *m.*	(a section of Paris)
marbre, le *m.*	marble
marcher	to walk
marier (se) *refl.*	to get married
marqué	marked
martyr, le *m.*	martyr
masculin	masculine
masse, une *f.*	mass
massif	massive
matin, le *m.*	morning, in the morning
me	me
méchant	mean
meilleure, la *f.*	the best
même, le *m.*	the same; the same one
merci beaucoup	thank you very much
mercredi	Wednesday
mère, la *f.*	mother
merveilleux	marvelous
message, le *m.*	message
mesure, la *f.*	measurement
métal, le *m.*	metal
météo, la *f.*	weather report
mettre	to put; to put on

mienne, la *f.*	mine
mieux	more; better
mieux est...	the best way is...
milieu, le *m.*	middle
milliers, des *m.*	thousands
minuit	midnight
Mirabeau	(name of bridge)
miroir, le *m.*	mirror
moi	I; me
moi non plus	me neither
mois, le *m.*	month
moitié, la *f.*	half
moment, le *m.*	moment
mon	my
Mona Lisa	(painting by Leonardo da Vinci)
monde, le *m.*	world; people
Monoprix	(a supermarket)
monsieur	"sir"
monter	to climb
montre, la *f.*	watch
monument, le *m.*	monument
mot, le *m.*	word
mur, le *m.*	wall
Muscadet, le *m.*	(a wine of the Loire Valley)
n'est-ce pas?	isn't it so?
nager	to swim
nappe, la *f.*	tablecloth
nationalité, la *f.*	nationality
Nationaux, les *m. pl.*	residents
ne	not
ne pas encore	not yet
ne plus	no longer
ne vous inquiétez pas	don't worry
nécessaire	necessary
neiger	to snow

neuf	nine
neveu, le *m.*	nephew
niveau, le *m.*	level
noir, le *m.*	darkness
nom, le *m.*	noun; name
nombreux	many
non	no
non plus	neither
nord, le *m.*	north
normal	normal
notre	our
nous	we
nous voilà	here we are
nouvel	new
nouvelles, les *f. pl.*	news
nuage, le *m.*	cloud
nuit, la *f.*	night
numéro, le *m.*	number
objet, l' *m.*	object
obstacle, l' *m.*	obstacle
odeur, l' *f.*	smell
oeuvre, l' *f.*	work
ombre, l' *f.*	shade; shadow
on	one; we
onze	eleven
or, l' *m.*	gold
organiser	to organize
origine, l' *f.*	origin
ou	or
où	where
oublier	to forget
oui	yes
ouvrir	to open
palais, le *m.*	palace
pantalon, le *m.*	pants (one pair of)

papier, le *m.*	paper
paquet, le *m.*	package, parcel
par	by
par ici	this way
parapluie, le *m.*	umbrella
parc, le *m.*	park
parc Montsouris	(a park in Paris)
parce que	because
parcmètre, le *m.*	parking meter
par-dessus	over
pardon	excuse me, sorry
pareil	alike
parfait	perfect
parler	to speak, to talk
pare-brise, le *m.*	windshield
partie, la *f.*	part
partir	to go
partout	everywhere
pas	no, not
pas encore	not yet
passeport, le *m.*	passport
passer	to walk by, to pass by
pâté, le *m.*	paté
patte, la *f.*	leg (animal)
payer	to pay
pays, le *m.*	country
peau, la *f.*	skin
peintre, le *m.*	painter
pellicule, la *f.*	film
pendant	during
pendulette, la *f.*	alarm clock
pénible	tiring; difficult
penser	to think
père, le *m.*	father
personne	nobody

personne, la *f.*	person
perspective, la *f.*	perspective
pervenche, la *f.*	periwinkle
petit	small; short
pétition, la *f.*	petition
peu, un *m.*	(a) little
peu de	little, few
peut-être	perhaps
photo	picture (photograph)
photomaton, le *m.*	photo booth
pickpocket, le *m.*	thief
pied, le *m.*	foot
pierre, la *f.*	stone
Pierre de Rosetta, la *f.*	Rosetta Stone
piétonne, la *f.*	pedestrian
pique-nique, le *m.*	picnic
place, la *f.*	seat; town square; space
plaire	to please
plaque, une *f.*	plaque, sign
plaques, les *f.*	license plates
plein	full
pluie, la *f.*	rain
plus	more
plusieurs	several
plus tard	later
poche, la *f.*	pocket
poème, le *m.*	poem
pointer	to point
pointures, les *f.*	shoe sizes
police, la *f.*	police
policier, le *m.*	policeman
politesse, la *f.*	politeness
pollution, la *f.*	pollution
pomme, la *f.*	apple
pomme de terre, la *f.*	potato

pomme verte, la *f.*	green apple
pont, le *m.*	bridge
population, la *f.*	population
porc, le *m.*	pork
porte, la *f.*	door
portefeuille, le *m.*	wallet
pot, le *m.*	pot
poularde, la *f.*	chicken (fattened)
poulet, le *m.*	chicken
pour	for, to, so that
pourquoi?	why?
pouvoir	to be able to
pratique	practical
premier	first
premier, le *m.*	the first
première, la *f.*	the first
prendre	to take
prendre l'habitude	to become used to
prénom, le *m.*	first name
préparer (se) *refl.*	to prepare oneself
près	close, near
présenter	to introduce
presque	almost
presse-ail, le *m.*	garlic press
prêt	ready
prix, le *m.*	price
probablement	probably
proche	near
produit, le *m.*	product
progrès, le *m.*	progress
projecteur, le *m.*	projector
promenade, la *f.*	walk
promener (se) *refl.*	to walk, to stroll
proposer	to propose

protéger	to protect
protestation, la *f.*	protest
protester	to protest
puis	then
puisque	since
Pyramide, la *f.*	Pyramid
quai, le *m.*	quay; platform (train)
quand	when
quand même	all the same
quartier, le *m.*	section, neighborhood
quatorze juillet, le *m.*	July 14th
quatre	four
quatrième	fourth
que	that
quel...	what a...
quel dommage!	it's too bad!
quelque chose	something
quelques	a certain number of; a few
quels	what *pl.*
quels drôles de...	what strange...
quel temps fait-il?	how is the weather?
qu'est-ce que	what, what is it that
qu'est-ce que ça fait?	what does it matter?
qu'est-ce que ça veut dire?	what does that mean?
qu'est-ce que c'est?	what is it?
qu'est-ce que c'est que ça?	what is that?
queue, la *f.*	line
qui	who; which
quoi	what
rabais, le *m.*	discount
raffiné	refined
raisonnable	reasonable
rangée, la *f.*	row
rapporter	to bring back

rapports, les *m.*	rapports, relations
récente *f.*	recent
recevoir	to receive
recommander	to recommend
regarder	to look
regrettable	too bad
reine, la *f.*	queen
remarquer	to notice, to observe
rempli	filled
remplir	to fill
rencontrer	to meet
rendez-vous, le *m.*	appointment
rendre populaire	to popularize
renseignements, les *m.*	information
répondeur, le *m.*	answering machine
réponse, la *f.*	answer
reprendre	to start again
réservation, la *f.*	reservation
résidence, la *f.*	residence
résolu	solved, resolved
restaurant, le *m.*	restaurant
reste, le *m.*	the rest
rester	to remain
restes, les *m.*	remains, leftovers
retrouver (se) *refl.*	to meet
réussir	to succeed
réveiller	to wake up
réveiller (se) *refl.*	to wake oneself up
revenir	to come back
revoir	to meet again, to see again
révolution, la *f.*	revolution
révolution industrielle, la *f.*	Industrial Revolution
riche	rich
ridicule	ridiculous

rien	nothing
ris de veau, le *m.*	veal sweetbreads
robe, la *f.*	dress
Rodin	(a famous sculptor of the XIXth century)
roi, le *m.*	king
Romains, les *m.*	Romans
rond-point, le *m.*	rotary, traffic circle
rose	pink
rouge	red
rouge, le *m.*	the red one
rouge violet	red-violet
rouleau, le *m.*	roll
route, la *f.*	road; path, way
ruban, le *m.*	tape
rue, la *f.*	street
sac, le *m.*	bag
sage	restrained, wise
saignant	barely cooked
salade frisée, la *f.*	curly endive
samedi	Saturday
sans	without
saucisse, la *f.*	sausage
sauf que	except that
sauge, la *f.*	sage
sauter	to skip
savoir	to know
sculpture, la *f.*	sculpture
sèchement	dryly
séjour, le *m.*	visit, stay
Seine, la *f.*	Seine river
sentir	to feel
sept	seven
sérieusement	seriously
sérieux	serious

service partiel, le *m.*	partial service
serviette, la *f.*	napkin
ses	his; hers; one's
seul, un *m.*	(a) single
seulement	only
si	if; so; yes
siècle, le *m.*	century
siège, le *m.*	seat
sieste, la *f.*	nap, siesta
simple	simple
six	six
soif, la *f.*	thirst
soir, le *m.*	evening
soldat, le *m.*	soldier
soldes, les *f.*	bargains
soleil, le *m.*	sun
solution, la *f.*	solution
sommet, le *m.*	top
son	his
sonner	to strike, to ring
sorbet, le *m.*	sherbet, sorbet
sortie, la *f.*	exit, the way out
sortir	to leave, to go out
souffler	to blow
source, la *f.*	spring, source
sourire, le *m.*	smile
souris, la *f.*	mouse
sous	under
sous-terre	underground
souvenir, le *m.*	souvenir
special	special
spécialité, la *f.*	specialty
station de métro, la *f.*	subway station
stationner	to park

statue, la *f.*	statue
suivant	next
superbe	very beautiful
sur	on
système métrique, le *m.*	metric system
table, la *f.*	table
tableau, le *m.*	display board
taille, la *f.*	size
tampon, le *m.*	stamp
tant	so many
tant de	so much of
tant mieux	so much the better
tapis, le *m.*	rug
tapis roulant, le *m.*	moving sidewalk
tarif, le *m.*	rate
tarte, la *f.*	pie
tasse, la *f.*	cup
téléphoner (à)	to telephone
tellement	so much
température, la *f.*	temperature
temps, le *m.*	weather
tendre	tender
tenir	to hold
tenir (se) bien/mal *refl.*	to behave well/badly
terrain, le *m.*	terrain
terrasse, la *f.*	terrace
terrine, la *f.*	paté
tête, la *f.*	head
théâtre, le *m.*	theater
Thermes, les *m.*	Roman baths
thermomètre, le *m.*	thermometer
tien, le *m.*	yours
tienne, la *f.*	yours
timbre, le *m.*	stamp (postal)

tirer	to pull
toilette, la *f.*	toilet
tombeau, le *m.*	tomb
ton	your
top	beep, signal (indicating time)
toujours	still; always
tour, la *f.*	tower
tour Eiffel, la *f.*	Eiffel Tower
tous	all
tout	everything
tout à fait	entirely
tout à l'heure	in a short time
tout autour	all around
tout ceci	all of this
tout de suite	right away
tout le monde	everybody
tout près	near by
traduire	to translate
tranche, la *f.*	slice
tranquille	leisurely; tranquil, calm
travail, le *m.*	work
travailler	to work
traversée, la *f.*	crossing
traverser	to cross
tremper	to dip
très	very
tricot, le *m.*	sweater
triste	sad
Trocadéro	(a subway station)
trois	three
trop	too much
trottoir, le *m.*	sidewalk
trouver	to find
trouver (se) *refl.*	to be placed, to be found

truffe, la *f.*	truffle
tu	you
Tu penses!	You bet!
type, le *m.*	guy; type
uniforme, l' *m.*	uniform
vague	vague
valise, la *f.*	suitcase
venant de	coming from
vendre (se) *refl.*	to be sold
vendredi	Friday
venir	to come
venir de	to have just
vent, le *m.*	wind
vérifier	to check
verre, le *m.*	glass
vers	toward
vert	green
veste, la *f.*	jacket
vêtement, le *m.*	clothing
vie, la *f.*	life
vieux	old
ville, la *f.*	city
vin, le *m.*	wine
visite, la *f.*	visit
visiteur, le *m.*	visitor
vite	quickly
vivre	to live
voici	here is
voilà	here is, there is
voir	to see
voiture, la *f.*	car
voix, la *f.*	voice
votre	your
vouloir	to want

vous	you
voyage, le *m.*	trip
vrai	true
vraiment	really
XIXème siècle, le *m.*	nineteenth century
XVIIème siècle, le *m.*	seventeenth century
y	there

ENGLISH-FRENCH VOCABULARY

In this section, gender and corresponding articles of nouns are indicated, as well as the masculine and feminine forms of the adjectives.

...ago	il y a...
A.D.	après J.C.
above	au-dessus de
absolutely	absolument
across	à travers
across the street	en face
active	actif/active
activity	activité, l' *f.*
(to) add	ajouter
address	adresse, l' *f.*
adhesive	collant(e)
(to) admire	admirer
advantage	avantage, l' *m.*
after; afterwards	après
after that	ensuite
agenda	agenda, l' *m.*
(to) agree	être d'accord
air	air, l' *m.*
airplane	avion, l' *m.*
airport	aéroport, l' *m.*
alarm clock	pendulette, la *f.*
alike	pareil(le)
all	tous (people); tout (everything)
all around	tout autour
all of this	tout ceci
all right	d'accord
all the same	quand même
alley	allée, l' *f.*

almost	presque
along	le long de
already	déjà
also	aussi
(to) amuse oneself	amuser (s') *refl.*
and	et
and then?	et après?
(to) announce	annoncer
another	un(e) autre
another one	encore un(e)
answer	réponse, la *f.*
answering machine	répondeur, le *m.*
apartment	appartement, l' *m.*
apple (green)	pomme verte, la *f.*
appointment	rendez-vous, le *m.*
arch	arche, l' *f.*
Arch of Triumph	Arc de Triomphe, l' *m.*
armchair	fauteuil, le *m.*
around	autour
arrow	flèche, la *f.*
article	article, l' *m.*
artist	artiste, l' *m.*
as, just as	comme
(to) ask to tell	faire raconter
at; to	à
at the; with; in	au
at the end of	au bout de
at the foot of	en bas de
at the house of	chez
at the top of	en haut de
Auguste Comte	(XIXth century philosopher; name of a street)
author	auteur, l' *m.*
avenue	avenue, l' *f.*
bacon bit	lardon, le *m.*

bag	sac, le *m.*
Balzac	(a famous writer of the XIXth century)
bar	bar, le *m.*
barely cooked	saignant
bargains	soldes, les *f.*
basin	bassin, le *m.*
bathhouse	établissement de bains, l' *m.*
bathtub	baignoire, la *f.*
(to) be	être
(to) be able to	pouvoir
beard	barbe, la *f.*
beautiful	beau/belle *m./f.*
(to) be awake	être réveillé
(to) be becoming	aller bien (of clothing)
(to) be buried	être enterré
(to) be called	appeler (s') *refl.*
because	parce que
(to) become used to	prendre l'habitude
before	avant
before; in front of	devant
(to) begin	commencer
beginning	commencement, le *m.*
(to) behave well/badly	tenir (se) bien/mal *refl.*
behind	derrière
(to) be hungry	avoir faim
(to) believe	croire
bell	cloche, la *f.*
(to) be placed, to be found	trouver (se) *refl.*
(to) be satisfactory	convenir
beside; close to	à coté de
(to) be sold	vendre (se) *refl.*
(the) best	meilleur, le *m.*/meilleure, la *f.*
(to) be tired	être fatigué
better	mieux
between	entre

bizarre, strange	bizarre
black currant liquor	crème de cassis, la *f.*
(to) block	bloquer
(to) blow	souffler
blue	bleu
boat	bateau, le *m.*
(to) boil	bouillir
bookstore	librairie, la *f.*
booth (telephone)	cabine (téléphonique), la *f.*
(to) bore	ennuyer
(to) bother	ennuyer
box	boîte, la *f.*
boy	garçon, le *m.*
bracelet	bracelet, le *m.*
breast of duck	magret, le *m.*
brick	brique, la *f.*
bridge	pont, le *m.*
bright yellow	jaune vif
brilliant	brillant(e)
(to) bring	amener; apporter
(to) bring back	rapporter
bronze	bronze, le *m.*
bubbly	gazeux/gazeuse
(to) build	construire
building	bâtiment, le *m.*
Burgundy	Bourgogne
(to) burn	brûler
bus	autobus, l' *m.*, bus, le *m.*
businessman, merchant	commerçant, le *m.*
but	mais
butter	beurre, le *m.*
buttered	beurré(e)
button	bouton, le *m.*
(to) buy	acheter
by	par

by airplane	en avion
café	café, le *m.*
calm	tranquille
camera	appareil de photo, l' *m.*
canal	canal, le *m.*
capital	capital, le *m.*
car	voiture, la *f.*
card	carte, la *f.*
carrot	carotte, la *f.*
cart (luggage)	chariot, le *m.*
cassette, la *f.*	cassette tape
castle	château, le *m.*
(to) catch a glimpse of	apercevoir
(to) celebrate	célébrer
center	centre, le *m.*
centigrade	centigrade
century	siècle, le *m.*
certain (some)	certain
certainly	certainement
chair	chaise, la *f.*
(to) change	changer
(to) change to	changer à
Charles de Gaulle-Etoile	(a subway station)
(to) check	vérifier
cheese	fromage, le *m.*
chicken	poulet, le *m.*; poularde, la *f.* (fattened)
child	enfant, l' *m.*
(to) choose	choisir
Christian	chrétien(ne)
church	église, l' *f.*
city	ville, la *f.*
class	classe, la *f.*
classical period	âge classique, l' *m.*
clear; light	clair(e)

clever	ingénieux/ingénieuse
client	client, le *m.*
(to) climb	monter
clock	horloge, l' *f.*
close	intime; près (near)
(a) close friend	intime, un(e)
clothing	vêtement, le *m.*
cloud	nuage, le *m.*
coat	manteau, le *m.*
coffee	café, le *m.*
coffee with milk	café au lait, le *m.*
color	couleur, la *f.*
(to) come	venir
(to) come back	revenir
(to) come free/off	détacher (se) *refl.*
comfortably	confortablement
coming from	venant de
(to) continue	continuer
contract	contrat, le *m.*
(to) control	contrôler
conversion	conversion, la *f.*
cooked	cuit(e)
corner	coin, le *m.*
corridor	corridor, le *m.*
country	pays, le *m.*
countryside	campagne, la *f.*
courtyard	cour, la *f.*
cousin	cousin, le *m.*
covered in	couvert(e) de
crazy person	fou, le *m.*
cream	crème, la *f.*
(to) criticize	critiquer
croissant	croissant, le *m.*
(to) cross	traverser
crossing	traversée, la *f.*

crust	croûte, la *f.*
crusty	croustillant(e)
cup	tasse, la *f.*
curly endive	salade frisée, la *f.*
cushion	coussin, le *m.*
custard with caramel	crème brulée, la *f.*
cut	coupé(e)
darkness	noir, le *m.*
date of entry	date d'entrée, la *f.*
day	jour, le *m.*/journée, la *f.*
(to) decorate, to garnish	garnir
decoration	décoration, la *f.*
Défense, la *f.*	(a section of Paris)
delicious	délicieux/délicieuse
department store	Grand Magasin, le *m.*
desk	bureau, le *m.*
dessert	dessert, le *m.*
(to) destroy	détruire
diary	journal, le *m.*
dictionary	dictionnaire, le *m.*
different	différent
difficult	difficile
digestion	digestion, la *f.*
Dijon	(a city in Burgundy)
(to) dip	tremper
discount	rabais, le *m.*
discovering	à la découverte
discovery	découverte
display board	tableau, le *m.*
dispute	dispute, la *f.*
(to) do	faire
(to) do good	faire du bien
don't worry	ne vous inquiétez pas
door	porte, la *f.*
down there	en bas

dozen	douzaine, une *f.*
draft	courant d'air, le *m.*
(to) drain	assécher
dress	robe, la *f.*
drink	apéritif, l' *m.*
driver	conducteur, le *m.*
dryly	sèchement
duck	canard, le *m.*
during	pendant
each	chaque
early years/childhood	enfance, l' *m.*
east	est, l' *m.*
edge	bord, le *m.*
eggplant	aubergine, l' *f.*
eight	huit
Eiffel Tower	tour Eiffel, la *f.*
elegant	élégant(e)
eleven	onze
employee	employé, l' *m.*
engineer	ingénieur, l' *m.*
English	anglais(e)
enormous	énorme
enough to	assez ... pour
entirely	tout à fait
entrance	entrée, l' *f.*
era	ère, l' *m.*
errands	courses, les *f.*
Europe	Europe
evening	soir, le *m.*
every; each	chaque
everybody	tout le monde
everything	tout
everywhere	partout
exact	exact(e)
exactement	exactly

except that	sauf que
excuse me	pardon
exit, the way out	sortie, la *f.*
(to) explain	expliquer
extraordinary	extraordinaire
exquisite	exquis(e)
fair	honnête
family	famille, la *f.*
famous	célèbre
far	loin
fat	gras, le *m.*
father	père, le *m.*
favorite	favori(te)
(to) feel	sentir
(to) feel like	avoir envie (de)
feminine	féminin(e)
filigree	filigrane, la *f.*
(to) fill	remplir
filled	rempli(e)
film (roll of)	pellicule, la *f.*
(to) find	trouver
(to) find one's way	débrouiller (se) *refl.*
finger	doigt, le *m.*
fire	feu, le *m.*
fireworks	feux d'artifice, les *m.*
first	premier/première
(the) first	premier, le *m.*/première, la *f.*
first course	entrée, l' *f.*
first name	prénom, le *m.*
five	cinq
flame	flamme, la *f.*
(to) float	flotter
floor, story	étage, l' *m.*
(to) flow, to run	couler
flower	fleur, la *f.*

foot	pied, le *m.*
for	pour; depuis
(to) forget	oublier
fork	fourchette, la *f.*
formal	formel(le)
founded	fondé(e)
fountain	fontaine, la *f.*
four	quatre
fourth	quatrième
free	libre
(to) freeze	geler
french	français(e)
French baguette (bread)	baguette, la *f.*
(a) Frenchman	Français, un *m.*
fresh	frais/fraîche
Friday	vendredi
friend	ami, l' *m.*/amie, l' *f.*
frog	grenouille, la *f.*
from	depuis
full	plein
gallery	galerie, la *f.*
gardens	jardins, les *m.*
garlic	ail, l' *m.*
garlic press	presse-ail, le *m.*
(to) garnish	garnir
geometric	géométrique
(to) get married	marier (se) *refl.*
(to) get up	lever (se) *refl.*
gilded	doré(e)
girl	fille, la *f.*
(to) give	donner
gizzard	gésier, le *m.*
glass	verre, le *m.*
globe	globe, le *m.*
glory	gloire, la *f.*

(to) go	aller; partir
goat cheese	fromage de chèvre, le *m.*
(to) go down, descend	descendre
going to	en allant à
gold	or, l' *m.*
good	bon(ne)
good morning, hello	bonjour
good-bye	au revoir
(a) good name	bon nom, un *m.*
(to) go shopping	faire des courses (achats)
(to) go to	aller à
green	vert(e)
green light	feu vert, le *m.*
grillwork fence	grille, la *f.*
guy; type	type, le *m.*
half	demi(e); moitié, la *f.*
half-liter	demi-litre, le *m.*
ham	jambon, le *m.*
happy	heureux/heureuse
hat	chapeau, le *m.*
(to) have	avoir
(to) have draw/n	faire dessiner
(to) have just	venir de
(to) have taste	faire goûter
(to) have to	falloir
he	il
head	tête, la *f.*
(to) hear	entendre
heavy	lourd(e)
height	hauteur, l' *f.*
hello	bonjour
here	ici
here is	voici
here we are	nous voilà
hill	butte, la *f.*, colline, la *f.*

his	son, sa
his/hers/one's	ses
historical	historique
(to) hold	tenir
honest	honnête
(to) hope	espérer
horrible	horrible
horse	cheval, le *m.*
hot	chaud(e)
hotel	hôtel, l' *m.*
hours	heures, des *f.*
house	maison, la *f.*
how	comment
how did it happen?	comment ça se fait?
how is the weather?	quel temps fait-il?
how many	combien
hundred	centaine, la *f.*
I	je; moi
idea	idée, l' *f.*
if	si
impressive	impressionant
in	en; dans
in a short time	tout à l'heure
in centigrades	en centigrades
in front of	en face de
in his time	à son époque
in the middle of	au milieu de
Industrial Revolution	révolution industrielle, la *f.*
information	renseignements, les *m.*
inscription	inscription, l' *f.*
instance, time	fois, la *f.*
interesting	intéressant(e)
interior	intérieur(e)
into Fahrenheit	en Fahrenheit
(to) introduce	présenter

(to) invite	inviter
is... (question)	est-ce que...
is this...	est-ce que ceci...
isn't it so?	n'est-ce pas?
it is necessary	il faut
it looks smart	ça fait chic
it's done, that's it	ça y est
itinerary	itinéraire, l' *m.*
jacket	veste, la *f.*
jet lag	décalage horaire, le *m.*
jewel	bijou, le *m.*
July 14th	quatorze juillet, le *m.*
June	juin
(to) keep	garder
kilo	(about 2 pounds)
kilometer	kilomètre, le *m.*
king	roi, le *m.*
Kir	(name of a drink with white wine and black currant liquor)
kitchen utensil	article de cuisine, l' *m.*
(to) know	connaître; savoir
lake	lac, le *m.*
lamp	lampe, la *f.*
(to) land	attérir
language	langue, la *f.*
large	grand(e)
late	tard; en retard
later	plus tard
law	droit, le *m.*
leaf	feuille, la *f.*
(to) learn	apprendre
learned	appris(e)
(to) leave	laisser; partir; sortir
leg	jambe, la *f.* (human); patte, la *f.* (animal)

leisurely, tranquil	tranquille
lengthwise	en long
let me introduce you to	je vous présente
let's go	en route, allons-y
level	niveau, le *m.*
liberty	liberté, la *f.*
license plates	plaques, les *f.*
life	vie, la *f.*
light	lumière, la *f.*; clair(e)
(to) light up	allumer (s') *refl.*
(to) like	aimer; désirer
line	ligne, la *f.*; queue, la *f.*
lion	lion, le *m.*
list	liste, la *f.*
(to) listen	écouter
lit up	illuminé(e)
liter	litre, le *m.*
(a) little	un peu
little, few	peu de
(to) live	vivre
(to) live, to inhabit	habiter
lobster bisque	bisque de homard, la *f.*
local	locale
long	long(ue); longtemps (time)
(to) look	regarder
(to) lower	baisser
luck	chance, la *f.*
luggage	bagages, les *m.*
lunch	déjeuner, le *m.*
macaroni	macaroni, le *m.*
machine	machine, la *f.*
magnificent	magnifique
mailbox	boîte aux lettres, la *f.*
(to) make a face	faire la grimace
(to) make shine	faire briller

man	homme, l' *m.*
many	beaucoup; nombreux; tant (so many)
map	carte, la *f.*, plan, le *m.*
Marais, le *m.*	(a section of Paris)
marble	marbre, le *m.*
marked	marqué(e)
(to) marry	épouser
martyr	martyr, le *m.*
marvelous	merveilleux/merveilleuse
masculine	masculin(e)
mass	masse, une *f.*
massive	massif/massive
maybe	peut-être
mayor	maire, le *m.*
me	me; moi
me neither	moi non plus
mean	méchant
measurement	mesure, la *f.*
(to) meet	rencontrer; retrouver (se) *refl.*
(to) meet, to cross paths	croiser (se) *refl.*
(to) meet again, to see again	revoir
membership card/ticket	carte d'abonnement, la *f.*
message	message, le *m.*
metal	métal, le *m.*
metric system	système métrique, le *m.*
Michelin guidebook	guide Michelin, le *m.*
midnight	minuit
milieu, le *m.*	middle
mine	mienne, la *f.*
Mirabeau	(name of bridge)
mirror	miroir, le *m.*
Miss	mademoiselle
moment	moment, le *m.*
Mona Lisa	(painting by Leonardo da Vinci)
Monday	lundi

Monoprix	(a supermarket)
month	mois, le *m.*
monument	monument, le *m.*
more	plus
more and more	de plus en plus
morning, in the morning	matin, le *m.*
mother	mère, la *f.*
mouse	souris, la *f.*
mouth	bouche, la *f.*
moving	émouvant(e)
moving sidewalk	tapis roulant, le *m.*
Mrs.	madame
much	beaucoup, tant
much talked about	fameux/fameuse
Muscadet, le *m.*	(wine of the Loire Valley)
mushroom	champignon, le *m.*
must	devoir
my	mon/ma
name	nom, le *m.*
nap, siesta	sieste, la *f.*
napkin	serviette, la *f.*
nationality	nationalité, la *f.*
near	proche, près
near by	tout près
necessary	nécessaire
(to) need	avoir besoin de
neighborhood	quartier, le *m.*
neither	non plus
nephew	neveu, le *m.*
new	nouvel(le)
news	nouvelles, les *f.*
newspaper	journal, le *m.*
next	suivant(e), prochain(e)
nice	gentil(le)
nice weather	faire bon/beau

night	nuit, la *f.*
nine	neuf
nineteenth century	XIXème siècle, le *m.*
no	non
no longer	plus
nobody	personne
none	pas
normal	normal(e)
north	nord, le *m.*
not	ne
(to) notice, observe	remarquer
not yet	pas encore
notebook	carnet, le *m.*
nothing	rien
noun	nom, le *m.*
now, right now	maintenant
number	numéro, le *m.*
object	objet, l' *m.*
obstacle	obstacle, l' *m.*
of; from	de
of course	bien sûr
of them	en
of which	dont
old	vieux/vieille
on	sur
on foot	à pied
on the way	en route
on time	à l'heure
one	un (number); on (3rd pers.)
only	seulement
(to) open	ouvrir
opposite	contraire, le *m.*
or	ou
(to) organize	organiser
origin	origine, l' *f.*

other	autre
our	notre
outside	dehors
over	par-dessus (on); au-dessus (above); fini (finished)
package, parcel	paquet, le *m.*
painter	peintre, le *m.*
palace	palais, le *m.*
pants (one pair of)	pantalon, le *m.*
paper	papier, le *m.*
parc Montsouris	(a park in Paris)
park	parc, le *m.*
(to) park	stationner
parking meter	parcmètre, le *m.*
part	partie, la *f.*
partial service	service partiel, le *m.*
party, festivities	fête, la *f.*
passport	passeport, le *m.*
passport control	contrôle des passeports, le *m.*
paté	pâté, le *m.*; terrine, la *f.*
path, way	route, la *f.*
(to) pay	payer
(to) pay attention	faire attention
pedestrian	piéton(ne), le/la *m./f.*
people	gens, les *m. pl.*, monde, le *m.*
perfect	parfait
perhaps	peut-être
periwinkle	pervenche, la *f.*
person	personne, la *f.*
perspective	perspective, la *f.*
petition	pétition, la *f.*
photo booth	photomaton, le *m.*
photograph	photographie, photo, la *f.*
picnic	pique-nique, le *m.*
pie	tarte, la *f.*

pink	rose
place	endroit, l' *m.*
plant	plante, la *f.*
platform (train)	quai, le *m.*
(to) play	jouer
pleasant	agréable
(to) please	plaire
pocket	poche, la *f.*
poem	poème, le *m.*
(to) point	pointer
police	police, la *f.*
policeman	policier, le *m.*
politeness	politesse, la *f.*
pollution	pollution, la *f.*
(to) popularize	rendre populaire
population	population, la *f.*
pork	porc, le *m.*
pork butcher	charcuterie, la *f.*
postcard	carte postale, la *f.*
poster	affiche, l' *f.*
pot	pot, le *m.*
potato	pomme de terre, la *f.*
pour	for, to, so that
practical	pratique
precisely	justement
(to) prefer	aimer mieux
(to) prepare oneself	préparer (se) *refl.*
present	cadeau, le *m.*
pretty	joli(e)
pretty as a "sweetheart"	joli(e) comme un coeur
price	prix, le *m.*
price tag	étiquette, l' *f.*
probably	probablement
product	produit, le *m.*
progress	progrès, le *m.*

projector	projecteur, le *m.*
(to) propose	proposer
(to) protect	protéger
protest	protestation, la *f.*
(to) protest	protester
proud	fier/fière
public garden	jardin public, le *m.*
(to) pull	tirer
purchase	achat, l' *m.*
(to) push	appuyer
(to) put	mettre
(to) put on	mettre
Pyramid	Pyramide, la *f.*
quay	quai, le *m.*
queen	reine, la *f.*
quickly	vite
quite enough	assez
rain	pluie, la *f.*
raincoat	imperméable
rate	tarif, le *m.*
raw	cru(e)
(to) read	lire
reading	lecture, la *f.*
ready	prêt(e)
really	vraiment
reasonable	raisonnable
(to) receive	recevoir
recent	récent(e)
(to) recommend	recommander
red	rouge
red one	rouge, le *m.*
red-violet	rouge violet
refined	raffiné(e)
relations	rapports, les *m.*
(to) remain	rester

remains, leftovers	restes, les *m.*
(to) remove, take off	enlever
reservation	réservation, la *f.*
residence	résidence, la *f.*
residents	Nationaux, les *m.*
(the) rest	reste, le *m.*
restaurant	restaurant, le *m.*
restrained, moderate	sage
réveiller (se) *refl.*	to wake up
revolution	révolution, la *f.*
rich	riche
(to) ride	circuler
ridiculous	ridicule
right (direction)	droite, la *f.*
right (legal)	droit, le *m.*
right away	tout de suite
right now	en ce moment
(to) ring	sonner
road	route, la *f.*
Rodin	(a famous sculptor of the XIXth century)
roll	rouleau, le *m.*
Roman baths	Thermes, les *m.*
Romans	Romains, les *m.*
room	chambre, la *f.*
root celery	celeri rave, le *m.*
Rosetta Stone	Pierre de Rosetta, la *f.*
rotary	rond-point, le *m.*
row	rangée, la *f.*
rug	tapis, le *m.*
run-down	décrépit
sad	triste
sage (plant)	sauge, la *f.*
same; the same one	pareil(le); même, le *m.*
Saturday	samedi
sausage	saucisse, la *f.*

(to) say	dire
scarf	écharpe, l' *f.*
schedule	horaire, l' *m.*
screen	écran, l' *m.*
sculpture	sculpture, la *f.*
seat	place, la *f.*; siège, le *m.*
section (neighborhood)	arrondissement, l' *m.*
(to) see	voir
Seine river	Seine, la *f.*
(to) sell	vendre
(to) send	envoyer
serious	grave; sérieux/sérieuse
seriously	sérieusement
seven	sept
seventeenth century	XVIIème siècle, le *m.*
several	plusieurs
sewer	égoût, l' *m.*
shade	ombre, l' *f.*
shadow	ombre, l' *f.*
shawl	châle, le *m.*
she	elle
sheet (of paper)	feuille, la *f.* (de papier)
sherbet	sorbet, le *m.*
(to) shine	briller
shirt	chemise, la *f.*
shoe	chaussure, la *f.*
shoe sizes	pointures, les *f.*
shop	boutique, la *f.*
short	court(e), petit(e)
side	côté, le *m.*
sidewalk	trottoir, le *m.*
sign	plaque, la *f.*
signal (sonorous)	top
(to) signal	faire signe
simple	simple

since	puisque; depuis
(a) single one	un(e) seul(e)
sir	monsieur
(to) sit down	asseoir (s') *refl.*
six	six
size	taille, la *f.*
skin	peau, la *f.*
(to) skip	sauter
skirt	jupe, la *f.*
sky	ciel, le *m.*
(to) sleep	dormir
slice	tranche, la *f.*
small	petit(e)
smell	odeur, l' *f.*
smile	sourire, le *m.*
snail	escargot, l' *m.*
(to) snow	neiger
so	donc
so much	tellement
so much of	tant de
so much the better	tant mieux
so that	pour (que)
soldier	soldat, le *m.*
solution	solution, la *f.*
solved, resolved	résolu(e)
some	du
some, a few	quelques; certains(es); des
something	quelque chose
song	chanson, la *f.*
sorbet	sorbet, le *m.*
sorry	pardon
souvenir	souvenir, le *m.*
space	espace, l' *m.*; place, la *f.*
(to) speak, to talk	parler
(to) speak to, to address	adresser

special	special(e)
specialty	spécialité, la *f.*
spoon	cuillère, la *f.*
spring, source	source, la *f.*
stairs	escalier, l' *m.*
stamp	tampon, le *m.*; timbre, le *m.* (postal)
star	étoile, l' *f.*
(to) start again	reprendre
statue	statue, la *f.*
(to) stay	rester
(to) step forward	avancer (s') *refl.*
(to) step out, get off	descendre
still	toujours
stomach	estomac, l' *m.*
stone	pierre, la *f.*
stop	arrêt, l' *m.*
(to) stop	arrêter (s') *refl.*
store	magasin, le *m.*
strange	bizarre, curieux/curieuse
street	rue, la *f.*
(to) strike, to ring	sonner
stroke	coup, le *m.*
(to) stroll	flâner
student	étudiant, l' *m.*
(to) study	étudier
(to) stuff	bourrer
subway	métro, le *m.*
subway station	station de métro, la *f.*
(to) succeed	réussir
suit	costume, le *m.*
suitcase	valise, la *f.*
sun	soleil, le *m.*
Sunday	dimanche
superb, very beautiful	superbe
swan	cygne, le *m.*

sweater	tricot, le *m.*
sweetbreads (veal)	ris de veau, le *m.*
(to) swim	nager
table	table, la *f.*
tablecloth	nappe, la *f.*
(to) take	prendre
(to) take someone to	emmener
tall	haut(e)
tape	ruban, le *m.*
(to) telephone	téléphoner (à)
temperature	température, la *f.*
ten	dix
tender	tendre
terrace	terrasse, la *f.*
terrain	terrain, le *m.*
thank you (very much)	merci (beaucoup)
that	ça, cela; que
that which	ce dont
the	le/la *m./f. sg.*; les *m./f. pl.*
The Bald Soprano	La Cantatrice Chauve (E. Ionesco play)
the best way is...	le mieux est...
the sun is shining	il fait du soleil
the weather is fine	il fait beau
theater	théâtre, le *m.*
their	leur
then	alors; puis
there	là; là-bas (slightly further); y
there is	voilà
there is...	il y a...
there is nothing to do	il n'y a rien à faire
thermometer	thermomètre, le *m.*
these	ces *m./f.*
thick	gros(se)
thief	voleur, le *m.*; pickpocket, le *m.*

thing	chose, la *f.*
(to) think	penser
thirst	soif, la *f.*
this	ce, cet/cette, ceci
this one	celui-ci/celle-ci
this way	par ici
those	ceux/celles
thousands	milliers, des *m.*
three	trois
(to) throw	jeter
Thursday	jeudi
ticket	billet, le *m.*; contravention, la *f.* (fine)
time	temps, le *m.*; fois, une *f.* (instance)
time period, era	époque
tiring; difficult	pénible
to	pour; à
today	aujourd'hui
together	ensemble
toilet	toilette, la *f.*
tomato sauce	sauce tomate
tomb	tombeau, le *m.*
tomorrow	demain
tongue	langue, la *f.*
tonight	ce soir
too bad	regrettable
too bad!, it's too bad!	quel dommage!
too much	trop
top	haut, le *m.*; sommet, le *m.* (peak)
to someone	à quelqu'un
toward	vers
tower	tour, la *f.*
to which	auquel *sg.*; auxquelles *pl.*
to whom	à qui
town	ville, la *f.*
town hall	hôtel de ville, l' *m.*; mairie, la *f.*

town square	place, la *f.*
traffic circle	rond-point
traffic light	feu, le *m.*
train station	gare, la *f.*
(to) translate	traduire
tree	arbre, l' *m.*
trip	voyage, le *m.*
tripe sausage	andouillette, l' *f.*
Trocadéro	(a subway station)
true	vrai(e)
truffle	truffe, la *f.*
(to) try on	essayer
twelve	douze
two	deux
umbrella	parapluie, le *m.*
under	sous
underground	sous-terre
(to) understand	comprendre
unfortunately	malheureusement
unicorn	licorne, la *f.*
uniform	uniforme, l' *m.*
unknown	inconnu(e)
up to	jusqu'à
(to) use	employer
vague	vague
various kinds	différentes sortes
vegetable	légume, le *m.*
very	très
visit	visite, la *f.*; séjour, le *m.* (stay)
visitor	visiteur, le *m.*
voice	voix, la *f.*
(to) wait	attendre
waiting line	file d'attente, la *f.*
(to) wake up	réveiller
walk	promenade, la *f.*

(to) walk	marcher; promener (se) *refl.*
(to) walk by, to pass by	passer
wall	mur, le *m.*
wallet	portefeuille, le *m.*
(to) want	vouloir
warm	chaud(e)
watch	montre, la *f.*
water	eau, l' *f.*
we	nous, on
weather	temps, le *m.*
weather report	météo, la *f.*
Wednesday	mercredi
well, good	bien
well-done	bien cuit(e)
well dressed	bien habillé(e)
what	quoi; ce que; qu'est-ce que
what, which	quel/quelle *sg.*, quels/quelles *pl.*
what a...	quel...
what are we thinking about?	à quoi pensons-nous?
what does it matter?	qu'est-ce que ça fait?
what does that mean?	qu'est-ce que ça veut dire?
what is it?	qu'est-ce que c'est?
what is that?	qu'est-ce que c'est que ça?
what strange...	quels drôles de...
when	quand
where	où
who	qui
why	pourquoi
wide open	grand(e) ouvert(e)
wife	femme, la *f.*
wind	vent, le *m.*
window	fenêtre, la *f.*
window (ticket counter)	guichet, le *m.*
windshield	pare-brise, le *m.*
wine	vin, le *m.*

(to) win out	gagner
wise	sage
with	avec
with a modern mind	à l'esprit moderne
with pleasure	avec plaisir
without	sans
woman	femme, la *f.*, dame, la *f.*
wonderful	épatant(e)
word	mot, le *m.*
work	travail, le *m.*; oeuvre, l' *f.*
(to) work	travailler
world	monde, le *m.*
World Fair	exposition universelle, l' *f.*
(to) write down	inscrire
year	an, l' *m.*/année, l' *f.*
yes	oui; si
yesterday	hier
you	tu (*inf.*), vous (*for.*)
You bet! (sarcastic)	Tu penses!
young	jeune
your	ton (*inf.*), votre (*for.*)
yours	tien, le *m.*; tienne, la *f.*

Hippocrene Beginner's Series

Beginner's Albanian
150 pages • 5 x 8½ • 0-7818-0816-2 • W • $14.95pb • (537)

Arabic For Beginners
231 pages • 5½ x 8½ • 0-7818-0841-3 • W • $11.95pb • (229)

Beginner's Armenian
209 pages • 5½ x 8½ • 0-7818-0723-9 • W • $14.95pb • (226)

Beginner's Assyrian
138 pages • 5½ x 8½ • 0-7818-0677-1 • W • $11.95pb • (763)

Beginner's Bulgarian
207 pages • 5½ x 8½ • 0-7818-0300-4 • W • $9.95pb • (76)

Beginner's Chinese
173 pages • 5½ x 8½ • 0-7818-0566-X • W • $14.95pb • (690)

Beginner's Czech
167 pages • 5½ x 8½ • 0-7818-0231-8 • W • $9.95pb • (74)

Beginner's Dutch
173 pages • 5½ x 8½ • 0-7818-0735-2 • W • $14.95pb • (248)

Beginner's Esperanto
342 pages • 5½ x 8½ • 0-7818-0230-X • W • $14.95pb • (51)

Beginner's Gaelic
224 pages • 5½ x 8½ • 0-7818-0726-3 • W • $14.95pb • (255)

Beginner's Hungarian
Revised with larger type
166 pages • 5½ x 8½ • 0-7818-0866-9 • W • $14.95pb • (308)

Beginner's Irish
145 pages • 5½ x 8½ • 0-7818-0784-0 • W • $14.95pb • (320)

Beginner's Italian
192 pages • 5½ x 8½ • 0-7818-0839-1 • W • $14.95pb • (208)

Beginner's Japanese
290 pages • 6 x 8 • 0-7818-0234-2 • W • $11.95pb • (53)

Beginner's Lithuanian
471 pages • 6 x 9 • 0-7818-0678-X • W • $19.95pb • (764)

Beginner's Maori
121 pages • 5½ x 8½ • 0-7818-0605-4 • NA • $8.95pb • (703)

Beginner's Persian
288 pages • 5½ x 8½ • 0-7818-0567-8 • NA • $14.95pb • (696)

Beginner's Polish
118 pages • 5½ x 8½ • 0-7818-0299-7 • W • $9.95pb • (82)

Beginner's Romanian
105 pages • 5½ x 8½ • 0-7818-0208-3 • W • $7.95pb • (79)

Beginner's Russian
131 pages • 5½ x 8½ • 0-7818-0232-6 • W • $9.95pb • (61)

Beginner's Serbo-Croatian
175 pages • 5½ x 8½ • 0-7818-0845-6 • W • $14.95pb • (138)

Beginner's Sicilian
159 pages • 5½ x 8½ • 0-7818-0640-2 • W • $11.95pb • (716)

Beginner's Slovak
207 pages • 5½ x 8½ • 0-7818-0815-4 • W • $14.95pb • (534)

Beginner's Spanish (Latin American)
315 pages • 5½ x 8½ • 0-7818-0840-5 • W • $14.95pb • (225)

Beginner's Swahili
200 pages • 5½ x 8½ • 0-7818-0335-7 • W • $9.95pb • (52)

Beginner's Turkish
300 pages • 5 x 7½ • 0-7818-0679-8 • NA • $14.95pb • (765)

Beginner's Ukrainian
130 pages • 5½ x 8½ • 0-7818-0443-4 • W • $11.95pb • (88)

Beginner's Vietnamese
515 pages • 7 x 10 • 0-7818-0411-6 • W • $19.95pb • (253)

Beginner's Welsh
171 pages • 5½ x 8½ • 0-7818-0589-9 • W • $9.95pb • (712)

Prices subject to change without prior notice. To order **Hippocrene Books**, contact your local bookstore, call (718) 454-2366, visit www.hippocrenebooks.com, or write to: Hippocrene Books, 171 Madison Avenue, New York, NY 10016. Please enclose check or money order adding $5.00 shipping (UPS) for the first book and $.50 for each additional title.